THE ORIENT

These are Borzoi Books, published by ALFRED A. KNOPF

PEOPLES OF SOUTHEAST ASIA

THE YOUNG HOPE OF THAILAND, TROPICAL ASIA'S
ONLY INDEPENDENT REPUBLIC

PEOPLES OF

SOUTHEAST ASIA

BY

BRUNO LASKER

PREPARED UNDER THE AUSPICES OF
THE AMERICAN COUNCIL OF THE
INSTITUTE OF PACIFIC RELATIONS

ALFRED A KNOPF

19 44

New York

ACKNOWLEDGMENTS

The writing of this book has taken more time than may be apparent to the reader. The author desires to thank the International Secretariat of the Institute of Pacific Relations and the Carnegie Corporation of New York for assistance rendered during part of that time. Neither they nor the American Council of the Institute which sponsors this book share his responsibility for statements of fact and opinion. The author also wishes to thank Elizabeth Allerton Clark and Dr. Karl J. Pelzer for the use of their photographs.

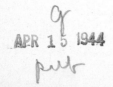

CONTENTS

ILLUSTRATIONS

PEOPLES OF SOUTHEAST ASIA

I

INTRODUCTION

THIS book is about the peoples of Southeast Asia, a hundred and fifty million of them. Today they are hostages in the hands of the enemy; tomorrow they must be our fellow workers in the building of a free world.

Soon American troops, with those of our brave allies, will fight and die to liberate these peoples. But the Japanese are bending every effort to estrange them from us. The record of the region's contacts with the West has made that task all too easy. Even today leading statesmen of the colonial powers claim that their soldiers, their merchants and industrialists, their civil servants and their missionaries have given peace and prosperity to countries which before their coming were wretchedly poor and haunted by fear. But the soul of man yearns for freedom, and blessings bestowed by aliens under the shadow of guns remain unappreciated. There are those among the brown and yellow peoples of Eastern Asia who understand the values of modern civilization and wish to be identified with it in every way. But there are also those who see its technical superiority only as a force that threatens all they hold dear. For them the white man's prestige rests on his arms and on his mastery of their use. The humiliating defeats suffered by the Western powers since December 1941 have destroyed much of that prestige.

If East and West are to resume their partnership it will

have to be on a firmer basis of common purpose. Military power will not be so greatly admired by the peoples of tropical Asia when we have to use it to bomb their own towns and villages in driving out the Japanese. The white man will have to show that the way of life which he cherishes and the human relations which he desires to create are really superior to those sponsored by the Japanese and their dupes, and cannot do this by liberating these countries merely to dominate them.

The old relations between East and West were already in flux; crude exploitation and brute force have given way to principles of trusteeship, of guardianship, and of voluntary co-operation. The progressive application of those principles has been interrupted by the war. Now, the campaign of reconquest and the re-establishment of orderly rule provide a unique historical occasion. Here is the chance, in one of the world's most important culture areas, to do something more than just continue where we left off. We are about to enter with purpose and determination a new era of international, interracial, and intercultural collaboration. But that is an enterprise which dare not be attempted in a cloud of ignorance and prejudice. We, the common people of the West, need to learn much more than we now know of the peoples and lands of Southeast Asia.

The region is one of continental plains and table-lands, rugged peninsulas and thousands of islands, bounded by China on the north, India on the west, Australia on the south, and the trackless Pacific on the east. Our forebears thought of it as a sort of outer court to Cathay, the Middle Kingdom; they explored the interior by following the rivers and the ancient routes of Farther India; they quarrelled over the right to trade in the Spice Islands. The region includes Burma, only recently a province of India, now a separate component of the British empire, with a population of about sixteen million; Thailand, better known by its former name, Siam, the only independent country of the region, with a population about as large as that of Burma; Malaya and the British possessions and protectorates on the island of Borneo, with approximately five and a half million people; Indo-China, twenty-four million; the Philippines, seventeen million; and the Netherlands Indies, sometimes called Indonesia, seventy-one million. The last named area includes Java, Sumatra, Celebes, the greater part of Borneo, the Moluccas, innumerable smaller islands, part of Timor (the eastern part of which belongs to Portugal), and the western half of the huge island of New Guinea.

Four centuries ago this region attracted the attention of the West as a source of valuable raw materials. Spices were sought not so much for their flavor as for their meat-preserving quality. Gems, pearls, ivory, and gold, brought by Arab traders from Farther India, had for many centuries found their way to Europe. Often, too, the traders brought costly works of art. But now for the first time sturdy vessels could make their way around Africa and made possible the export of these riches in larger quantities. Soon wares not quite so precious became common articles of trade: tea, coffee, coconut, jute and other fibers, woods that would take a fine finish, rice and sago, skins, and the products of many crafts. Seas which have once more become accustomed to the volleys of men-of-war then saw broadsides not only from the fleets of nations competing for monopolies but also from pirates and adventurers.

Gradually the great Western powers settled their differences: wharves and warehouses rose on beaches once strewn with the wreckage of war. Soldiers and sailors elbowed their way through streets busy with the traffic of foreign commerce, kept in order by agents of the civil government. Homes and churches were built. Missionaries sent to convert the "heathen" went inland and discovered primitive cultures in unspoiled savagery, elaborate Asiatic civilizations still flourishing, and the remains of great historic epochs. Scientific explorers who followed them traced to their origin the glamorous sculptures and rites of palace and temple, took inventory of the tropical abundance of field and forest, eventually dug up evidence that here may have been the cradle of the human race, or at least the home of that branch which, emerging from the foothills of the Himalayas, later spread over a large part of the world.

By the end of the nineteenth century, one of the Western colonial empires, Spain, was but a memory, and another, Portugal, barely retained a foothold. Yet, in the Philippine Islands a fragrance of Spanish tastes and ideas remains after forty years of American rule, and at least one of the major industries still is in Spanish hands. The Portuguese, having been the first to arrive, have left a lasting imprint on the construction of native ships and on urban architecture. The Dutch controlled all of the Indies; but their administrative machinery had not penetrated very deeply the more recent and less exploited of the island acquisitions. The French controlled Cambodia, Cochin-China, Laos, Annam, and Tonkin, although the latter remained for some time under Chinese suzerainty. The British were firmly established in Burma, the Malay Peninsula and North Borneo, but they, too, continued to rely as much as possible on "indirect rule" — often little more than nominal rule of native princes.

The first world war widened the scope of the struggle for colonies and brought Japan to the fringe of the region as heir, under a League of Nations mandate, to Germany's scattered island possessions in the western Pacific. The second world war has given the region an entirely new significance. For centuries it was the scene of rivalry between the rising empires of the West for the right to dominate the declining empires of the East. Now East and West are united against a common foe who combines the most cruel features of the old despotism with a mastery of modern weapons. Joint international purposes now span the globe, transcending former conflicts. For the first time, the democracies of Europe and America bring the full force of their liberal traditions to bear upon a contest between irreconcilable concepts of human rights and human destiny. With victory for the allied cause — which none can doubt — a new prospect opens up in Southeast Asia. It is one of the great centers of military and naval strategy today. Tomorrow it will be one of the world centers of social and economic strategy and a testing ground of enlightened political principles.

New Maps for Old

A few years ago, such a book as this would have had to start with a description of the major geographical features of the region which we are about to discuss. Today, thanks to the Japanese war lords, almost everyone is familiar at least with its location and general outlines.

We have been re-educated in our geographical thinking. Our school geographies usually place the continents in the center of their maps, with margins of ocean around them. We now know that the oceans unite; we think in terms of Atlantic and Pacific strategy, and not of European, Asiatic, and American strategy. The South China Sea, like the Mediterranean and the North Sea, is a body of water on which important routes of sea trade meet. Its control insures political power. But while former wars in this region have been contests between alien empires, in the present war most of the peoples of the region have allied themselves with the protagonists of a democratic world order to defeat a return to the rule of force.

The active phases of war in this region often take place in some partly enclosed sea so that the inhabitants of the surrounding coast lands become participants or innocent victims of campaigns that may have little relation to their own political fortunes. The South China Sea was one of the first maritime regions to feel the brunt of the second world war; and with the gathering strength of the United Nations it is bound once more to become a major theater of war.

Centuries ago this region was the scene of great international events, even though the movement of ships and of men then was, compared with that of today, like a camera set for slow motion. Mountains, rivers, many branches of the sea, and a ring of volcanoes had created in prehistoric times an almost ideal setting for the mingling of racial groups and cultures. Like a great stage, the region has its exits and its entrances. From at least two wings the actors have entered it in a succession lasting through centuries. On this stage they have fought out and made up their differences. Some of them have been driven onto barren mountain ridges and isolated islands. Some, like the Thai, the Annamese, the Javanese, have grown strong and have incorporated remnants of weaker groups. Some branches of the Malay race have ventured to distant lands and there built richer civilizations of their own.

The political boundaries of this region have often changed. The empires of India and China have swept over it, adding portions of it to their own realm or retreating and leaving behind peoples with more than a trace of Indian or Chinese blood, and cultures deeply imbued with Indian or Chinese traits. Even in modern times each period of famine or unrest in the borderlands of China, Tibet, and northern India has started a trek across the surrounding mountains. The great ships have disgorged their millions of Asiatic steerage passengers at the docks of new port cities: Saigon, Singapore, Bangkok, Rangoon. Africa and western Europe have made their human contributions, and Islam has continued its ancient contact with its own former Far Eastern colonies.

It is difficult to give such a region or its peoples an inclusive name. The principal native stocks are Malay. They show predominantly Mongoloid traits. But some of them can claim part-Caucasian descent; less numerous are the more primitive Negritos and Papuans. All these groups and their sub-groups are distributed very unevenly, and everywhere intermixed. Negrito and Papuan features are more often seen among isolated island and mountain peoples — the former in the Philippines, the latter in the Moluccas, Timor, Flores and New Guinea. Comparatively pure Malay are the Dyaks of Borneo, the Bataks of Sumatra, and the older groups of Celebes and the Moluccas.

Despite their many differences, the peoples of Southeast Asia have a fundamental unity of culture, partly conditioned no doubt by the tropical climate or even, in the case of the majority, by a remote biological kinship, but mainly because of a similarity in social history and economic organization. Dragged into the orbit of world economy, forced to abandon many of their accustomed ways, some of them are now in a state of cultural ferment, and this the present war no doubt is quickening.

The general reader is perhaps better acquainted with the ancestors of the inhabitants of Southeast Asia than with the present generation. For their ancient arts and beliefs, the vestiges of their cultural heritage have been the subjects of many romantic books. Books tell us much about the small remnants of primitive hill people but less about the masses of peasants and workers who are not nearly as picturesque. Many aspects of the traditional ways of life are, indeed, worth knowing because of the light they throw on human nature, on the growth and decay of human institutions. We stand in awe before the grandeur of the great monuments left behind by peoples now represented by only small population groups. We also admire the craftsmanship of simple people who, with the tools of former ages, still bend the natural materials of their immediate environment to their own needs. But all that remains of the past gains even greater significance when we study it as the source of living societies, as starting points and milestones of human progress. In estimating past civilizations we too often substitute palace and temple for the huts of the people. Here in tropical Asia we can often see side by side the old and the new, the timid beginnings of that way out of the jungle which leads to settled community life and the dignity of modern men freely associated for common ends.

A subconscious search for relief from the more sorry aspects of our own civilization has made us dwell overmuch on the bronzes of Cambodia, the brocades of Annam, the music of Java, the temple ceremonies of Bali, the Buddhist classics of Burma, the gabled houses of the Menangkabau in Sumatra, and other evidences of great culture epochs. The same search has glorified the beauty of the human form as seen in the lithe temple dancers or even on the rice fields and on the roads. We hear much less about the beauty of character, of thought, of craftsmanship, displayed by many of the groups now on the threshold of modern civilization. Contemplating the glories of descending old-world cultures we are liable to overlook the nascent genius of those who, already on an ascending intermediate stage of world culture, are heirs not only of their own past but also of ours.

Therefore, in this book we shall concern ourselves largely with the dynamic of inward growth which so many of these Asiatic peoples display, despite their reputation for conservatism and love of tradition. Our interest in them is a practical one, for their welfare now affects that of people in every part of the world. Their striving for a higher plane of existence — not in material comfort alone but also in knowledge and artistic creation — is no longer only their own concern and that of their rulers. They are our fellow workers in a global movement. The Japanese appeal to them as sharers in a common past; we appeal to them as sharers in a common future.

With the exception of small groups of political opportunists whom Japan has seduced, the people of these lands, about one fifteenth of the world's population, are our allies in this war, although relatively few of them have had the chance to enter into active fighting or even to defend their homes against the common enemy. The character of these populations, no less than the region's material wealth, is a vital factor in the prosecution of the war. As the dark cloud of enemy occupation is rolled back by the combined effort of many nations, there will begin a new chapter in the peace-time relations of all these peoples. The day of imperial rivalries in tropical Asia is coming to an end; the opportunity for world co-operation in the use of the globe's material resources, in the protection of its weaker population groups, and in the establishment of a vigorous exchange of goods and ideas is at hand. Southeast Asia, perhaps more than any other part of the world, has the chance to become a scene of a great experiment in international guardianship. Perhaps more than any other region it invites the civilized world to work together for the welfare of peoples not yet ready to take their full share in the defense and advance of world civilization.

The emphasis in these pages on internal situations in the society of Southeast Asia does not indicate a lack of appreciation of the importance of its economic relations with the rest of the world but is intended merely to balance the excessive attention generally paid to the stake other countries have in this region. After all, a democratic new world order will have to concern itself first of all with the interests of the inhabitants of a given region and not with those of their alien rulers or of aliens who carry on business in the region.

More especially, however, shall we try to steer a middle course between those who discuss the problems of Southeast Asia without regard for its geographical distinctions — for example, the hot and moist climate of most of it and its influence on man — and those who dwell on environmental factors as though they represented so many natural barriers to mutual understanding and collaboration. The monsoon rains, the dry winds from the Himalayas, the matted forest growth, the savage typhoons, the live volcanoes, the deadly swamps — all these are not to be underestimated as influences on human destiny, but they do not in themselves determine human character. Our business will be to look at the peoples as they are today. And most of them, we shall find, are already in part emancipated from the fetters of their wild environment. Not even the jungle dwellers of Malaya are quite as hemmed in by nature today as our novels and motion pictures make them out to be.

Few even of the city dwellers in tropical Asia have as yet grown to the full stature of world citizens. Wanting to know these peoples as they are, we are concerned not only with their past and present contribution to world civilization but also — and perhaps even more — with those nascent abilities which circumstances have not yet enabled them to unfold. What happens when the simple Filipino peasant, the Javanese plantation worker, the Ambonese soldier, and many other groups are brought into contact with this or that aspect of modern civilization?

First, Ask the Right Questions

This book, in short, is intended to give some of the information which an intelligent world citizen will wish to have if he is to think realistically of the political future of tropical Asia. It is not intended to give all the answers. Indeed, until we have the help of the indigenous peoples themselves, until we have expressions of their experiences and desires through organized channels of representative public opinion, we are hardly in a position even to ask all the pertinent questions.

There is sometimes, even among persons who have lived in tropical Asia, only the vaguest appreciation of the difficulty of adjusting a traditional Oriental way of life to the requirements of a modern industry or a modern urban environment. The difficulty is even greater, of course, when we ask ourselves what is required to adjust such tribal cultures as those of the Indo-Chinese borderlands, hitherto able to survive only because they were somewhat cut off from the main avenues of world intercourse, to an intricate series of modern international connections and influences. One need only think of the recent history of Japan to recognize how much more is involved than just learning some new skills or acquiring an inkling of the natural sciences. There must be changes in attitude, too, and these are all the more difficult when the advantages of innovations are by no means clear to the people.

In most of Southeast Asia, centuries of despotic rule have stunted any sense of social responsibility beyond the confines of family and tribe; in more favorable circumstances this might have grown into something akin to a sense of citizenship. Nor have contacts with the international world of modern civilization favored a rapid expansion of the individual's sense of social obligation. Disregard for the welfare of wage-earners and share-cropping cultivators of commercial crops was the rule not so long ago in the large economic enterprises of the tropics. Increased participation in world economy meant an increased scramble for land and, among the disinherited, for jobs. Use of money, at first a pleasing key to new pleasures hitherto undreamed of, brought new, utterly incomprehensible, hazards. What could a rice grower in Cochin-China do when a shift on

the Paris exchange suddenly depreciated the money which
he had received for his crop? What could an Indonesian
rubber-grower do when a new agreement among the large
producers suddenly closed to him a market on which he had
long relied? Only the speculator benefits from price fluctuations, and he is usually a foreigner. Even the relatively large
Filipino, Thai, or Indonesian grower who considered himself a member of the commercial world community did not
know what was happening to him when dealers in Amsterdam or elsewhere drastically reduced the price of leaf tobacco to get rid of old stocks, or when American cottonseed growers got Congress to raise the tariff on coconut oil.
Population groups which only recently had carried the
brunt of economic unfreedom could not, when the world
economic depression began in 1931, feel that they had a
common cause with the large foreign enterprises, even
though the more modern governments had feebly tried to
protect them. Some of them, on the verge of becoming absorbed in a world economic system, drifted back to the relative security of their tribal and local associations — even
to barter and abstention from the use of imported commodities. The native side of Southeast Asia's dual economy
took on new life.

No proposal for the future of Southeast Asia has much
value that does not recognize the pluralistic character of
society in the Asiatic tropics, and the hold of tradition on
the various segments of that society. Their divisions of language, of customs, of religious beliefs may seem relatively
unimportant to the military administrator, the politician,
or to the industrial manager who has to work with mixed
groups: similarity in conditions and the same disciplines
will keep even a heterogeneous group of people in step. But
each group carries with it into the modern setting its own
attitudes shaped by past experience. Its response to one
wage incentive or another, to one form of treatment or an-

other, to one kind of environment or another, will be characteristically its own.

Before setting out on any elaborate project for political or economic reconstruction in Southeast Asia, Occidentals would also do well to re-examine their own views as to the nature of the indigenous populations. Behind the reference to the hundred and fifty million as an "oriental society" there may hide a good deal of misunderstanding, even prejudice. Peoples of Malay or kindred origin often are pictured in travel accounts as happy and childlike. More than one writer has told us that the natives of the Asiatic tropics do not desire a life much different from that which they now live, that their standards of living seem low to us only because we do not understand how little material comfort they require. Observed inadequacies in their economic and social behavior, always from a Western point of view, are explained as deficiencies in racial character or sometimes, more charitably, as effects of the hot climate; but no mention is made of the net effect on social attitudes of centuries of oppression.

The ease with which these peoples have been subjected by the Japanese, and in former times by other Asiatics and by Europeans, may be a sign that they are physically inferior to the hardier stocks bred in dry or temperate climes. But we must not forget that in every case the contest was an uneven one: the conqueror invariably had better weapons, and the superiority of Hindu, Arab, Chinese, and Western civilizations was not in physical endurance but in the application of greater science to the arts of war. Where attention has been paid to the nutrition and health of native troops, as for example in the Philippines, they have shown an extraordinary sturdiness under adverse conditions.

A peculiar contradiction sometimes characterizes descriptions of these peoples: on the one hand we are told that they are so peace-loving and indolent that they could never be made into a first-rate army. But we are also told that foreign rule over them is necessary because without the imposition of superior force to keep them at peace, they would soon be engaged in armed strife with their neighbors and with each other. In pre-colonial days, warlike conflicts in tropical Asia, as in other parts of the Pacific, often resulted from competition for land. In particular, the peoples of the arid highlands bred too fast to be supported by the natural resources available to them. The land they fought for was not always the most fertile but always that most favorable to their accustomed occupations. The relatively primitive conditions that make for such competition and wars have given way, in the greater part of Southeast Asia, to permanent agricultural settlement and to a general acceptance of law as the guarantor of peace. Settled peasants throughout the world love peace. Overpopulation, unless encouraged in the interest of an aggressive tribal leadership, finds its outlet in intensified production, in migration, and here and there in planned resettlement.

For the most part the peoples of Southeast Asia are in a transitional stage between a backward-looking pre-industrial and a forward-looking technically equipped civilization. In that stage many of the mental attributes formerly observed are undergoing change, many of the fears and hopes have taken on a changed complexion. Their minds are more flexible; and those Occidentals who sincerely wish to help them in their difficult adjustment to the integrated world community of the new era will find the native people responsive even where in outward appearance they seem conservative and aloof. But that help, whether given by the Occidental trustees of a given dependency or by members of the larger world citizenry, must be based on understanding and on mutuality.

For many of the Asiatics now under the heel of Japan

the war of liberation will provide a harsh experience in mental growth. On them will fall the responsibility not only for some of the fighting, but especially also for the maintenance of order and the salvage of lives and property. Already, some of their rulers have admitted members of the indigenous community to services long withheld from them. When all are helpless before a strong foe, supposed differences in innate abilities fade away; real ability alone holds authority. No doubt, the unschooled peasants of the Asiatic tropics need us in their struggle for freedom; but we should not forget that we need them, too.

Part I.

IN FORESTS AND FIELDS

II

OF MANY ROOTS

THE LAW of the survival of the fittest operates in both primitive and advanced societies. If the Dyaks and the Javanese today differ greatly from each other it must be partly because for some hundreds of years the sort of Malay who could lead in battle and secure a large number of enemy heads would have been a misfit in the best Javanese circles. He might even have become an outcast and ended his days as a homeless wanderer. Among the Dyaks, on the other hand, a Javanese — or, what comes to the same thing, a coast Malay — who was wise in counsel but slow in action, whose comfort and efficiency depended on many little things which the forest does not afford, and whose talents as a craftsman had found no suitable materials to work upon — such a man might in vain ask for the hand of an eligible maiden. He might even be ostracized and die without leaving either fortune or heirs.

These, you may say, are mere speculations. Let us look, then, at some of the evidence of the remarkable adaptations of ethnic groups in this region to the setting which nature provides for them.

For our first sample we might take the P'u-Noi, a mountain tribe in the Phong Saly area of Indo-China. There are only ten or fifteen thousand of them, distributed through some forty villages and over an area of about twenty-five square miles. There, in almost complete isolation, they carry on their traditional way of life. They are said to have lived at one time on the upper Mekong, in a Burman kingdom. But when the Chinese invaded their former home, they fled. They are the remnant of a group that was much larger, but they have never had a chance to increase again because their neighbors — the Burmans, the Laos, the Annamites, and others — were constantly at war with them and with each other, so that the P'u-Noi barely escaped annihilation. Their present physical characteristics reflect their survival by flight and their ability — at least that of the surviving remnant — to adapt themselves to less and less favorable living conditions. They are sturdy, short, and able to carry heavier loads than almost any other tribal group in that part of the world. Survival by escape is reflected also, of course, in their way of living. Travelers have observed that their women are more timid than those of the neighboring groups. When a stranger enters their village, they make off in a body. Yet their villages are larger and more easily defended than most villages of that region's uncivilized tribes. Their houses are built on stilts, though they are high up in the mountains where there is no danger of floods; indeed, lumber for building often has to be carried up from below.

Much the same thing may be heard about the Moi of Indo-China. They, too, have taken refuge in the mountains. Their ancestors, according to one authority, have come from the Malay Peninsula. Not many years ago they were reported as wearing few clothes, as not being overclean, as building their houses on stilts or in trees, and as being altogether "savage." The Annamites who now make up the dominant native population of most of Indo-China say of the Moi much the same things that Filipinos say about Ifugaos (non-Christian peoples of central and northern Luzon), coast Malays about the Dyaks of central Borneo, Burmans about Kachins — the same things that

Greeks said about the barbarian tribes of Macedonia, Romans about Britons, New Yorkers about Iroquois, Chinese about Mongols. Always these more primitive peoples are hunters who if they go in for agriculture at all do only a little of it, afraid to take root in an area from which at any time they may be ousted by superior force. Always the "superior" people call them savages and deny that they have any culture or religion. Like others in the same situation, the Moi were hostile when strangers from the distant West first penetrated their territory in search of treasure. And since their subjection they are reputed to be sullen and shy. They are poor and yet unwilling to accept the blessings of civilization, unwilling to learn despite their ignorance. That is what unsympathetic outsiders say of them — Annamites or Chinese or, occasionally, a Frenchman. Some of their equally primitive neighbors, the Sedang, the Stieng, the Ruong, at least have occasionally rebelled; but the Moi, as one writer says of them, "wait for misery, sickness, and alcohol to bring about their ultimate extinction."

Not knowing the Moi at first hand, one may not quarrel with observations such as these. But they are strangely familiar. Native peoples disturbed in their accustomed ways of life by a stronger power, thrown out of their habitat by the encroachment of foreign enterprise, even enslaved or subjected to conditions resembling slavery, always have a reputation for lacking spirit. At one time anthropologists even invented a new disease for them: *la grande misère psychologique*. These people just pined away, we were told, because they had nothing to live for.

And yet, the same ethnic groups have shown themselves altogether adaptable to new circumstances when brought into contact with another civilization under conditions that leave them some dignity and some hope. On the Chinese side of the border, for example, they have responded of late to friendly overtures on the part of the national gov-

ernment, a government which has opened schools among
them and appointed magistrates to protect them against
the greed of Chinese land speculators. Everyone has read of
the heroism with which whole Moi villages, including the
women, have helped build and defend the Burma Road.
In Indo-China there are Moi who, though they have never
seen a white man or a modern city, take part in the same
civilization which we think of as our own. And this quite
directly, too. We read, for example, of a Moi woman who
operates a telephone exchange; or of a Moi mechanic who
finds the leak in an automobile engine and repairs it. Moi
tribesmen replace the telephone poles knocked down by
wild elephants.

Refugees All

Such a leap over centuries is no longer exceptional.
There are today in the valleys and coast towns of Southeast Asia thousands of people whose relatives still live in
the mountains very much as they did before the coming of
the white man. In Farther India there are many such tribes.
Their languages usually differ from valley to valley or,
more often, from one plateau to another, for they live
high up on the shoulders of a naked mountain where their
enemies cannot reach them. Although they have almost no
intercourse with each other, there are similarities as well
as differences between the tribes. The reason is that they
have all had much the same historic experience. They have
all, in the course of centuries, been driven out of larger and
richer areas by the expanding Chinese empire. This process
reached its height under the Mongol rule and made it possible for Marco Polo in the thirteenth century to travel
from Peking to central Burma without having to enter an
alien realm.

In addition to the Miao (whom the French call Méos),
there are the Lolo and the Man peoples. They arrived at

different times in their present mountain habitats. There was much sporadic fighting, both among themselves and between them and the Thai and Annamites, before they divided into the peculiar mixtures in which we now find them. The Man like to build their villages on mountain slopes, not too far from the valleys where they exchange their produce for Thai-grown rice. The Lolo have more or less come to terms with the valley people, too, but most of them continue to live in the hills. The Miao, who came last and had to fight hardest for survival, stayed in the higher altitudes.

It has been suggested — for example by the Harvard zoologist, Harold J. Coolidge, Jr., who spent some time in the border region between China and Indo-China — that this horizontal accommodation, from the fertile valley bottoms to the barren mountain tops, represents not so much the result of a struggle for existence during which the latest comers and the weakest had to take what was left over, but rather a voluntary choice: each group made its home where the natural conditions were similar to those of the area from which it came and in which it knew best how to make a living. There may have been some such selective adaptation in the final settlement, especially in a tropical region where the differences in temperature at various altitudes are very great. But the history of human migrations suggests that this is not the full explanation. The first few generations of a sturdy mountain people may well have preferred the relative hardships of life on their bare hill tops to the heat and humidity of the valleys. But unless they could keep the valley people in subjection and force them to minister to their needs, they must in time, as their numbers grew, have overcome their reluctance. After all, these were warrior tribes whom the far better equipped Chinese and Mongolian armies had never been able entirely to subdue. It is unlikely that they refused for any length of time to take advantage of the more luxuriant vegetation and the more diversified fauna of the lower slopes and the river valleys. That the Thai — themselves descended of hill peo- ple — are ten times as numerous as the Man or the Miao would seem reason enough why we find the former en- trenched, along with the Annamites, wherever the soil is most productive. And it is not surprising either that to this day, despite much suffering from diseases caused by cold and by meager diet, both the Man and the Miao are re- puted to be more vigorous than the two dominant groups which own the rich bottom lands.

If we go to neighboring Burma, we find a similar con- trast between the physical characteristics and the habits of the majority and those of the immigrant minorities that live in the hill country. Sir James George Scott, an acknowl- edged authority on the peoples of Burma, said of the Kachin that they were "the only temperamentally war-like race in the province." (When he wrote, in 1924, Burma still was a province of India.) He thought that the British Army command during the first world war had made a great mistake in sending contingents of this people to Meso- potamia where, unaccustomed to flat country, a march of only a few miles tired them out, whereas at home they could go all day on the steepest hills and then sprint the last hundred yards. Another army officer of great experi- ence, Major C. M. Enriquez, takes issue with people who complain that Kachin, when brought down from the high- lands and settled among the Shan, are liable to deteriorate through easy living in a rich, low-lying country. He is not at all alarmed by the prospect — for one thing because, even after three generations of settlement, the lowland Kachin still intermarry with the highland Kachin. These Kachin, resettled after their subjugation, like the Miao in northern Indo-China, still seem to prefer living on the hill tops. But in their case, too, the difference in climate may not suffice to explain their preference for a more difficult way of making their living. As for the physical ability of the Kachin settled around Lashio, the Japanese who made their acquaintance as guerillas when they fought there for the first stretch of the Burma Road into China, probably are willing to give them a flattering testimonial.

In passing, it may be worth noting that these defenders of one of the world's famous highways once were greatly feared as bandits. They levied blackmail on caravans passing between Burma and China and exacted fees for the "protection" of Shan villages. The recruiting and training of these people, both for the regular army and for the policing of this unruly corner of the British empire, has been highly successful. Nevertheless, on the higher levels of this mountainous country, where most of them still live, we get the same picture that we have of the Miao in Indo-China: that of a minority making a last stand in self-defense. Their villages are on exposed mountain crests, almost unapproachable by an enemy force; even so, they are fortified with stockades, the timbers for which must be brought up from the woods below. For even greater safety they live several families together — that is, in larger kin groups than is usual — under one roof. In short, their reported bravery, their preference for a fortress-like home environment, and their banditry are all part of the same pattern. They are a refugee people, not strong enough numerically (two hundred thousand or less, all told) to invade the richer of the Shan states — especially since the latter have come to be protected by British arms. The Cham likewise have learned how to subsist on barren rocks and heaths where the soil is shallow and the undergrowth is thick — land that nobody else wants.

The Shan people among whom the Kachin have to some extent been settled are also an immigrant minority, but a much larger one — more than a million strong and about one-tenth of the Burmese population. They are racially identical with the Thai of Indo-China and Thailand and are related also to a number of minorities in China itself, which, under the Ming empire, were driven from their homes in the mountainous southwest. Some of these have settled on the coast of south China. Some have been driven off the land altogether and live on rocky islands off the coast and even on the water itself. The famous boat people of Canton are the descendants of such a refugee group. Even in Manchu times, right into the twentieth century, they were not allowed to own land and so subsisted as best they could by fishing and piracy, more recently as highly efficient mariners and pilots through the mazes of the Pearl River delta. There, in a village of these boat people, I witnessed a religious ceremony, performed by an itinerant priest or magician on a torchlit square. Young men of the local fisher folk who assisted him were hypnotized into a state of trance; and the martial gods of the people in their ancient mountain home of the distant West were called upon to give them strength and prosperity.

Sir George Scott says that the Shan are not only identical with the Thai but are also of the same stock as the Pai-i, the Moi, the P'o, the Han, the Nung-jen, the Ming-shia, and groups known under yet other names. No ethnologist, Chinese or Occidental, has as yet been able to disentangle the kinship relations of all these different groups. They have spread from their homeland in Yunnan and Kwei-chow east into Kwangsi and Kwangtung, south into Laos (partly in Thailand and partly in Indo-China), and west into the Shan states of eastern Burma where, in the seventh century, they were combined into a powerful kingdom whence they have repeatedly invaded the lower plains. The Thai of Siam, or Thailand, have long been known for their independent character.

In addition to fairly large and constant migratory move-

ments over land and over narrow sea passages, there has
always been in Southeast Asia a sprinkling of maritime
contacts; and these have taken place over thousands of
years, leaving their residues not only in physical traits but
also in additions to languages and customs and folklore. In
this milling of peoples a migratory stream may even reverse
itself. Of this you can see a sample if you visit some of the
small towns and villages in southern China from which
men have gone forth for many generations to make their
fortune in one of the rich countries of the *Nan Yang*, the
South Sea, as the Chinese call all of Southeast Asia. In
these Chinese towns and villages you will occasionally come
across a boy or girl of pure Malay looks, as clear-skinned,
large-eyed, straight-backed, and small-boned as any youth
or maiden to be found in Java. Despite their finely modeled
heads, full lips, and graceful bodies, these are the children
or grandchildren of Chinese emigrants who have married
overseas and sent their offspring back home to receive a
Chinese education in China. The youngsters usually are
the children of second wives, the first wife having been
left by the young emigrant to look after his parents and
perhaps a child or two of his own. Such stepchildren of
alien mothers from overseas are as a rule received with open
arms because their coming signifies that the husband and
father, although he has founded a new family in Thailand
or Java or the Philippines, still thinks of China as his fa-
therland and will return to his hometown, perhaps when
the first son of his overseas marriage is old enough to take
over the business he has established.

Until recent times, life in one of the tropical countries
to the south was so much more secure and so much more
profitable for the Chinese emigrant that it did not occur
to him to take or send his foreign-born children to China,
even when the mother was not Malay but of Chinese blood.
So, all around the South China Sea and in Malaya and

Farther India, we see today large populations of "native people" who look like Chinese and, in fact, are the descendants of Chinese immigrants with an admixture of other stocks. But as China itself grows more united and stronger, her sons abroad — who have always felt proud as the carriers of a superior culture — will be prouder still; in another hundred years or so, the streets of Canton, Swatow, and Amoy will be as crowded with different racial types as the streets of Bangkok, Singapore, and Macassar were in the days before the war.

Indeed, out of the Caucasoid and Mongoloid mixtures that have peopled southeastern Asia, a common fate and common aspirations are now blending a new hybrid type. Varying in skin color, in head-shape, in stature, and in other features, different racial strains here converge. Soon the differences in natural equipment between the various groups will be no larger than those between Europeans. Of course, there are people who can tell you at a glance that this man has Papuan blood in his veins and that one has a Hindu somewhere in his family tree. If your informant has made a study of racial types, you can take his word; but more likely he is just trying to pose as an expert when he really knows no more about the matter than you do.

Measurements have shown that ethnic stocks adapt themselves in the course of several generations to new environments. Italians in the United States grow taller on the average than they are in Sicily or Calabria, or wherever they come from, even when they do not intermarry with other groups. It is the same in the Asiatic tropics. One scientist tells us that "the Thais are a thickset race of middle height and well adapted to mountain traveling." He is talking about the Thai highlanders in Indo-China. But in their present major habitat and national home, Thailand, the Thai are "well adapted" to life in the rich river valleys.

Physical differences developed among the Malays as, in

the course of their varied history, they made their homes in different environments. The Dyaks of Borneo and the Javanese come originally from related stocks, but looking at them you would hardly think so. The Javanese — a Mongoloid deutero-Malay group — have for centuries been living a rather highly civilized life. They are lithe, have beautiful smooth skins, and well molded features. Some of the young Filipinos you see as busboys in American restaurants and in our Navy uniforms are much the same type, though perhaps a little shorter. The Dyaks — a Caucasoid proto-Malay group — are, on the other hand, large-boned, tall, heavy, and sharp-featured.

Speaking of the Devil

Now, it is an interesting thing to learn that at one time the inhabitants of Java must have been much more like the Dyaks than they now are. The Hindu invaders called them devils — or called the devil after the Javanese, which comes to the same thing. This devil is misshapen, has big teeth and protruding oblique eyes. There is, in fact, a certain resemblance between this Hindu devil who takes his likeness from the wild Javanese, and the European devil of the middle ages who, as the artists saw him, so often looked like a Hun. As a matter of fact, the Malays and the Huns may originally have been branches of the same family, the main difference being that the Huns, moving westward over the wide Asiatic plains, remained nomadic horsemen, while the Malays were forced to proceed on foot. These Malays, to quote Cabaton, "driven from Central Asia by fiercer or more mobile enemies, or by some unknown catastrophe, such as a disease, a blight, a cattle pest, or by a prophecy or a superstition, found their way across the Himalayas, through the forests and the uplands of India, down the Burmese border, finally reaching the Malay Archipelago and perhaps the regions to the east thereof."

When Europeans began to know the Malays, there still seem to have been vestiges of an earlier nomadic way of life. There still remains the practice of "shifting cultivation" — moving on when the fertility of a particular piece of cleared forest land has been exhausted — a primitive form of agriculture which manifestly has grown out of the habits of people accustomed to move around. Early chroniclers reported that the peoples in various parts of Farther India were always moving in hordes from one place to another, and that on these occasions the chief was either carried in a litter or borne on the back of an elephant. Even more conclusive to some anthropologists is the report that these migrations were usually directed by an omen — the flight of a bird.

Be this as it may, it is well known that the devil is of no known race but appears to every people in the guise of that racial group which it most fears. Since the people who have grown prosperous and lazy in the rich river valleys of the world are usually more timid than those who inhabit the infecund highlands, and since they look for possible invasions from the hills, the devil most often is pictured as a wild man of the mountain, with the attributes of the beasts among which he dwells. Hence horns and hoofs. Hence also the frequent location of temples and shrines in southern Asia on the most exposed side of the town, usually upon a height overlooking it (the location also of David's temple in Jerusalem). But there are other devils who come by sea, and ferocity dominates their features, too. The sculptors of Bali who have shown themselves so adept at incorporating modern scenes and portraits in their temple decorations no doubt will leave for future generations their impressions of the Japanese intruder.

On the other hand, if there are any artists in the Japanese armies of occupation they will if they survive perhaps produce devil-masks resembling the native guerilla soldiers whom they fought in the hills and forests of Burma, Malaya, and the two Archipelagos. Press dispatches informed us in January, 1942: "Borneo head hunters, masked with fright-instilling war paint and with their ancient spears sharpened, are ready to go on the war path." At one government station in the jungle, "several hundred natives, armed with their ancient guns, spears and knives, suddenly approached the settlement, scaring the wits out of the residents. They had come prepared to defend the Great Mother (Queen Wilhelmina)." What sort of a composite Satanic picture the Japanese artist will draw of the Burma guerillas remains to be seen. Here some thousands of Karen villagers in the mountains were organized by a British officer so tall and thin that among his comrades he goes under the name of "Spooky." The arsenal of these hillmen included shotguns, Italian rifles, a few tommy guns, and crossbows with poison-tipped arrows. They took wireless sets along with them into the woods, mounted on elephants. The four British officers wore skirts and turbans like the natives.

"What makes the Moro wild?" I once asked an anthropologist. He laughed. "Believe it or not," he said, "it is because he is a pacifist. He is an earnest believer in the Koran. And the Koran says, 'Thou shalt not kill.'" He waved aside my unspoken protest. "I know what you are going to say. A Moro does not kill except to validate his religious faith, and that faith is in humanity. Tagalogs and Ilocanos never were internationalists. You may say, they are the Moro's brothers. They share the same physical inheritance — except that there is more Arab blood in the Moro stock and more Chinese blood in that of the Christian Filipinos. And that, perhaps, explains their mutual dislike. I do not mean," he added hastily, "anything like instinct or physical aversion. But the majority of the Filipinos face west, and the Moro faces south. Those others have missed the great civilizing influence of Islam that spread over the

Indian Ocean to Java and Celebes and Borneo, then to the
Sulu Archipelago and Mindanao."

"Was not Mindanao at one time governed from Borneo?" I asked.

"From Java. It was part of a great empire cemented by
goodwill, piety, and trade."

"But piracy . . ." I interrupted.

"You forget, my friend, that piracy has become a crime
only in modern times. Among the Greeks and Phoenicians
— even in Elizabethan times — it was as respectable as any
other calling. Until the advent of modern navies, merchants and fishermen had recourse to it in all parts of the
world when they could not make a living in more normal
ways. Such an occasion arose when the Spaniards tried to
monopolize the trade of the Indies. The Moros fought for
their survival and for the glory of the Prophet in the only
way they knew — just as they did in the Mediterranean.
The disinherited do not fight with gloves."

When I looked puzzled, he added, "You know, I suppose,
that the word 'Moro' simply is the Spanish for Moor. The
Spaniards found the same sort of resistance in the Sulu
Sea that they had earlier experienced nearer home." He
thought for a moment, then repeated: "For three hundred
years these Moslem internationalists have defended the
freedom of the seas against the imperialists."

"But long after the defeat of the Spaniards, after the
establishment of American rule in the Philippines, there
have still come reports of ghastly atrocities committed by
Moros."

"That is true. They did not recognize us as their de-
liverers. To them we were at first simply another bunch
of white men. Like the Spaniards, Americans identified
their interests with those of the Christian Filipinos who had
done so much to keep the Moros in poverty and subjection.
It takes more than one generation to learn that we mean

well. They certainly are not yet convinced that the Christian *politicos* from Manila mean them well."

"Remember," my friend concluded, after a few illustrative instances of the trickery that has given a bad name to the Christian Filipinos among the Moros, "these fellows are as much feared by the Moros as they fear the Moros."

He came back to this conversation on another occasion when I told him of my theory concerning the representation of the devil. We agreed that there are really three kinds of devil-image, corresponding to three kinds of experience. The ferocious devil, when the fear that has given rise to him has vanished, becomes a funny devil — still with some traces in features and bearing of the ethnic group that at one time threatened the security of the peace-loving people, but now in a more humorous guise — perhaps a figure to frighten children with, but a ludicrous fellow. You can see such figures among carved temple decorations in Bali. There are, I believe, in a Japanese temple court some seventeenth-century figures of Dutchmen that answer this description. And they certainly exist on the Chinese stage.

But it was the third devil-image that especially interested the anthropologist, because neither of us could remember ever having seen it perpetuated in Oriental art. This is the image of the cunning, deceitful, usually alien group which simple people see on the outskirts of their own society — and have reason to fear. The devil of Goethe's Faust and of Stephen Vincent Benét's Daniel Webster, always ready to take advantage of less clever people and to betray them, has his counterpart among the less advanced people of the Malay world. They hate the Indian or the Chinese moneylender, the Arab or the Coast Malay trader (less often the European) who has insinuated himself into their midst and fleeces them. This figure is not feared because of his physical strength or agility or even because of his superior weapons, but because he can always turn the ignorance and even the simple virtues of others to his own account. He conveys favors with a smile and, when it is least expected, pulls the noose and leads his prey into slavery.

Sometimes the mighty falls. The foreign moneylender is chased out; the native one finds his power curbed by lawmakers intent on the protection of the common man. He falls on evil days, knowing no other craft with which to sustain his accustomed way of life. His plight may even invoke sympathy — but the "poor devil" rarely figures in folk art.

III

NATURE AND NURTURE

WE SET out, a good many pages back, to show that what is called racial character is not some mysterious innate quality. It would always have a simple explanation if only we knew enough of the original homeland of a people and the experiences through which it has passed. We found that populations reported to be savage, warlike or primitive usually are the remnants of refugee groups. Unable to find or to conquer a territory rich enough in resources to meet their needs, they have learned to make a more precarious living on less hospitable lands. Such people, even when they are relatively secure, usually lack three things necessary to develop an advanced state of civilization: wealth, leisure, and stimulating contacts with the outside world. Racial kinship may make for a certain likeness in the physique and in the modes of living of diverse groups that originally have come from the same area. But similarity of experience, producing the same selective influence on survival, is at least as potent a force. So we get a peculiar repetition of descriptive details about isolated mountain peoples in various parts of Southeast Asia even when their origin is as different as that, say, of the Moi and of the Kachin.

Mention has also been made of the Dyaks of Central Borneo. They are not the original inhabitants of that vast interior maze of mountains and jungles, of roaring rivers and all but impenetrable virgin forest. They are kin, rather,

of the Bataks of Sumatra, and of half a dozen or more
groups in Malaya and even in Indo-China, with names spelt
in a variety of crazy ways. The aborigines whom they replaced in all but a few isolated spots, are stunted little people, dark-skinned, with woolly hair. These, like their kins-
men in the Malay peninsula, have at times been libelled
by Malay invaders who classed them with the apes and
credited them with the possession of a tail — a caudal ap-
pendix of which explorers anxious to find the much discussed "missing link" have in either country been able to
discover not a trace. On the Asiatic mainland, mountain
tribes are usually of stocky build. But the Dyaks are slender
and strong. They share with other Caucasoid proto-Malay
groups a fair skin, full lips, a flattened or stubby nose, and
rather pleasing facial features — that is, pleasing to Europeans. While the blood of the Malays of the coast is
strongly blended with that of seafaring Chinese, Buginese,
and Arabs, the tribes of the interior are less intermixed.

Not All Wild Fruits Are Sweet

Like some of their continental kin, the Dyaks have until
recent times been head-hunters. Sympathetic investigators
have found that deplorable habit not inconsistent with a
highly socialized and relatively peaceful way of life. Even
in the European middle ages neighboring villages occasionally resorted to force in boundary disputes, in revenge for
actual or fancied wrongs, in the taking of brides, and for
other causes. The trophy room of a successful British big-
game hunter and the display of heads on the wall of a Dyak
men's house serve the same purpose — prestige and evidence of prowess or manliness. For both circles the occasion on which, and the manner in which, a head — and
thus incidentally a life — may be taken is governed by a
binding etiquette. The Dyaks are, in fact, noted for traits
that make them attractive to people with high moral stand-

This hunter and fisherman, member of a Sakai tribe of mixed Mongol and Negroid origin, manages to make a fair living in the jungles and highlands of Malaya.

This Dyak hunter's blowpipe, short sword, and amulet are works of art. He is a man of noble lineage; his evident intelligence has never been applied to agriculture.

A "shifting cultivator" of Mindanao, working on the family's temporary dry-rice patch (ladang) in a forest clearing.

A peasant woman of Panay, P. I., weaves piña cloth in the cool open space under her house.

ards. Colonial officials and visitors speak in glowing terms of their honesty and of their hospitality. An American scholar who recently sojourned among them compared them with our own early settlers: despite their fierce struggles with the primeval forest, and a hand-to-mouth existence which made every day a day of adventure, they were generous to a fault and did not know what it was to lock up their possessions. Since everything a man in the forest owns is the product of his labor and of his risks, the sense of private property is strongly developed, and theft is, accordingly, the cardinal sin.

The reverse of the Dyak's love of independence is an often exaggerated shyness, a hostility to strangers of whose motives and purposes he is not sure. The explanation probably is — as it is also among some of the forest and mountain peoples of the mainland — that they themselves are refugees who seek survival in an inhospitable environment because access to richer lands has been denied them. They are hunters and food gatherers, with little skill in the cultivation of the soil. This is made difficult by the continual encroachment of jungle or forest on what little land may have been cleared, and they see no virtue in drudgery. Since they are unable to accumulate treasure, they do not achieve the higher forms of civilization, forms made possible only by thrift and foresight. Surrounded by perils, their spiritual universe is peopled with ghosts who must be appeased. Neither Mohammedan nor Christian missionaries have succeeded in converting them to trust in an all-loving deity.

The inhabitants of central Celebes have a reputation similar to that of other forest peoples of Malaysia. On a visit to that island a few years ago, that excellent reporter, Bruce Lockhart (of *Return to Malaya* and *Retreat from Glory* fame), found that they retain their warlike character and their quick temper in spite of everything a benevolent

government has done to bring law and order into their
midst. They, too, combine a highly socialized community
life with a fierce jealousy of outside interference. The tribes
of central Celebes have, in fact, been subjected to foreign
rule for only a generation, although the Netherlands came
into possession of the islands in the seventeenth century.
For example, the Posos, a Toradja tribe, do not like to
leave their highland fastnesses. In one instance, when the
government was determined to resettle them for their own
good in a river valley, and employed force to carry out this
policy, the people lost all interest in life, their resistance to
lowland epidemics proved feeble, and the death rate among
them was high. The hope that they would soon be won over
to modern agriculture by its obvious reward of a much
larger yield proved illusory.

The Toradja of central Celebes are distinct in character
but not in origin from the two majority groups of the
islands, the Macassars of the west and the Buginese of the
south. But they have given more trouble to the authorities.
As is so often the case, an inferiority is attributed to them
which, when the situation in which they find themselves is
analyzed, is seen to be the result of circumstances. To begin with, they have until quite recently been — and some
are believed still to be — head-hunters. That means that
they are always under suspicion. But as in the case of the
Dyaks of Borneo, head-hunting with them is a traditional
method of settling differences and not a perverted taste for
blood. They engage in it only on special occasions and for
special purposes prescribed by their own law. Some of them
have embraced Christianity, but it is doubtful whether
their acceptance of the faith goes very deep. The coast people, with their cosmopolitan background and higher standards of living, consider the Toradja dirty, stupid, and savage. And they fear them.

And so we might go from island to island, always finding,

wherever there is a fairly large and unreclaimed central plateau, some mountain tribe that shares in the general indictment of the civilized coast people. The Achinese of the mountains in the northernmost part of Sumatra are brothers of the lowland Achinese, but there is no love between them. Through the centuries the latter have developed trade relations overseas, at first mainly with India but then also with the Arab world; the former are known as fanatical isolationists who long succeeded in resisting the rule of the Netherlands. The coastal Achinese share with other, racially very different, coastal peoples of Netherlands India a reputation for greed, flattery, and a tendency to think more of high living than of high morals. The Achinese of the mountains are feared as bandits with no interest at all in peaceful trade or in the proprieties that go with good neighborly relations. I have no doubt that if the reader and the author were to pay a visit to the Achinese they would find redeeming and, indeed, pleasing features in the life of both branches of the family; but never having been in northern Sumatra, I can here only summarize what respectable Netherlands, British, and French writers say about them.

This reminds me that old Raffles himself — Sir Thomas Stamford Raffles, the man who governed Java for a time and founded Singapore in 1819 — was nettled by the defamation of the character of the Malay peoples. Of these inhabitants of Sumatra he said in his *Memoirs:*

> "The Bataks are not bad people, and I think so, notwithstanding they eat one another, and relish the flesh of man better than that of an ox or pig. You must merely consider that I am giving you an account of a novel state of society. The Bataks are not savages, for they write and read, and think full as much and more than those who are brought up at our Lancastrian and National Schools."

Raffles himself gives currency to the then widespread belief that the Bataks "relished the flesh of man. . . ." In
connection with head-hunting, throughout the Malay
world, there are traces of a rite in which the blood of the
slain man is sipped or even a bit of his flesh is consumed,
obviously a symbolical act designed to transfer something
of the strength and vitality of the victim, and common to
many races throughout the world.

The Bataks, though relatively few in numbers, are, indeed, one of the most interesting peoples of the whole of
Malaysia. According to Raymond Kennedy, they were the
only true cannibals of the Indies (*The Ageless Indies,*
1943). Arab merchants reported that the Bataks were particularly fond of eating their aged grandparents so as to dis-
pose of their bodies in an honorable way, and of making ban-
quets of their criminals, of prisoners of war, and of aliens.

Now, as among the Dyaks of Borneo, the Malays of the
Malay Peninsula, the Achinese, and the Buginese of Celebes, so also among the natives for Sumatra it is well to make
a distinction between those who live on the coast and those
in the interior. The former, first to be brought into contact
with foreign trade, are largely Mohammedan, the latter
are still largely pagan but also Christian — and good Christians at that. At least this would seem to appear from the
fact that in 1941 the Netherlands Indian Government,
after the internment of the German Protestant missionaries
who had been largely responsible for keeping up the
churches, schools, and hospitals among the Bataks, allowed
the latter to take over most of the institutions and to run
them under an independent Batak Church. But the Christians make up only about one-half of the Batak population.
The rest continue to live according to their ancient traditions. Like other peoples of Malaysia, they are greatly influenced in their every-day life by the insecurity and perils
of their existence. Their animistic beliefs arise from fear.

A long history of subjection to Hindu rule, before the advent of the Moslems and then of the Europeans, has given these beliefs a mystic universality which they did not previously possess, but has not fundamentally altered them.

We need not pursue our comparison of the peoples of the plains and those of the mountains through every part of Southeast Asia. But let us try a glance at the Philippines. Western civilization has here penetrated much deeper than in the countries mentioned so far. One would expect to find less sharply drawn the contrasts between "civilized" and "savage" population groups — between those who have had good opportunities to advance and those who have not. But it is remarkable to what extent the lack of easy communications perpetuates ancient differences that have their origin in geographical separations. This is especially true on the island of Luzon where some of the most advanced and some of the most backward elements of the Philippine population live in close proximity. A patient and foresighted administrative attitude toward the pagan highland people of the island — usually classed together under the inclusive name of Igorots — already has shown that the striking contrasts between the various ethnic groups are not innate but derive from differences in geographical environment and historic experience. School and army have been the two instruments, not so much to obliterate the cultural diversity of the Philippine peoples as to provide all of them with opportunities for cultural growth.

Long before the war with Japan or active preparations for it, American army officers reported that the Igorot recruits made excellent soldiers. One of these officers told me that it was "almost unbelievable what a difference even a few months in an army camp can make in those fellows." He emphasized physical training, cleanliness, and good food as the major means of transformation. Discipline, too, of course, he hastened to add, but discipline is not everything. The army has for many years now been the Igorot's most successful training-school. Many things which we, and the citified Filipinos of Manila, take for granted, which our children learn even before they go to school, are entirely outside the experience of the mountain people, and this in spite of the fact that they have a highly developed agricultural and social system of their own. You may have seen pictures of their terraced rice fields, rising tier upon tier from the bottom lands of their valleys to the highest crests. These unlettered "savages" have created a system of water supply and irrigation that is the admiration of every visitor. Less visible is their traditional law without which the operation of such a system would be impossible. As in Java and other areas devoted to wet rice cultivation, there goes with it a practice of co-operation and a high degree of social thinking; and these predispose for other forms of community activity. But these people, or many of them, have never worn clothes. Many of those who join the army have never seen an engine or a stove, have never built a wagon or driven a horse. They learn all this and much more; and the knowledge is beginning to revolutionize — not their homes which in the main meet their needs, but their attitudes.

In Luzon, as elsewhere, the regional and local environment will continue to exert its influence on the thoughts and habits, the desires and the abilities of men, but it will control them less and less. The teachers of the more advanced techniques and the merchants of the new tools of civilization, instead of trying to force these upon unwilling and seemingly backward people, are learning to adapt their offerings to the needs of these groups. It is only, however, as the fears of injustice at the hands of the dominant group are laid that the aborigines are drawn into partnership. And this, with the unfortunate history of their exploitation, takes time.

Romance and Reality

Americans like to applaud peoples and cultures that are a long way off and can be viewed through the rose-colored glasses of romance. Southeast Asia has been no exception. Any tired European novelist could take a quick trip to tropical Asia and be sure that, however commonplace his itinerary, his travel notes, when properly padded out and "illustrated with photographs by the author and decorations by Madame de Plume," would find a receptive American market. If he could get in a champagne party with an Annamite prince or a big game hunt with a Malay sultan, so much the better. We just revel in quaintness when it is thousands of miles away. No author has yet been able to lay it on too thick to suit the American taste. We do not, on the other hand, like to be reminded of squalor and dirt and smells. But if the returned traveler wished to tell the truth about Malaya or Siam or Cambodia or any other of the ancient countries of Southeast Asia, he would be obliged to say something also about the symptoms of neglect and about cruelty in the every-day relations between man and man, about lack of foresight and excessive conservatism.

We have long been familiar with the same romanticism in our own regional literature. Though the fashion has changed in favor of realism, some writers still ask us not to believe the evidence of ragged shirts and of cabins all but falling to pieces in the cotton fields. There is, they tell us, a song beneath those shirts and laughter under the leaky roof. In a similar strain our guides to Southeast Asia tell us about the happy nature of the Thai and the Malayan's freedom from care. We are informed that the Kachin or the Miao or the Dusun or the Murut values his freedom more than a full stomach. Look at the gay clothes of the Macassar Buginese — must we not envy them? Some go so

far as to say that it is a crime to interfere with the happiness
of peoples that have not yet developed a taste for soap,
trousers, and pencils. I have even read about the Filipino
that he is "congenitally merry"; and it is sometimes pointed
out that the glum-looking men one sometimes meets on
the roads of Java are over-sophisticated. "You should see
the peasants back in the hinterland, they laugh and tell
stories all day long."

Now, I am quite willing to admit that the Malay, and
especially the lowland Malay peasant, is a cheerful person;
we cannot contradict so many observers who have lived
with him for many years. But I have found the same sort
of happiness in the slums of English cities, among Mexican
laborers in Arizona who lived in makeshift huts made of
packing cases and twigs, among Chinese coolies with an
income of less than ten cents a day, among Rumanian and
Latvian workers with large families which never have
enough to eat. It is well for us to recognize that the simple
life has its compensations for even the neediest. That is no
reason for salving our conscience in so far as there may be
some relationship between our material security and the extreme poverty of those millions whose life has come under
the domination of our Occidental technical superiority. It
is no reason why we should not try to discover the causes of
the tremendous differences in the enjoyment of material
satisfactions which now divide the human family as much
as do differences in religious beliefs.

Some people will say, there is no difficulty here. All of
Southeast Asia, after all, is in the tropics. The climate itself
limits the human capacity for enterprise and cultural
growth. Let us abstain from making the peoples of color
dissatisfied with their lot. For their lot is in many ways
easier than our own; nature smiles on them and to live in
reasonable comfort they need not exert themselves as much
as we must. They have shown themselves incapable of de-

veloping a high type of civilization. Why not leave it at that?

This view, which is widespread, is itself a product of Europe-centered values which we in America have inherited along with so many other incorrect judgments. Actually, the tropics have given the world some of its greatest civilizations. The fact that in modern times large parts of the tropics have been subjected to the domination of peoples originating in the northern temperate zone has led us falsely to assume that the nordic peoples have a monopoly on creative enterprise. Because hot countries are not as rich in durable materials as colder ones, the records of achievement are fewer. But our men of science, probing into the past of the human family, are accumulating proof that Central America, Africa, Arabia, India and Ceylon, Farther India and the Malay Archipelago have given rise to great civilizations which have deeply influenced the rest of the world. Long before Columbus discovered America — if, indeed, that attribution still stands — Polynesian seafarers had conquered much greater distances in the Pacific. Malay and Arab mariners, as well as Central Asian caravans, had linked China and Imperial Rome in trade. Centuries before any of the Gothic cathedrals were built, Hindu masons had constructed the lofty and intricate structures which only a generation ago came to light in Cambodia and Java.

The Asiatic tropics, then, to some extent are — and to a much greater extent can be made — habitable for populations that combine high standards of living with the energy requisite to achieve and maintain them. It so happens that much of the land area of Southeast Asia is exceptionally fertile. Often, as in Java, it is composed of young volcanic rock which disintegrates rapidly in the warm and moist climate. The growth is so luxurious that, as long as the population is not too large, crops can be harvested with relatively little labor. Or perhaps it would be more correct

to say that in the tropics, generally speaking, more food and
fiber can be produced in a shorter period than in the temperate zone; but whatever work is necessary — the planting
and cultivation of rice, the maintenance of irrigation
ditches and terrace walls, for example — must be done
diligently and systematically to insure results.

Now, you have often heard that the Malays are lazy people. Magellan was perhaps the first to make that remark,
telling it to his chronicler while describing his voyage to
the Moluccas in 1519. Travelers always comment upon the
idleness of natives in tropical countries when they see them
take a nap in the middle of the day. You may take it for
granted that these natives do not go in much for physical
exercises in order to keep slim, and that, like the rest of
us, they work no more than is necessary to provide themselves with those things which for them are the means to
a decent sort of life. They do not often find it imperative
to work overtime so as to be able to pay instalments on a
vacuum cleaner or to pay off the mortgage on a two-and-a-
half-story brick house. But when their numbers grow or
the natural fertility of the soil lessens from gradual exhaus-
tion, they do work hard, and they inculcate in their children the habit of regular labor with the same zeal as do
peasant peoples with long winters and short growing seasons. All day long small boys help in the fields, small girls
wield the heavy pestles with which the rice is hulled. No,
they are not brought up in idleness.

The reputation of tropical peoples generally, and of
Malays in particular, for being lazy and easily contented
is explained not only by physical factors but also by the
relative force of incentives that arise from political and
social circumstances. To understand those circumstances,
we must look into the ways in which the natives of different parts of Southeast Asia derive their livelihood from
the soil.

Winds and Weathers

First, we have to distinguish an important geographical influence which sharply divides the economies of the region. On part of it rain falls throughout the year; on others it is regulated by a seasonal change in the direction of the air currents. The explanation for this is so simple that I may as well try to indicate it in a few words before I discuss the effect on human activities of this difference in climatic conditions. The northern winds, having passed over the vast interior plains of Asia, are almost dry by the time they reach the Himalayas. Thus no large glaciers are formed which would cool the atmosphere over a wide area. On the other hand, the moisture-laden south winds are at their strongest in summer when the high temperature does not permit of the formation of snow. As a result, no atmospheric conditions exist that would modify the sharp contrast between the moisture-laden summer air and the clear air of winter. Some small parts of the region — the western tip of Java and some of the lesser Philippine islands among them — are not touched by the continental winds; here the annual seventy inches or so of rainfall are fairly evenly distributed over the year. The trees are always green and bear buds and fruit at the same time. The greater part of the Malay Peninsula, Sumatra, Borneo, Celebes, and most of the Philippine islands, also have a high rainfall; but, as the reader knows from a number of motion pictures in which the characters appear dripping from head to foot, the beginning of the rainy season is often sudden and upsets both the normal routine and the normal temper of the participants in the human comedy. The periodicity of the monsoon rains will be remembered also because of its importance for military strategy in the present war. Even before the Japanese invasion of Indo-China, China's reliance on supplies from the west made it a question of dramatic significance whether the Burma Road could be finished before the beginning of the wet season and whether, when finished, it would withstand the drenching of the monsoon rains. In northern Burma, northern Thailand, and northwestern Indo-China, the higher elevations and greater remoteness from the wide river basins, which keep the climate of the lowlands somewhat humid all the year around, make for the greatest relative contrast between the seasons. Weather conditions here verge on those in the higher latitudes, and agricultural developments similar to those in the temperate zone have been undertaken with success though hampered by lack of adequate communications.

Practically all of Southeast Asia was at one time covered with forest. But in the area with more or less even rainfall throughout the year the forest is exceptionally dense; and this, together with the high degree of humidity, has made human settlement difficult. On the other hand, in those sections which have a pronounced dry season, the clearance of the forest has been much easier; and the denudation of the land in itself has somewhat influenced the climate. Here population is denser, for the most part, than in the rain-forest area, at least until absentee capitalism moves people about in complete disregard for the amenities of life. As we have seen in a previous chapter, people do not necessarily migrate in largest numbers to those areas where things grow most quickly and most easily, even though it may be taken for granted that an adequate supply of food is always the first consideration. We have to take into account also the question whence the migrant masses — often groups driven out of their homeland by conquest or by natural calamities — have come. Most of them, especially in the long ages of migration prior to recorded history, were not agriculturists at all. They were hunters and food gatherers who had to move on when, through their own exertion, the food resources of the land within their reach had become insufficient to support them.

Just before the war Dr. Karl J. Pelzer of Johns Hopkins University went to Southeast Asia to study the uses to which the different land areas of that region are put. He noted people on the Malay Peninsula (both on the Thai and on the British side), on Sumatra and in the Philippines engaged in the primitive kind of life I have just mentioned. If he had gone farther he would also have found such a recent migrant group in Borneo, the Punan. These people are now in a stage through which others passed some time ago. They make no effort to cultivate the soil. Although the women use sticks with which to dig up edible roots, they have not yet discovered that their sticks may be put to even more profitable use, that of assisting nature to place the seeds of wild cereals where they are more likely to take root than when permitted to go with the wind. These hunters and food gatherers do not know what it is to have a permanent residence. They claim as their own the area which they happen to be occupying, until they have exhausted it of game or fish or fruit-bearing trees, and so are obliged to move on. It has not yet occurred to them that they might burn some of the heavy forest growth and clear the ground for a more assured supply of food. Surrounded by potential wealth, they are poor.

However, the remnants of these shy forest dwellers are small. Much larger are those populations which, like the Indians on the Pacific slope of the Rocky Mountains at the time of the white man's coming, combine their hunting, fishing and food gathering with a primitive form of agriculture. Horticulture came first in the forest clearings of Malaysia. Its most primitive form consisted in taking the kernels of fruit one had been eating, carrying them a short distance from one's hut, and digging them in so as to insure a growth of new trees.

So the digging stick became a planting stick, and by stages there developed what anthropologists call "hoe-culture," that is, not only the planting of roots and grains but also the regular cultivation of the ground. The planting stick is still much in evidence in many parts of Southeast Asia. But it would be a mistake to conclude that the natives who use so primitive a tool are unintelligent. The truth of the matter is that for the forest dwellers the cultivation of food plants remains supplementary to their main resource, food gathering. Their inventive genius has gone into the making of hunting weapons — both of the shooting and the blowing kind — and of traps.

Economists sometimes overlook the important part which hunting and fishing still play in the livelihood of peoples on the threshold of entry into a modern money economy. Take, for instance, Laos, that mountainous part of Indo-China where the rivers still teem with an apparently inexhaustible supply of fish. The Moi fishermen catch this, their most reliable food supply, with line, net, and spear. They construct dams of bamboo across the deeper river channels and have learned to smoke and preserve the haul for several months. The same people are also skilled trappers. Captain Henri Baudesson, who was engaged in survey work in this country thirty years ago, admired the inventiveness and skill that had gone into the construction of their snares. "We found," he wrote, "apparatus of different kinds all over the country, its form apparently being determined by the seasons of the year and the particular region." He then went on to describe in detail some of the devices used, devices evidently requiring a precision of construction which we sometimes falsely imagine to have been introduced only by modern science. Indeed, "the construction of these snares calls for a degree of skill and experience to which few Europeans can attain." Similar testimony comes from expert students of native hunting and trapping methods in Borneo and Mindanao, including also the preparation of various poisons used in the killing of game, and the processes developed — by the Dyaks of central Borneo, for example — for drying the meat of deer and other game.

In passing, a word may be said also about the high technical perfection of native coastal fishing in many parts of the Malay Archipelago. We have become accustomed to think of this pursuit as archaic or to regard it as superseded by that large-scale and destructive exploitation of the Pacific Ocean's food resources in which the Japanese have outstripped all other nations. But we must not forget that millions of people still make their living by methods of fishing that are unsurpassed in the ingenuity of pre-scientific observation and invention. The Moros are especially adept in this. Though the money value of his catch may not exceed six American dollars a month, a Moro fisherman in southern Mindanao often is both a navigator and an ichthyologist of the first rank.

Or take the Buginese of Celebes. They have never been farmers. Their culture is little different from what it was when the Portuguese first introduced them to world trade in the sixteenth century. Their seamanship is unsurpassed, though they steer their *prahus* by the stars. If they do take a compass along it is more for its magical effect than for any practical use. Yet these sailors can make Singapore in less than a week; and the Netherlands steamship company not so long ago complained that, with their lower freight rates, the Bugis were taking most of the rice trade of Celebes away from them.

It should not be forgotten, either, how closely in primitive life the arts of food gathering and food production are connected with other arts. We are too prone to think in categories and thus fall into the error of regarding the often highly developed household crafts as incipient industries

and not also as the high points in processes of food production, usually classed with agriculture. A tribe that may
seem to live in an early stage of agriculture, as regards
methods of securing food supplies, may in a hundred ingenious ways and with the simplest of tools work up the
products of forest and jungle and sea into an elaborate
household economy. Some of the weapons, garments, carved
ornaments, and other materials which we display in our
museums are merely the most artistic examples of means
employed to adapt the gifts of nature to the needs of man.
It is as unrealistic to measure the cultural achievement of
a tribe by its rudimentary agriculture as it would be to
measure our own by the crudeness of those aspects of our
culture which we do not take very seriously — say, the
"victory gardening" of apartment dwellers. However, to
the inventiveness and skill shown by the Malay peoples in
matters that are important to them, we shall return in a
later chapter.

The anthropologist of this day no longer follows a blue-
print of human advance. There is no set series of stages
through which each branch of the human family must pass
in its cultural advance. It all depends on circumstances.
For example, when first they entered into any sort of economic relation with our Western civilization, primitive
groups in Southeast Asia were by no means encouraged to
abandon their primitive agricultural implements and to
produce more expeditiously with modern ones. Quite the
contrary. It was not at all in the white man's interest to
make life easier for the natives. He wanted them to go more
alertly after those natural products which he had come with
his fleet of ships to carry away. If he offered any suggestions
for technical improvements — which was seldom, since the
natives knew much more about the matter than the newcomer — these would probably relate to the collection of
trade goods rather than to their production. The foreign

trader might be able to show the simple people how to get nuts, furs, hides, and lumber undamaged to the trading station, and perhaps how to preserve certain gums, plant extracts, barks, spices, or animal products. He might show them how to cut valuable trees most advantageously. Some of the skills thus co-operatively worked out survive. Malaysia has many trades today that have developed directly from the indigenous economy of forest and sea and have entered the modern world economy without passing through any intermediate culture stage.

IV

TILLERS OF THE SOIL

FROM forest horticulture came knowledge of that greatest of life's mysteries, the seed. The use of the digging stick as planting stick was not the only early invention. To know how to improve on nature's crude and wasteful method of disposing of plant seed was not enough. Means had to be found, too, of increasing the cleared area where seeds might be dug in. Accidental fires probably showed the way. To cut away the underbrush around a few favorite trees was slow work and did not get rid of the larger shrubs, especially not in a country where, because of the great humidity, many of the prevalent species send out almost innumerable roots from their many-branched crowns.

In the famous botanical gardens at Buitenzoorg, in Java, it seemed to me that the typical forest of the Asiatic tropics grows down quite as much as up. In the course of time, the main trunk of many trees almost disappears in a maze of gigantic feelers that make new contacts with Mother Earth, as though the tree did not feel well enough anchored to withstand the tropical storms. To cut away all these roots and the vines interwoven with them is quite an undertaking. But a forest fire, while it does not entirely destroy them, will damage the bark or the outer layers, and, after a time, the wood will rot away and the tree will fall.

So the women, whose business it had become to plant rice in the fertile virgin soil of the clearings, got the men to burn down level sites that seemed well suited to their primitive cultivation. Millet and, especially, upland rice thus assumed an importance in the diet and economy of the Malay peoples which in time superseded all reliance on the digging up of roots and tubers or, even more, reliance on the hunt. Or rather, two developments took place. In some parts of Sumatra and the Moluccas, the increased root crops proved so attractive that, through many generations, the natives continue to cultivate them; and there, to this day, several cultivated tubers, together with a few vegetables but no grains, form the principal diet. The cultivation of cereals demands a more advanced discipline: the seasons and the best locations for good results have to be studied, and the hoe culturist must acquire regular habits in order to take advantage of the best times for planting. The Toradja of Celebes and the people of Timor, according to Pelzer, have reached this stage and, incidentally, have learned to orient themselves by the stars, so as not to miss the proper time of the year for preparing the ground and planting. In Western Borneo, a branch of the Dyaks who inhabit the coastal plain have learned to utilize the wet land. They too have learned to watch for the change of season by the stars and do not sow until the Pleiades have reached a certain height above the horizon before daylight. One of the tribes makes use of a sun dial. From the length of the sun's shadow at noon they know whether it is the right time of the year to plant, that is, the time when the monsoon rains will help the rice stalks grow but not destroy the ripening grain.

The greatest discovery of all, however, was that it was possible to control the supply of water in the fields in such a way as to secure the balance between moist and dry conditions most suitable to the raising of rice at different stages of its growth. Today there are marked distinctions between what is called "wet" and "dry" cultivation of rice.

In the lowlands, where water is plentiful, much higher yields can be obtained because the fields can for months be left standing under a thin cover of water. But even in the higher altitudes, and especially on mountain slopes where without man's help the falling rain waters have carved their own pools and channels, irrigation is also possible; but the water must be used more sparingly since it continues to fall to the bottom lands and some of the streams cease running altogether during part of the year.

The irrigation of dry lands as a means of increasing the yield seems to have been an accidental discovery when men sought to protect their cleared fields from erosion. For instance, the **Dusuns of Borneo** deliberately leave some of the tree stumps and lay logs against them horizontally in steps down the steep mountain slopes in order to prevent the humus from being washed away by the monsoon rains. The remarkable terraces of the Ifugaos in northern Luzon may have had a similar origin; sometimes the retaining walls are higher than the fields are wide.

Today, native agriculture in tropical Asia may roughly be classified as either wet or dry. Each predisposing condition has produced not only its own techniques but its yearly occupational cycle as well, and hence also its modes of living and its social customs. In the lowlands, the work of planting and reaping is concentrated on a relatively short part of the year, when all the man-power of a given village must be concentrated upon the job at hand. This necessity to economize the available labor, so as to get the largest yield, has led to a high development of co-operative arrangements. If after re-occupation there should be lack of food and need for relief, the officials of the United Nations' relief organization will find that the common storage of grain for just such purposes is an old custom in many parts of the region. Of course, the existence of such stores cannot be relied upon, as the Japanese are quite capable of destroying what they cannot carry away with them. And hidden stores do not keep long in a tropical climate.

The cultivation of grain foods does not necessarily make for permanent settlement. Those tribes which learned to make use of fire did not always have the opportunity of also learning to make use of water by regulating its supply to their fields. On the contrary, running water often was their enemy. When they had cleared the ground and dug into it, torrential rains came and carried the loose soil away. When this had happened several times, the ground was exhausted: the yield grew poorer with each season, and finally starvation grimaced around the corner. So the peoples accustomed to the cultivation of dry rice and other cereals have in some cases remained nomads to this day — at least to the extent that they feel obliged every once in a while to move off, burn down some more forest and jungle growth, and start all over again.

This moving from place to place would long since have proved disastrous for land and people alike if the native peoples had possessed more effective tools. Perhaps it is fortunate that the Western colonial governments have so long remained indifferent to the improvement of native agriculture for home consumption. Had they tried, during the centuries of the people's ruthless exploitation, to teach them how to increase the output of their fields, they would almost certainly have drained off the resulting surplus yields and starved the land by doing nothing to renew its fertility. As it was, the deterioration of the soil has been serious in spots. But the heavy rainfall and the prolific growth of vegetation in most sections of Southeast Asia have so quickly repaired the damage inflicted upon the soil that often the same tribe would return to its former habitat which, having lain fallow for a number of seasons, would have recovered something of its former response to sun and rain.

Shifting Cultivators

Between the primitive semi-nomadic tribe which leaves a district or neighborhood when this can no longer support life, and the fully settled agricultural community, large numbers of people in the Philippines, in Netherlands India, Malaya, Thailand, Burma, and Indo-China occupy a middle stage. They are what is called "shifting cultivators" or, as the Chinese say, "slash-and-burn agriculturists." They deliberately let some of the land they use lie fallow for a given period and clear a small forest area of corresponding size and so very gradually, by regulated steps, move over from a deteriorating to a fresher soil. They, too, use rather primitive tools. They, too, clear the ground with axe and fire, and do not bother to remove roots and stumps. But they go about their job more systematically. For example, the ashes from the cleared area, or as much of them as can conveniently be gathered, are used to prolong the fertility of the land. As the upland rice, the vegetables, or root crops which they plant, diminish in yield or fail to make headway against encroaching weeds, the "shifting cultivators" get ready to abandon that particular field, having already prepared another. Through trial and error they often learn exactly how long it takes for a piece of land to be so depleted of its natural fertility as no longer to be worth planting. In this way, a regular system develops, with a cycle of years during which fields are first planted, continued to be planted, allowed to revert to their natural state, and, after a lapse of perhaps ten or fifteen years, cleared once more.

During the first year of planting, the soil is little disturbed. During the second, it is necessary to dig a little deeper, and some hoeing is imperative to get rid of weeds. During the third year, these labors increase further. And yet the yield will gradually diminish.

Originally, the division of labor between the sexes was

such that he planting and cultivation of the land was
w°   :; but with diminishing returns the area under
         nd more and more the men are called upon
         ground. Then, if there is a limit to the flat
         e cleared without going too far afield, it be-
         to make use also of sloping ground, so that
         ee huntsman and trapper finds himself com-
         terraces. Not only this, but a choice bit of
         quite a way from the settlement, and it is im-
         the women to go there often enough to weed
         nd finally to harvest it. So some of the men have
         ere in temporary huts, as the Swiss do when they
         eir herds to the summer pastures.
         itually the day may come when practically all the
         near the village has been exhausted of its fertility. It
         es not necessarily follow that the whole community will
         move. The best land now available for cultivation may not
be at all agreeable as a place of residence. So a decision has
to be made as to which of a number of available sites for
dry agriculture is the most promising, and the elders will
appoint those who are to go in advance and do the work
of clearance in preparation for those who plant the seeds.
This is a vital business for the whole community. Omens
are consulted to make sure that so important a decision is
in accordance with the will of the presiding spirits or — if
the people are Mohammedans — the will of God.

With the growth of population as a result of inter-tribal
peace and the beginnings of modern health provisions the
devastation of large areas by this wasteful sort of agriculture
 as become a serious danger to the security of native populations. Several of the governments concerned have reached
 une point where they question the wisdom of permitting a
large section of the indigenous population to continue a
self-sufficient but decidedly primitive hand-to-mouth kind
of life. It is always a hazardous thing to interfere with the

basic livelihood of such simple people as the "shifting cultivator." But with due precaution it has been found possible,
in parts of Sumatra and Borneo, to persuade that individual to introduce among his food crops — that is, his rice
or corn or tubers — a cash crop or two, perhaps a few rubber trees or coffee or pepper or coconut. Planted as soon
as the land is cleared, such trees are left standing, free from
choking weeds, when in the third year the site is abandoned
as no longer yielding a sufficient food crop. When the cultivator returns to the same site a few years later, the trees
will have grown enough to bear fruit, or yield sap, for
which there is a market. If this goes on for several decades
the once destitute cultivator, never more than a sprint
ahead of starvation, may own a number of such tree-planted
sites. If he is fortunate, he may, as the owner of a miniature
orchard or plantation, live entirely from his cash crop and
buy his food.

There is, however, a fly in the ointment, which the Netherlands Indies officials have not been slow to recognize:
who is to guarantee that, when all these scattered lots have
been planted with trees, there really will be a market for
their crops? The answer is that the growth of the area
planted to such tree crops will be gradual, so that changes
can be made in the choice of things to be grown if this
should prove desirable. Moreover, for some of the products
there is little competition in other parts of the world, and
the market may be supposed to be fairly regular. In any
event, these cultivators will not be worse off, except that
they may have wasted some of their labor.

From Planting Stick to Plow
It should not be thought that native agriculture in Southeast Asia is still *predominantly* carried on by such primitive means as have been described. The region, after all,
has long been in touch with the outside world and has

adopted some of the most advanced methods. The plow
seems to have been introduced both from India and from
China. Now, the wooden plow is not of much use to break
up heavy clays; but it is good enough on wet rice fields.
These fields are usually left to cake in the burning sun after
the harvest, and no attempt is made to plow them up until
just before planting time, when enough water has been allowed to trickle in to soften the surface. In the cleared forest areas, too, the use of a wooden plow is quite practical
if care is taken to break the ground before it is overgrown
with weeds. The roots and stumps soon disintegrate under
the onslaughts of the microscopic fauna of the tropics. You
have seen pictures, no doubt, of the use of water buffaloes
(*carabaos*) as draft animals. Usually a small boy will be seen
sitting on the amiable bovine whose broad back provides
protection from snakes and other crawling creatures. The
animal is the Malay peasant's most prized possession. He
does not grudge him long hours of leisure in some tree-
shaded pool.

The great majority of Malay agriculturists have passed
through the stage of shifting cultivation to that of permanent plow culture. When a man has cleared a piece of land
and tilled it so that its fertility has a chance of renewing
itself, when he has trained animals to help him in the heavy
work of turning over the soil, when he has built walls and
ditches to insure just the right amount of water needed for
his crop, when he has, perhaps, surrounded his home with
fruit-bearing trees and helped his womanfolk to plant a
few favorite vegetables — when he has done all that, he
does not lightly relinquish his land to take up virgin soil.
He will have learned what each small plot requires in the
way of special care to bring forth all that it is capable of
yielding. Like an observing father of many children, he will
know how to evoke in each a maximum of response. And
so, in the course of time, not only do the denizens of every

valley and every hillside specialize in their own major crop,
but within the area which the community calls its own
there will be specialization according to the nature and the
exposure of each field.

Often all three of the major categories of arable land
are to be found in the same community: irrigated land or
land naturally flooded by some stream during part of the
year; dry land; and garden land, close to the homes of the
people and cultivated with special care to provide the table
with a variety of fruit and vegetables. This variation in
the uses of land by one and the same community is, perhaps, the most civilizing of all influences. It means that
habits of work and life must adapt themselves to many different needs. Physical effort must be matched by mental
effort if advantage is to be taken of each season of growth,
if the labor of men, women, and children is to be dove-
tailed so as to neglect no opportunity of adding to the material enjoyments of all.

Out of this enriched vocational cycle of the year, often
including a double crop of the staple food, or of rice in rotation with some root crop, there arises a new versatility
in dealing with problems in human relations as well as with
problems in the mastery of nature. The rights of individuals and of families assume a new importance. Monopolies
arise; and against these the community must defend itself.
The more precious of the crops must be protected, and this
too requires joint and organized effort. A palisade or a
living hedge may be built around the village itself with
its home gardens. Or some may be appointed as guards
to watch the fields and to operate the often ingenious
and elaborate contrivances for frightening away predatory
birds. Some will become specialists in laying traps for wild
hogs or elephants that destroy the crops, or for tigers and
other carnivorous jungle animals that endanger the livestock. Some will become hydraulic engineers, directing the

Rice terraces on a mountain side. The water has been drained from the lots at the left for a dry crop, to renew the fertility of the soil. Note the smallness of the cultivable area in proportion to the height of the mud walls that have to be kept in repair.

In the villages of East Java, the seed rice needed for next year's planting is preserved in a public storehouse zealously guarded by village officials. Note the shape of the supporting pillars designed to keep out rats.

Filipino town house, showing the use of movable hardwood window frames with small square panes of shell.

A Cambodian home built on stilts over a stream, as are many homes in the Asiatic tropics both for sanitary reasons and for protection against floods.

construction and repair of those irrigation ditches and waterworks on which the economic safety of the community now depends.

And so the homogeneous community begins to take on a class structure. Different kinds of land are differently taxed. Only those are admitted to the vote who own some of the more valuable kinds of land: irrigated fields and gardens. The status of woman rises when with physical labor in the fields she combines an increasing variety of skills in and about the home. Old men, always honored for the wisdom that comes with long experience, even in nomadic days and in the uncertainty of shifting cultivation, now are the custodians of established law which they expound with the knowledge of many precedents. A growing disparity in wealth creates a new desire to assert status through lavish hospitality. There begins an accumulation of material goods that serve no useful purpose other than that of advertising the prosperity of their owner. Soon the whole community is ruled by prestige.

Foresight now is indispensable to well-being. With a permanent residence and permanent land occupation, the peasants cannot allow their fields to become eroded but must take proper precautions. So, long before there has been any conspicuous improvement in the tools used, we find the sloping hillsides terraced and the water kept in, either with low stone walls or, where no stone is available, with walls made of clay and grass. Even bricks may be baked solely for the purpose of constructing such walls. There is a progressive increase of fields and gardens as population increases. More and more, poorer and poorer land is brought under the plow.

Governments are beginning to learn that to remove populations from crowded and exhausted lands to some other location is not always the best solution of their problem. Unless there is a change in methods of production, the new clearings, too, may soon be worked out and their soil be washed into the river valley and into the sea. This happened when a group of villages were removed from rolling land in Cebu to similar land in Mindanao. They threw themselves with enthusiasm into the task of growing three crops of corn a year on the virgin soil of their new home. Before long, the soil had disappeared. On the other hand, in Java and Madura, the villagers have been encouraged to build new terraces near their old homes, so as to utilize some thousands of acres that had never been cultivated. And those acres have become a permanent addition to the arable land.

Another way to increase the food supply is to introduce new crops, or a better variety of an old one, or a new rotation of crops. As the uplands of Java which had yielded a sufficiency of rice became impoverished with over-use, the poorer peasants started to grow a root crop along with the cereal — not because it was more nourishing but because they could grow more of it. Agents of the Government tried to persuade them to grow something else next year — perhaps a crop of beans or anything that would help to fertilize the land. But the peasants only asked, what shall we eat in the meantime?

There is, of course, no satisfactory answer if the available area of arable land is really too small to feed a given population, or if rents and taxes are so high that the peasant cannot retain enough of what he grows for the use of his family. But conditions rarely are so desperate that with the satisfaction of hunger there cannot go some small improvement. Usually it is possible to engineer at least a gradual shift away from a land use that utterly destroys the basis of livelihood to one that will maintain and even increase it. The difficulty lies not so much in the peasant's conservatism as in the urgency of the demands he must meet: taxes and interest on loans.

Farming as Business

Roughly speaking, the dividing line between primitive and modern farming lies between production for subsistence and production for trade. As soon as the peasant employs a moderately effective plow and follows it up with a rake of some sort, he is likely to think of disposing of some of his harvest in exchange for things which he cannot himself produce. The American farmer typically considers himself a business man. This idea would be strange to the great majority of Malay peasants. There is, however, a transition by imperceptible grades from a mainly self-sufficient to a mainly commercial system of production. Most of the agriculture of the Philippines is in this transitional stage: its primary purpose is that of raising food for home consumption, but despite the impending severance of the country from its assured market in the United States, production for export has increased with each recent decade. Even since 1935, when there no longer was any question about the Islanders' early obligation to stand economically on their own feet, the production of all the principal export crops has increased, while that of rice for home consumption — occupying nearly one-half of the country's cultivated area — has somewhat decreased. Rice in the Philippines is the principal food for about two-thirds of the population, and yet the country does not raise enough of it for its own needs. One-third of the cultivated land before the war was planted to cash crops.

The Filipinos have definitely entered a stage in which their own economy must fit into that of some part of the outside world — not necessarily the United States. As a matter of fact, their economic dependence is primarily on other parts of Southeast Asia. While the Filipinos pay for their imports in a roundabout way, chiefly through exports to the United States, it is the surplus rice production of Thailand and Indo-China on which they rely for their living: some four million bushels in 1941 out of a total consumption of fifty-eight million bushels. The year before, with a rather better harvest, the import of rice amounted to only two and a half million bushels. Toward the end of 1941, when Japan grabbed all the rice available in Indo-China and Thailand, the Philippines turned to Burma for some of its staff of life. How the people have managed since that country, too, was overrun, and especially since their own country became the prey of its northern neighbor, I do not know.

Rice is not the only food which the Philippines normally import. Large quantities of wheat, of dairy products, and of meat also were imported in the pre-war years. But these foods are in a somewhat different category from rice: they could not easily have been produced in the Philippines and therefore represent an enrichment of the plane of living — more especially of townspeople — made possible by the country's exports, particularly of sugar, coconut oil and copra, hemp, tobacco, minerals, and such manufactured articles as embroideries, cigars and cordage.

The change-over from a simple subsistence economy to a modern commercial one depends on many circumstances and cannot be accomplished very quickly. This is shown also by what has happened in Indo-China, though here the general situation is very different. The country is an exporter of rice which, in addition to forming four-fifths of the native diet, makes up about seven-tenths of the export trade. This colony has been prosperous for generations because of the exceptional fertility and productivity of much of its soil. But even here the methods of production have lagged far behind those practised in the West. Poor seed selection, insufficient fertilization, and the use of primitive implements, despite years of effort on the part of the administration to improve matters, combine to make the total yield of the cereal per acre the lowest of any country in the Pacific.

The causes of retardation, then, are primarily social. If peasants continue to use outmoded methods, it is not — as some unimaginative foreign commentators suggest — because they are too indolent to try anything new and too easily satisfied with what they have. It is not because the limits of productivity at a remunerative cost have been reached — a modern plow would pay for itself in a very few years, even on a rather small farm. It is not because the market is limited. It is because there has not as yet been enough education or enough of an incentive to make the people feel that a larger effort and a larger yield would be for their own benefit.

In large parts of Indo-China, the people do not have enough to eat. And yet, while enterprises dominated by foreign capital — the growing of rubber and the mining of coal, for example — have increased by leaps and bounds, not only rice production but that of all native food crops has lagged behind the growth of the population.

There are several reasons why the Annamite, the Thai, or the Burmese farmer is not more progressive — why, for example, he goes on using the same inefficient plow that has been used for two hundred years or more, when a plow that cuts more deeply and throws the sod up obliquely can easily be had. It is not merely ignorance. The man who refuses to purchase an improved plow often has actually seen a demonstration of what it can do for him in his own village. One explanation is that the so-called "primitive" tools and methods, after all, are not so ineffectual considering the kind of land the peasant has and the kind of tillage he has to do. He can get along. And if despite all good advice this same peasant refuses to diversify his crops it is mainly because he knows that there is a market for his staple crop but is by no means certain that he could get a worthwhile price for the small amount of maize or beans or cowpeas which he as an individual could produce.

The one thing which experts often find it so hard to understand is that the farmer and his family must eat. The peasant knows from long experience — that of the community if not his own — that with the traditional methods he can in normal years gain food enough, even after his rent and interest on his running debt have been paid. But when he departs from these time-honored methods and tries something different he is quite uncertain of the results in terms, not of market price, but of food. He is too poor to make experiments. When he does make them — perhaps to please some government official — he is half-hearted about it; and this explains why he so often fails. In short, he behaves much as poor farmers behave everywhere.

As one looks deeper for the psychological causes of the prevailing conservatism, the answer is found in the poverty and exploitation of the common farmer. In Thailand, the middleman, the creditor, and sometimes the landowner, often is Chinese and not of the farmer's own nationality. The general picture of landlordism and its effects is the same everywhere. The peasant can take no advantage of rising prices when the market happens to be good, and suffers grievously when it is not. He is chronically in debt and, owing a large part of his harvest in payment of interest, has no inducement to improve the quality of his rice or whatever else he produces for the market.

Land prices were forced up by speculation when, at the beginning of this century, the Government of Thailand opened up its part of the peninsula to exploitation. Some of the land was soon exhausted by the first settlers, largely Chinese, who cleared the jungle, so that it was a poor buy when it got into the hands of Thai peasants who came to settle there and make a home for their children. In central

Thailand, where the quality of the land is much better, its price reflects relative distance from one or other of the many waterways over which the produce has to be sent to market. Hence, the necessity of continually shipping rice, in order to pay the high rents, and not the suitability of the soil for one crop or another, determines what the farmer does with the land. In the depression years, 1931 to 1933, many of the poorer farmers lost their savings, their draft animals, and what little land they still owned.

The situation in Thailand is less serious than in some of the neighboring countries — especially Burma with its influx of competitors from land-hungry India. Sometimes the inability or unwillingness of native cultivators to introduce improvements of methods when these have been explained and demonstrated to them has its cause not so much in present discouragements as in a historical experience that has left its mark. For instance, there is reason to believe that the Khmer and the Cham peoples of Indo-China at one time engaged in far more elaborate and thorough forms of cultivation than they do now. Their indifference today is the outcome of the terrible injustices to which they were subjected when their great empires fell, and as the power of the Annamites continued to grow. It is also possible, of course, that in the course of wars and rebellions the most enterprising and intelligent of the people either fell or were enslaved. Others who were moderately successful may voluntarily have become assimilated to and intermarried with the dominant ethnic group. In short, what is left is a backward mountain village proletariat with a cultural heritage which today survives only in a few of its crafts and in the practices of its medicine men.

In the Philippines, too, a good deal of neglect and seeming lethargy is unquestionably a result of intertribal strife in the past. We find evidence of this both among the Moros and among some of the non-Christian mountain tribes which still remember how their best lands often were, in Spanish times, appropriated by Christian Filipinos who enjoyed the backing of the government. The island of Luzon has a long history of trespasses by land-hungry Ilocanos upon the inherited domains of the Ifugaos. As a result, the latter have even in recent years been slow to register their lands, lest the legalization of their ownership might only produce another wave of spurious claims and disputes in which they would expect to be the losers.

Modern Improvements

An American farmer usually would jump at the chance to make a few extra dollars by growing a crop of groundnuts or of soy beans if he were shown how it could be done, and especially if at the same time he were doing something to improve the soil. But the Thai, Annamite or Malayan farmer is, first of all, concerned with the question of how such a departure from established usage would affect his relations with his fellow villagers. And these relations are firmly fixed by tradition. To do a little better this year than last is nice, but it does not affect his standing in the community. A man attempting to set himself off from his fellows by what our economists call conspicuous consumption would by that very fact proclaim himself of no account. He would be a rebel, not an honored first citizen. What raises a man in the eyes of his neighbors may be an unusual accomplishment if it is for the benefit of all; but even such a distinction has its limitations. For the Asiatic, the sort of security which we are prone to seek as individuals by bettering our economic status, rests much more in the ties that bind his community together; and those ties are strong because they are steeped in tradition. The security afforded by the bonds of family and community weighs far more with the individual in simple societies than do private possessions. The folklore of many peoples contains stories of misers who could not protect their wealth or their persons. In a tropical climate it is, of course, even more difficult than in the temperate zone to store for one's own needs. The individual may be more aware of his helplessness as he faces the dangers of the jungle, of torrents, or earthquakes. But I do not believe that climate explains the difference between the Malay's attitude to self-reliance and our own. After all, we have passed through the same stage. If it were not for the remnants of familial and tribal bonds in our own present-day society of "sturdy individualism," it would long since have collapsed — or given way to a collective system.

The most advanced of the colonial governments in Southeast Asia, that of the Netherlands Indies, has found that it cannot force the pace of modernization in the agricultural systems and methods of its various subject peoples, and that no great harm is done if a few innocent survivals of magic slow up progress. The various systems and methods of agricultural production which flourish side by side in Indonesia are proof that there has been and continues to be a realistic adaptation of ingenuity and skill to many kinds of natural environment and many new demands in the social and economic situation. There is need for little more. Progressive changes to insure survival and prosperity are not uniformly needed throughout the social fabric. They are needed mainly where there is considerable alteration of the environmental conditions — for example, where jungle gives way to cultivated fields and where modern highways penetrate a formerly isolated mountain plateau. But this raises another question: why should not the great majority of Javanese peasants, and for that matter simple peasants anywhere, be allowed to go on as they have done for ages? After all, their welfare is determined by the ideas in their own minds of what is good and what is evil, what constitutes happiness and what misfortune — not by objective standards. Do they not, on the whole, manage quite well to provide themselves with those material aids to well-being which they appreciate? Is it not, perhaps, outside interference that is responsible both for the material destitution of so many Asiatics (growth of population without corresponding growth of resources for their sustenance) and for the mental anguish of those among them who oscillate between loyalty to the old civilization and admiration for the new?

It is true that throughout Southeast Asia conquest and the victory of foreign ideologies have interrupted the age-old rhythms that controlled the growth of population in relation to available resources. It was outside interference that laid new and often crushing burdens on the people for "improvements" from which sometimes they gained nothing at all. Imperialism, to take the most charitable view, helped millions to survive who otherwise would have died, but it robbed them of the old certainty that there was something worth surviving for. The fortunes of the humble peasant were linked to the stock quotations on the exchanges of London, Amsterdam, New York; and at the same time the Occidental giants who seemed so powerful that even the native princes could not stand up against them, permitted the wealth of the forest and of the sea to be filched from those who had depended on it for a living. Here and there the wilderness was tamed, but for millions life was made more precarious in new ways against which the wisdom of the fathers and of the scriptures did not prevail.

The question, then, is pertinent: by what divine dispensation is it ordained that the people of tropical Asia must be brought into what we proudly call world economy, though actually it is the economy of a small alien minority?

One answer, difficult to controvert, is that it is altogether too late seriously to consider putting a stop to a historic

Native rubber growers in Sumatra use portable hand-mangles to press the viscous latex into sheets.

On Negros Island, rich in sugar plantations, many of the Filipino hill people are too poor to buy a wheeled wagon. Their rice is pulled to market on sleds.

The girls of Palembang, Sumatra, probably do not know that harvest time is flirting time the world over.

A Javanese farmer and his wife shred and wash cassava roots. The starch stays at the bottom of the vat and, when dry, is exported to the United States, where it becomes tapioca pudding. The man's attire is typical for the younger generation of workers.

trend. It is no more possible to leave any part of the world alone, in the sense of permitting its inhabitants to work out their own salvation without regard to the rest of humanity, than it was possible for our own country to withdraw behind the imaginary curtain of its ocean fronts. The question is not really whether a substantial portion of the world's population shall be forced against its will to take part in an all-inclusive world economy and world civilization. Except, perhaps, for small remnants of tribes, so isolated that they have practically no knowledge of the outer world, there are no peoples content to go on as they have in the past.

Agriculture in by far the greater part of the world has become commercialized. It is no longer an incidental adjunct of activities primarily directed toward the satisfaction of personal wants — as it is with the suburbanite who spends a few minutes in his garden to gather strawberries for his breakfast. To talk about the possible self-sufficiency of Thailand or of the Philippines makes little more sense today than to talk about the self-sufficiency of the individual village community. Even if such self-sufficiency were possible it would be so only by virtue of a deliberate renunciation of those higher standards of life which men have striven to achieve with much sacrifice of immediate comfort.

Whatever may be said about the deficiencies, even the aberrations and cruelties, of colonial and semi-colonial systems, it cannot be denied that at least they have accelerated the progressive advance from lower to higher levels of civilization which could not automatically take place within the old civilizations which they found. They have, through a commercial self-interest often in sharp defiance of the social good, shown the way to a higher productivity of man's own resources when applied to the abundant resources of nature in tropical and subtropical regions. And while higher productivity is not everything, without it the enjoyments, the comforts, and the security of the millions are limited to a level which, in retrospect, appears to have been amazingly low through countless ages.

We turn, therefore, from the relatively modern transitional stage which agriculture has assumed in most parts of tropical Asia, compared with the traditional stage of native agriculture which preceded it, to an even more advanced stage, that of commercial agriculture. That stage, although it predominates in all discussions of colonial economics, as though it were the only one that mattered, actually affects the lives of but a minority of the native peoples. The majority, while they contribute in part to world economy are not functionally part of it. They are essentially peasants and not "agriculturists" — a term which, to my mind, involves at least a modest interest in agricultural economics beyond that in the occasional sale of small surpluses of produce in the local market. Or perhaps one may explain the difference between the peasant and the agriculturist by comparing it with that between the artisan and the industrialist. It is not so much a difference in scale of operations or the use of modern machine tools, though these factors are part of the picture, as one of attitude. The artisan produces for immediate purposes intimately known to him, whether he be a wheelwright who repairs the carts of his fellow villagers or a weaver who sells his wares in the local market. He knows how to do certain things and does them for whatever remuneration his efforts may gain him. The industrialist thinks of the demand first and not of what he has to supply. He is ready if necessary to change his methods and his implements and the character of his output itself, if by such means he can increase his profits. In the same way, the peasant, whether he consumes most of his produce or markets a large part of it, has his eyes fixed on the particular piece of land he has, what crops it has been customary to grow on it, and the customary way of growing it. It is precisely because he thinks more like an artisan than like an industrialist that it is difficult to make him adopt a new crop or a method of cultivation very different from that to which he has been accustomed. When he allows market prices and costs to determine his choices of crops, and the methods of producing them, he has ceased to be a peasant.

V

MERCHANT FARMERS

TOWARD the end of the last chapter we spoke of the dualism that runs through the agricultural economy of most of Southeast Asia. The simplest way of looking at it is to regard one side of the dividing line as essentially peasant farming and the other as essentially commercial farming. There is a good deal of overlapping, of course. Through large sections of the region rice is grown by small cultivators with an attention to detail and with means as intensive as those of any cantaloupe grower in the Imperial Valley. The individual holding may be small, but the trade as a whole is organized to gear into the machinery of world supply. That the cultivator and his family also live on rice is incidental, although without the traditional reliance of the local population on that grain the industry would probably not have developed. There is overlapping also when we find in certain areas that large estates under foreign management, devoted to a single commercial crop, have got into the habit of setting part of their holdings aside to permit the production of food for local consumption.

Nevertheless, the distinction is sound. Commercial agriculture develops in areas where the population has grown too large to be self-sustaining. Such a community may bethink itself of some crop which it is in an especially favorable position to produce, and specialize in that. And if this stratagem succeeds, the tendency will be to grow more and more for cash and less and less for the kitchen. After a time, the community, without giving up its dependency on agriculture for its livelihood, will have become quite incapable of going on without trade. If they specialize in some crop that is not food they will have to buy elsewhere a large part of what they eat. So food production itself may become a specialty. Let us envisage two areas, *A* and *B*. *A* produces tobacco, the larger part of which it sells to *B*. Before long, the people of *B* have become so accustomed to the use of tobacco, which they can only get through purchase, that it becomes a necessity for them to produce far more rice than they can consume. Now both districts have become dependent on exchange — but with a great difference: district *A*, which specialized in a non-essential crop, must continue to find customers for it or engage in some other trade or export labor power in order to live; district *B*, which found it easy to produce more food, must sell merely to maintain a higher standard of living. In the course of time, district *B* with its good arable land may have so increased in population that even the sale of a large part of its rice harvest every year no longer suffices to support the people in the mode of life to which they have become accustomed: now it is district *B* that has become "over-populated." And, as a matter of fact, most of the complaints about over-population in Southeast Asia today come from regions with an exuberant vegetation, lands that regularly produce two crops a year and flow with milk and honey, so to speak.

Take Burma, for example. Lower Burma is a country made up of the rich soil deposits of its great rivers, the Irrawaddy, the Sittang, and the Salween. This fertile valley is considered by many the best rice-growing land in the world. The crops were large enough to feed a sizable population and much of the land remained jungle because there was no necessity to reclaim it. Though there were crowded

populations in India and China, the international trade
in rice was necessarily small before the advent of the steamship. The cost of transportation was too high in relation to
the cost at which food could be produced elsewhere. But
in less than a hundred years Lower Burma had become
one of the great granaries of the world. Its rice exports
amounted to three and a half to four million tons a year.
Rangoon in the late 'thirties was one of the two or three
busiest ports in the world. The population of Lower Burma
had increased in proportion with the growing rice trade,
or perhaps a little more. The area under rice almost trebled
between 1891 and the middle 'thirties; and although the
country swarmed with immigrants from the northern
mountain districts and from China and India, almost one-
half of the total rice crop was exported. Then came the
depression. In April 1934, the price of rice was only two-
fifths of what it had been in 1929. The teeming population of Lower Burma no longer was the envy of the world.
"When paddy commands a good market," says a Rangoon
editor, "Burma is glad and prosperous; when it is not she
is sad and impoverished. Over 90 per cent of her people
are dependent on rice for a living." Instead of reducing the
area of land under rice, there was talk, just before the out-
break of war, of reclaiming more swamp land, though this
would have meant costly construction of river embank-
ments and drainage canals.

Now, let us look for a moment at Upper Burma, a poor
mountainous country, some of it rocky and some exces-
sively dry. The contrast between this area and Lower
Burma may be compared with that between New England
and Virginia in colonial days. In the north, possibilities of
large-scale cultivation were strictly limited. But many different crops that could not be grown so well in the warmer
lowland or which the lowland people, with their immense
staple crops, did not have the patience to cultivate, would

do moderately well. In Burma this meant, among other things, tree crops versus rice. Thus, although chronically over-populated in the past, Upper Burma became relatively prosperous in modern times, with exports of tea, oranges, lac, tung oil, cotton, beans, and tobacco. Just before the war broke out, promising experiments were going on with the cultivation of sugar, silk, peanuts, and a variety of fruits. As it diversified its agriculture, Upper Burma also went farther than the southern part of the country in developing small industries. Like the New Englanders in colonial days, the hill people were pushed by circumstances in the direction of progress. Visitors to northern Burma and the Shan States in the years just before the present war sometimes wrote about the orchards, the small farms, and the prosperous little towns as though we might expect a new California, a realm of intensive horticulture interspersed with industrial crops, to emerge there at any moment. Some of these pictures may have been overdrawn, but there are interesting possibilities; and these possibilities will depend a good deal on whether capital can be attracted for road building and other investments.

Similar contrasts are to be found in neighboring Thailand. There, also, rice has long been the principal crop and is now the basis of the country's economy. Most of it is grown on land watered by the great river system. In ancient days the Khmer people, who built the magnificent temples of Cambodia, had an extensive system of wet farming on the level lands. Being northerners originally, like their predecessors, the Thai did not quite know what to do with the enormously fertile inundated lands around the river deltas. Some of them they never reclaimed, although now the pressure of population in the central plain and in the delta areas is considerable.

For centuries the Thai cultivated only as much rice as they needed for their own food and left the rest of the land under jungle and forest. Then exports through Bangkok increased. And now the whole country depends on them. Rice cultivation became so profitable that the Thai no longer took the trouble to grow other foods. They got so taken up with their vast stretches of level rice paddies that they almost forgot what to do with sloping land or with land that was not flooded once a year. For the people of Lower and Central Thailand, rice growing has become a business. They are in it to make money. And so, when the world economic depression came, they were hit — not as the small farmer is hit who has his vegetable garden, his orchard, and his wood lot, to fall back upon, but as a business man is hit who has put his all in ostrich feathers a week before ostrich feathers go out of style. In this part of Thailand, the effect of the depression was similar to that in Burma. Up to the time when the war upset everything, the agricultural experts looked feverishly for new crops that might be introduced to make the growers less dependent on the unreliable world price of rice. The Government, thoroughly alarmed, sent its agents around to preach the growing of more food for home consumption. Their pamphlets on the homely virtues of beans are worthy of the best American models in that field of literature; their commendations of the dairy industry are poetry.

In Indo-China, too, we have something of the lowland-upland contrast, the contrast between a rural life sustained by large-scale production of a staple crop and one diversified by the requirements and uses of different soils and exposures. Rice provides four-fifths of the people's diet and seven-tenths of the country's exports. If you think of farming as pottering around in fields and pastures, growing this and that, cutting hay one week and picking apples another, then most of the people in Cochin-China and in Annam can hardly be called farmers. One kind of crop is all they have ever learned to raise. If for any reason the export market for their product were to drop out they would be as helpless as a bus driver in a horse stable.

In Indo-China, too, "over-population" first developed in the river-delta regions. The density of land occupancy here is in some places greater than that of a Chicago suburb. Yet no other industries have grown up to keep the people employed. Just as in Burma and in Thailand, there is a tendency now for the highland populations to grow beyond the numbers which the traditional land uses can support. Since the fields are not naturally flooded or of the same fertility as the river-deposited lowland soils, here too poverty can be combated only with skill, willingness to experiment, and investment of capital. None of these three things has thus far been available to a sufficient degree. There are not even good enough transportation facilities to bring rice from the lowlands to the uplands. So, although all sorts of valuable crops are grown in the rolling country, none of them is produced in large enough quantities to become an important article of export, even to neighboring China.

There is, then, an inner maladjustment in the agricultural economy of each of the three countries of Farther India. Its cause is only in part geographical; and it has nothing to do with the character of the populations, which are different from each other in origins and in their present ways of living. Rather, the cause lies in the fact that all these countries south of China have been warped in their economic development by the commercial expansion of Europe. They have come under the influence of European powers later than the island archipelagos of the South China Sea. Burma until 1937 was an outlying province of India. Indo-China was occupied by France more as a next-best since France could not secure for herself a slice of China. Thailand, the former Siam, escaped being attached altogether since neither Great Britain nor France cared to make war on the other for its possession. Nevertheless, it was European trade, European ships, and European capital which first gave all three of these countries the impetus to that concentrated production of rice which has pretty nearly come to be their undoing. In all three countries, the governments were constantly in need of more revenue and encouraged those types of enterprise from which a toll could be collected most easily. In all three countries labor immigration was favored until it became a threat to the safety of the state. Absentee landlords, absentee capitalists, contract laborers who sent most of their wages away to their homeland — even absentee governments — these were the forces that shaped the economic development of the three countries.

When during the recent world economic depression reliance on a few export crops led to inevitable disaster, it was too late to right what was wrong in the economic setup. Foreign laborers might be sent home. Agricultural agents might be sent around to preach the gospel of rotation of crops. A few promising peasant sons might even be sent to school to learn new agricultural methods. Plans might be laid for new credit institutions, for curbing abuses, for the construction of roads and railroads and great waterworks. None of this could make up for long years of neglect. Despite the great natural wealth of the region, the people of all three countries are poor, ignorant, unaccustomed to co-operation beyond the confines of the community, distrustful of their respective governments.

Economic Dualism

The "dualism" of Netherlands India's economy cannot be charged altogether against its foreign rule. Thailand, which has never been subjected to a Western power, is even more definitely chained to the world market. Even if no profits were drained off to enrich European investors, the two economic systems — the native and the commercial —

would continue to exist side by side. And it really makes little difference to the overburdened small man whether the landlord and the middleman who get the lion's share of what he produces live in Amsterdam or in Bangkok. The returns from peasant production suffice if they provide an adequate but modest livelihood for the cultivator, but the returns from commercial production must in addition support the inflated standard of living of those whose main function is precisely that of swelling — of waxing fat on the blood they suck from the workers. In this sense the great port cities of Southeast Asia are as parasitical as those of Europe.

Of course, many merchants are hard workers; and there are loafers among the peasants. All categories overlap; you cannot say of one class that it is purely creative and of another that it is purely vegetative. It would be difficult to say whether a Javanese farmer who sells a large part of what he grows in order to pay his taxes and to purchase manufactured articles, but who has never seen a city and has no idea what becomes of his rice after he has sold it, does or does not belong to the capitalist system. Perhaps we had better let him decide that for himself: if he shows no hankering for things much different from those his grandfather has enjoyed and is happy to spend his life pottering around the village and its immediate environment, then he probably is pre-capitalist in his functions and in his thinking even though he makes use of money. The man who lives in a pre-capitalist world is not thereby excluded from world civilization. He may be linked to millions of people through common language, religion, consciousness of race, fear of the same demons and enjoyment of the same puppet-shows. Indeed, some of the most complex social arrangements for agricultural production — in the matter of irrigation, for instance — may belong to the non-capitalistic side of the dual economy.

On the other hand, take one of the native sultans under
the British or the Netherlands flag. He may live in Oriental
splendor, enjoy the arts and pleasures native to his land,
scrupulously observe the rites of Islam, keep away as much
as possible from Europeans, and know little of any European language. Yet this man, with a fortune enlarged a
thousandfold through its investment in sugar or rubber
or tobacco plantations established in his territory by foreigners, certainly belongs to the capitalist system, is in
fact one of its chief beneficiaries. The Sultan of Johore
ruled over a jungle before rubber was introduced. The Sultan of Deli (in Sumatra), also grown fabulously wealthy
from rubber, and this in a single generation, hears the
cash register ring each time you light a cigar with a Sumatra
wrapper. His father lived little better than a peasant though
his subjects prostrated themselves when he came down the
road, which by the way they no longer do.

These subjects, and those of all the other potentates, remain poor. They may be a little more secure; but they can
hardly be unperturbed as the plantations extend farther
into the forest, and hordes of immigrant unbelievers are
settled among them to make wealth for white foreigners.
Once these woods were theirs. The Sultan was one of them
though elevated high above them by his rank. Now they are
no longer even in the center of the scene. They are poor
relatives, kept out of sight. And like poor relatives some
of them have sneaked among the wage-earners, undigni-
fied though it be; and some have wandered off to join the
footloose proletariat.

What distinguishes the Netherlands Indies and the
Philippines from the other countries of Southeast Asia is
that the native peasant is somewhat better protected by
anti-foreign land laws as he gradually gets drawn into the
modern commercial system. The dualism will be there as
long as some of the people work on the land to earn wages

while others work on it as part of their way of life. Now, the first consequence of the existence of the two economies side by side is that what is good news for the one may be bad news for the other. In the United States, when there is a good year for cotton — high yields and an attractive world demand — everybody is the gainer: northern farmers, who do not grow cotton, cash in on the prosperity of the southern farmers by selling them more wheat, fruit, meat, cheese, hides, and a hundred other things that grow better or are produced more cheaply in the north than in the south. But when the coconut growers of Netherlands India get a good price for copra, large numbers of native peasants are the losers, because they are consumers of coconut oil and have to pay approximately the world price for it, but have nothing to sell to the coconut growers. There is nothing a government can do about this or about even more serious discrepancies between the price fluctuations of what the common peasant has to sell and must buy. But it can protect him somewhat against the danger that large-scale foreign enterprise will cut in on his resources for making a living. Above all, it can protect him in his enjoyment of the land itself. And the two governments of which we are now speaking are doing that with fair success.

Foreign ownership of land is not, of course, the only factor that determines the extent to which capitalism encroaches upon the native economy. The distribution of land ownership as between the native users of the soil may be equally disturbing. Out of five Filipinos only two own land and house, and two more own the houses they live in — more aptly described as shacks — but not the land they till. In the richest sugar-cane district, only one in ten of the families owns any part of the occupied land, and almost one-third own neither house nor land. This may not be so bad if you think of a country where it is customary for farmers to rent their farms. But we are speaking here of a

purely agricultural country cultivated for many generations by the ancestors of those who now live there, all of
them simple peasants with no property worth mentioning
if they do not own a piece of land. In the province of Nueva
Ecija, in central Luzon, artificial irrigation at public expense has made a fertile soil available for rice cultivation.
But less than one-third of the families supposed to benefit
from this public improvement own any of the land. It is
in this province that a number of peasant uprisings have
taken place in recent years; and the main cause of discontent is that the people who at one time owned the land
they tilled now have to pay exorbitant rents for it. One
cause of increased tenancy is the growth of population.
For several generations, now, there has been a reduction in
death rates without a corresponding decline in birth rates.
As a result, the demand for land goes up and with it the
price of land. In the more crowded sections of Java, of
Indo-China, of the Philippines, the married son no longer
can buy land enough to bring up a brood of children of
his own. So he rents additional land, and rents rise pro-
portionately. It is at this point that the peasant falls into
the clutches of the usurer. He has to sell or mortgage what
little land he has in order to pay his debt, and sometimes
merely the interest on his debt. Land ownership gets concentrated in the hands of a few wealthy local squires or of
corporations whose large-scale enterprises soon transform
the once free farmer into a wage-slave. The Philippine
Government has tried to stem this trend by breaking up
and selling the large estates which it had taken over from
the Church. However, these did not provide enough land
to fulfill such a purpose, and it was difficult to prevent the
land from falling again into the hands of large owners. In
fact, most of the sales have been made for the growing of
sugar and other industrial crops, not for mixed farming.

In Cochin-China, rents of one-half of the rice harvest are

common. As a result, many of the small tenants there, too, are permanently in debt to their landlords. Immigration has added to the natural growth of population a pressure on land values and sent them sky-high. Again, the measures taken by the Government are insufficient: a little construction here and there to drain and irrigate more land for rice-growing, or a start with the establishment of rural credit banks to make the peasants a little less dependent on the moneylenders. As it is, they can barely afford to eat of the rice they grow.

In Lower Burma and in southern Thailand, the best rice land is in the hands of absentee landlords. Tenants must renew their leases from year to year. If they are successful in raising a good crop they have to pay that much more rent the next year. In one district near Bangkok more than four out of every five farmers are tenants — an unusual proportion in a country where commercialized farming is so recent. Naturally, a large proportion of these people are in debt, both to alien (Chinese) and to native usurers.

In British Malaya, no serious development of commercial farming by native Malay peasants has taken place at all. Instead, the Government has invited Indians and Chinese to come in to man the big plantations. Many of these have settled down and are now in possession of most of the medium-sized farms. It may be said of Malaya that it is part jungle and part industrial plant, with farming, as we understand the term, only as a side-show.

In Netherlands India more attention has been paid to the improvement of native farming than in any of the other countries of Southeast Asia. Serious and successful efforts have been made to hold in check the tendency to concentration of ownership. Considering the density of population in many districts, the proportion of tenant-farmed land is not large. Where tenancy does predominate because of exceptional population pressure, as in Central Java and around Batavia, rents usually rise as high as one-half of the harvest. Naturally, the Javanese who pay these rents are poor. In the so-called Outer Islands — that is, everywhere except Java and Madura — relatively simple traditional peasant farming still prevails amid huge estates devoted to commercial crops, crops owned, of course, by non-natives and often manned if not with immigrants then with contract laborers brought in from the crowded sections of Java.

Sometimes those who talk about the troubles of Asiatic peasants blame their difficulties on their thriftlessness. The peasants would not have lost their land, they say, if they had not fallen into debt. And they have fallen into debt because they are lacking in foresight. I think it would be more correct to say that they have fallen into debt because it was in the interest of some people that they should. In the older Malay society there was no particular advantage in having a man in your debt. You would rather he paid you off as soon as possible. Islam prohibits taking interest because of its anti-democratic tendency. But under the new dispensation, with the importance which cash crops have attained in the economy, you can go on making the debtor work for you year after year simply by seeing to it that he never produces quite enough to make both ends meet and so must borrow each year to keep himself and his family going. If the interest on the debt is made high enough, such a man can never keep enough of his product for his own use to see the year through.

Usury and indebtedness seldom go alone. Once a man has had to sell his land and must pay rent in order to live, the landlord and the moneylender between them can squeeze him dry. He gets as little, or less, for his labor as though he worked for them on a wage basis. And when this has gone on for some time and enough farmers have been

reduced to that state, the landlord and the moneylender —
often two-in-one — may be rich enough to move into town
and lead a gentleman's life.

Factories in the Fields

In addition to the distinction between peasant farming
and commercial farming there is also a distinction between
commercial and industrial farming. Rice cultivation, as
carried on in Farther India, is commercial farming, even
when the grain is hulled and sorted in a local mill before
it is exported. The method of producing the crop still is
traditional, though now applied on an enormous scale.
Industry is a matter of refinement and mechanization of
methods in accordance with scientific principles, above all
of specialization of functions. The scale of operations is
immaterial. Some of the large plantations in Southeast
Asia are simply overgrown farms. Many more belong, together with the factories, the shipyards and the mines, in
the realm of industry. It just happens that they make use
of rural labor; but so did the early cotton mills, and so do
the canning plants of the United States to this day.

The sugar plantation with its crushing mill, the coconut
plantation equipped to dry the kernels and press out the
oil, the tobacco plantation with its drying and sorting sheds,
the tea garden, and many other large-scale enterprises in
tropical Asia to some extent re-create the synthesis of primitive peasant farming: they employ skill to assist nature and
skill to fabricate her gifts into things useful to man. There
still are gaps. The products of these establishments do not
appear on your table all wrapped in the original cellophane. But already the rubber people of Akron own and
run some plantations, and some of the sugar centrals in the
Philippines are financially connected with the great American refineries. More industrial than agricultural is the
production of sugar, rubber, tobacco, teak — and in some

parts of the region coconut, palm oil, coffee, tea, tung oil, gambier, spices, pineapples and other fruit.

There is, of course, no clear division between industrialized and ordinary commercial farming. The same kind of crop, not only coffee but also sugar, for instance, may in one place be produced mainly by peasants in small lots and near-by in huge quantities on scientifically managed estates. A combination of the latter with production on estate-supervised peasant-owned farms is today the most characteristic form of large-scale enterprise in the Asiatic tropics. You get the general idea when you think of the clothing industry in America in the latter part of the nineteenth century: it had not yet emerged altogether from the home-industry stage — which itself was a development from the pre-industrial tailor shop. There were few factories, and these were at the same time the employers of a multitude of small shops that contracted either for the making of whole garments or only for some particular operation on the garments. But the introduction of more costly machinery, more extensive use of power, and what you may call scientific management, destroyed the advantages of low rents, long hours, and starvation wages, that had kept the sweatshops going for many decades; and today when you buy a ready-made suit you may feel fairly certain that it has been produced under tolerably decent conditions. Of course, the small man who receives his materials and his instructions from a big concern — sometimes also his implements which he either rents or pays for in instalments — is in a very different position from the independent producer. He does not know the market; often he does not understand why one method rather than another is insisted upon, or how the price or piece rate offered him is arrived at. He is already half-way to the status of a wage-earner who merely does what he is told.

Thus the peasant who makes a contract with a neighboring estate. There is, for example, the Javanese who grows coconuts and sells them to a nearby mill which dries and presses the kernel (copra) to prepare the oil for export. This man formerly grew coconuts for his own use. Then, being perhaps more successful than others or having a little more ground around his house, he specialized in growing coconuts. He sold the surplus of his crop in the market where it was bought by wholesalers who sold what they collected to even larger dealers. Then these dealers, dissatisfied with the quality of the nuts, or for other reasons, set up estates where they could experiment with the growing of trees on a larger scale and under scientific supervision. But the demand for copra and coconut oil kept on growing, and so the same people went on buying from the peasants. At first, it made no difference to the small man that now he was on the outer edge of a very large business. While the market kept up, he still got his price — around 1921 about twenty-five guilders for a thousand nuts, from which the mill could produce about 200 kg. of copra. Then, for reasons about which he knew nothing, the world market collapsed. All prices went down, but especially those of colonial products that competed with home products in the industrial countries. Under our own tariff law, for example, coconut oil was imported free of duty until 1921. It was used to make soap and in its refined form served as an ingredient in various margarines and lard substitutes, and in the making of confectionery. American producers of cottonseed and other vegetable oils after the World War wanted the American market for themselves. So a duty of two cents a pound was imposed on coconut oil, and our imports dropped from sixty-three million pounds in 1920 to three million pounds in 1922. By 1927, the imports of this oil were so small that they were not even listed separately any more. But the Oriental and South Seas producers still had other customers, in both Asia and Europe. These

customers some years later also got frightened by the shrink-
age of world trade and either tried to substitute other products for coconut oil or to limit their purchases of it to their
own colonies. The economic depression from which all the
world began to suffer in the late 'twenties was an inevitable
result of all the tariff walls that had been built up in this
period of growing economic isolation. For large producing
countries with no privileged market of their own — such
as the Philippines had in the United States — the situation
became calamitous. They might eat more of their own products, but they could not suddenly change from a diet of
rice, which had to be partly imported, to one of coconuts,
tea, rubber, and mattress stuffing (kapok).

To return to our peasant on the southeast coast of Java
— he had to go on selling his coconuts because he needed
the money to buy food: rice and corn and cassava. He could
eat a little less rice which was brought from a distance and
a little more corn and cassava which were grown locally.
But he had to have money. Therefore, he sold his thousand
nuts, which had netted him twenty-five guilders in 1921, for
seven and a half in 1935. He could not buy enough food
with that, though the price of rice had gone down from
about seven guilders in the fall of 1921 to not quite two
in that of 1935, and other prices in proportion. So, after
many prayers which remained unanswered, he at last decided to sell his buffalo. In 1921, an animal of its years and
strength would have brought one hundred and twenty
guilders; now he could get only ten for it, and that was
more than some of his neighbors got for theirs. What else
did he have to sell? He had been making roof tiles off and
on, and for these he used to get eleven guilders per thousand in the local market. But now his neighbors were as
poor as he, and there was little building. He was lucky
when a local mosque bought his titles at a guilder and a half
per thousand.

Our peasant was no longer able to buy anything but necessary food for himself and his family. The wall-lamp which
he used to keep burning all through the night he now filled
with vegetable oil, made in the neighborhood, because he
no longer could afford kerosene. That, too, cost money; so
he made himself a smaller lamp consisting of a bottle and
a tiny wick, and this he blew out before he went to bed.
He no longer bought matches but made fire once a day
with an old-fashioned flint and tinder from the sugar palm.
The family now practically lived on cassava and *gaplek* —
which is the dried root of cassava. He also grew a little corn,
but that was still saleable, so it went to the market despite
its relatively high food value. Sometimes his wife travelled
all day to the market town and back again all the next day,
because she could get a few cents more there for the baskets
of corn and pepper she had to sell. But even so, the holiday
season approached, and for the first time in their lives the
family had to go without new clothes.

This Javanese peasant and millions like him in the Philippines and in other countries of Southeast Asia, too, are
in a position comparable with that of the sweatshop workers
in our own country before manufacturing industry became
organized and threw off the chrysalis of its humble origin
in home industry. The small man's unstandardized products do not command a high enough price to repay him
for his labor. In Netherlands India, the livelihood of millions of peasants was, if not wiped out, at least made extremely difficult by the world economic depression. All
their Government could do for them was to resettle some
of those from the most densely populated districts (where
they could not get land to grow more food for themselves)
in the Outer Provinces where land was still to be had for
the clearing; and to show many more how they might re-
establish themselves as independent farmers without rely-
ing on cash crops at all. But the great majority of small

cultivators in Netherlands India have not found it easy to return to the ways of their fathers, which meant doing without many manufactured articles to which they had become accustomed. Nor could they help seeing that their children did not prosper on the vitamin- and mineral-poor diet which was all they could now afford.

Peasants in the other countries of the region whose existence has become partly dependent on foreign trade and on the large enterprises that bought their cash crops fared even worse than the Javanese. They can neither go back to the old ways of self-sufficiency nor, unaided, go forward into an age of thoroughly commercialized and industrialized agriculture. The only possibility of improving their lot lies in the absorption of many of them in enterprises so large and so well financed, so important for the economy of the distant mother country, that their government cannot allow them to go down but in one way or other will prop up prices.

VI

CRAFTSMEN AND ARTISTS

MODERN industries have grown from the modest rice fields, gardens, and orchards of Malay peasants. Others of the commercial staple crops, like coffee and rubber, were introduced from outside for the purpose of feeding foreign trade; and some of these, too, have given rise to industries. In the same way, it is possible to distinguish between industries that have grown out of old-established native handicrafts and others introduced full-fledged, either to save the importation of manufactured articles or to give additional value to local raw materials before they are exported.

When people speak of the "industrialization" of Indo-China or Netherlands India, they usually have in mind the heavy industries and other power-using industries, such as cotton mills, where manufacture is from the start on a large scale and has no direct relation with previous forms of production in the country. These new industries are the most important from the standpoint of foreign trade, of public finance and even from that of national defense, as in the case of metal and cement works. But from the standpoint of the native people the mechanized industries that are closely linked with the traditional crafts may have a greater immediate importance. They affect the lives of the people more closely, offer opportunities to larger numbers, and more directly affect standards of living.

We have become accustomed to think in such polarities
as town and country, agriculture and industry, and so forth.
These are simplifications, used to help us in our social
thinking. Actually, there are no such sharp contrasts. Towns
are overgrown villages, for the most part; and industry has
its origin in the needs of men living close to nature. The
principal occupation of early man was that of pottering
about. Sometimes he invented a tool, and then he discovered that it had more than one use. The same chipped
piece of flint which served as a spearhead with which he
could fish could also be attached to an arrow with which
he could shoot birds. A knife fashioned to cut meat could
also be used to dress the skin. A hatchet shaped to fell small
trees could, in case of need, serve as a weapon of defense.
The present war has forced on us a similar multiple use of
utensils.

In tropical Asia to this day a single knife often fulfills
an astonishing variety of agricultural and household uses.
Not only the primitive tribesman in the mountain but the
Filipino townsman, too, would rather go without any of his
other possessions than without his knife. He has a hundred
uses for it and feels lost without it. Of this, General Mac-
Arthur gave an interesting bit of testimony in a report to
the War Department on March 6, 1942. He referred to a
Japanese order to Filipinos in occupied areas to surrender
all their weapons, including ornamental and utilitarian
knives of every description.

> "This order," wrote the General, "would operate to
> deprive the Filipino of his *bolo* which, while some-
> times used as a weapon, customarily serves as a tool. It
> is universally used as an industrial and agricultural
> implement. With his *bolo* the Filipino farmer builds
> his house, fences his stock and harvests his crops.
> Hence, if he surrenders his *bolo* he will find it difficult
> to earn a living."

We cannot, then, distinguish between different kinds of human activity merely by the tools they employ. The foundations of industry lie in the home, in the fields, in the jungle, and on ships. The hunter and nomad, the squatter, the herder of animals, the sailor, the merchant, and the settled agriculturist — all have contributed to it. To them goes the credit for the basic inventions.

In a region still for the most part inhabited by simple peasants, with more primitive groups in the uncleared forests and on rocky mountain slopes, all the stages of industrial development can be seen. And, interestingly enough, we can trace industrial growth backward and forward: there are mechanized industries grafted on the older crafts, without roots in them; but there are also the beginnings of industries that have been transferred long ago from the Orient to the Occident and seen their greatest development there. An example of the first would be the metal shops where you find Orientals bending over their benches to reproduce as best they can and with inferior tools such Occidental objects as flashlights or enamelware. An example of the second would be the shop where puppets are cut from animal skins, predecessor of all our motion picture studios.

But most significant are those budding industries which have both their beginnings and their maturity in the minds and hands of the Asiatic craftsmen. For example, in the Philippine pavilion at the San Francisco International Exposition of 1939, the most impressive exhibits and those most certainly pointing to a great industrial future for the Islands were those which represented new and advanced uses for local materials through ingenious developments of old-established local crafts. Some of these manufactures may owe their introduction to foreign initiative, but most of them, except for the use of power equipment, have remained Philippine in character.

An illustration of the former is the construction, in 1940, of the first of a number of cellulose factories in the Philippines, to utilize bagasse, the fiber by-product of sugar cane when the juice is extracted. What to do with it has always been a problem. American sugar growers in Hawaii worked on that problem, too, some years ago. At that time, the material — in quantity about one quarter of the cane milled — was used as fuel or was exported to the mainland for the making of a rough cardboard. The sugar people thought it should be possible to find a more valuable use for it. In the Philippines, two other basic materials, salt and lime, also are abundantly available, and because of the high cost of importing cellulose articles, such as cellophane, paper and cardboard, rayon, and film, the door seems open to a variety of new industries. The husks of coconuts, used as fuel, represent another potential raw material which only modern industry with its elaborate chemical processes can utilize. The same company which started to make cellulose in 1940, that year also started to use the coir fiber of the coconut husks to produce a fabric strong enough to take the place of jute and burlap imported from India. Both industries, when fully developed, may employ large numbers of Filipinos and also help to bring down the cost of packing other Philippine products.

Another incipient industry is that of shell-craft. As you walk down the streets of Manila, you see many windows made of small squares of thin, opalescent shell, set into wooden frames. The shells are obtained at low tide, and the flat squares are cut out nowadays with the aid of machine saws which make the product one of standard sizes. I do not know whether Filipinos or Spaniards originally discovered this advantageous use of sea-shells: they let in enough light but effectively shut out the heat. Sometimes a window is made like a large screen, composed of hundreds of these little squares, and folds back after the heat of day to convert the room into an open porch. These panes are now made also into lamp shades and screens in modern designs, are already becoming popular in other countries and ought to be a regular export article — along with their hardwood frames — to southern China and other warm countries. In this respect, the shell-pane business is more promising than the shell and pearl buttons of which we imported nearly a million gross from the Philippines in a recent year but for which it might be difficult to find substitute markets when the special import privilege enjoyed for a few years more under the Independence Act will have disappeared.

Philippine rattan work, too, though still carried on almost entirely by hand, promises the growth of an important industry once it is adequately financed for large-scale production. Well-designed rattan porch furniture still is an expensive luxury in the Occident; but with the changes in our living habits — and especially the large increase in outdoor life and the construction of homes with less enclosed and more open space — the demand for sturdily constructed furniture that will stand outdoor or semi-outdoor wear is growing. The Philippine product is less delicate than some other types, and answers the purposes of a mass supply. But to bring the price within reach of the masses, manufacture will have to be on a larger scale than hitherto, and standardized machine processes will have to be substituted for some of the hand labor. Even with the elimination of much of the hand work that goes into the making of this furniture, it still provides work for many thousands and may do so for many tens of thousands.

That this is the result of cheapened production and larger sales is shown by the recent history of Philippine straw-hat manufacture. Likewise deriving from a native craft, this industry has evolved simultaneously in two directions: for connoisseurs it has remained a source of what can only be described as an art product, a hat of exceedingly fine weave; for mass consumption it has developed into a partly mechanized industry supplying a serviceable article in standardized models at low cost.

From Household Craft to Industry

This tendency of twofold evolution, on the artistic and on the industrial side, is rather general throughout Southeast Asia. In Netherlands India, the commercial possibilities of native crafts are better understood than in the Philippines. For a good many years, improvement of the household crafts has been a recognized part of the educational system. Teachers of home crafts are trained at Bandoeng, the center of technical education in Java. These specialists conduct institutes and extension courses elsewhere. While no attempt has been made to westernize such crafts as weaving or pottery, improved processes have been introduced, and inexpensive handlooms of an approved type are sold at cost price. The Department of Economic Affairs has a special bureau charged with the encouragement of the native industries. The Government utilized the depression years to intensify the improvement of native agriculture. In connection with this it also promoted an intensification of native industries, so as to make the islands less dependent on imports of manufactured articles and to pave the way for new export industries. Partly as a result of these efforts, about a million and a half guilders' worth of batik textiles were exported in 1939 to Singapore for distribution in Malaya. At the same time, weaving, pleating, umbrella-making, zinc and tin work, soap, ceramics, hide and leather tanning and dyeing, furniture and woodwork, and tobacco manufactures in the late 'thirties took a new lease on life. Exports, until the Japanese occupation put an end to all this economic growth, went mainly from Java to the outlying islands and to Malaya.

During the depression years, the Netherlands Indian authorities made a great effort to stimulate the production and export sale of Javanese batiks. You may remember having seen batik sarongs (for use in place of bathing trunks) and shawls sprouting all over Fifth Avenue at that time. By the way, the prevalence of blue in Javanese batiks and *kains,* as also in the dyed fabrics of China, is not an inherited preference but results from the salesmanship of that ubiquitous blues-maker, the Deutsche Farben-Industrie Gesellschaft.

Left to themselves, native home crafts do not, of course, produce an over-supply for sale abroad. Usually they are carried on for local consumption. The weaver, dyer, potter, silversmith, wood carver, and blacksmith know exactly what the market will absorb, if they do not, in fact, produce only to order. In the larger towns of Southeast Asia it is customary for the workers in each trade to combine in a trade guild. As in medieval Europe, such a guild keeps an eye on the quality of its members' work, so that standards of workmanship — and prices — shall not decline. Unfortunately that has happened nevertheless, especially in those crafts which were swerved from their loyalty to traditional standards by the rather sudden growth, since the World War, of an indiscriminating tourist and curio business. However, in justice to the authorities charged with the expansion of foreign — especially American — trade in art goods to relieve the economic depression in Java, it should be added that the Javanese wood carvings, jewelry, batik and other wares that have appeared in such greatly increased quantities on the counters of our department stores are usually still, despite their low prices, of honest workmanship.

Judgments differ as regards the influence of widened trade relations on the native crafts. Some take a pessimistic view. Imported manufactured articles, they say, are so much

liked by the natives that they overlook their obvious de-
fects, such as poor construction and lack of durability in a
tropical climate. Objects that reflect Western civilization,
even when they come from Japan or from Chinese factories
in Singapore, are deemed superior to the traditionally
home-made or locally made articles which they replace.
Whole areas of native production have been evacuated before such importations and before the competition of immigrant Chinese and Indian artisans and small manufacturers. In Johore Bahru, the capital of Johore, I noticed
that even the repair of Malay buildings of native construction was being done by Chinese carpenters; and all the furniture for sale was Chinese. This predominance of immigrant labor in the skilled trades may be seen in all the
countries of Southeast Asia.

The contact with modern civilization, both Western and
Far Eastern, makes the indigenous people rely on the work
of others. It also sometimes makes them ashamed of the old
things they used to cherish, and over-anxious for new things.
So I was told again and again. But this is a one-sided picture. Even from the standpoint of those who deplore the
natives' "laziness," it may be a good thing for them to have
new wants — for, in order to satisfy them, they will work
more regularly. The restless man is precisely the one who
will soonest overcome the prejudice against the discipline
required by modern enterprise of any sort. He knows what
he wants and is willing to work for it. It is true, some of
the old crafts may go by the board, but is not that the way
of progress? What is happening is that the Malay people are
advancing along the road of specialization. They have not
yet gone far on it; but then they are not very far advanced
in their use of manufactured articles either. They are too
poor.

You must not overlook, I was told on one occasion, the
fact that those crafts which you so much admire as tradi-

tional and as closely adapted to the needs of the people are
not always indigenous and may be the results of earlier culture importations. Often the characteristic handiwork of
a particular population group or district is a mixture of arts
brought by that group from an earlier home and of arts
found among their peasant neighbors. Thus, for example,
the textile arts of the Thai in what until recently was a part
of Indo-China seem to be entirely their own; but what they
know of carpentry, iron work and jewelry made of precious
metals, they have learned from the Chinese or the Annamites. Again, all over Southeast Asia you can find the
large pottery jars of Pegu in Burma. They are deservedly
popular because they hold more liquid or grain than any
vessel the potters of Java or of Malaya can contrive. But
if it is a good thing for the Burmese to export these jars,
should we not remember that they would not have had this
industry at all had they not earlier imported their pots from
China and eventually learned from Talaing captives how to
make them? Moreover, the use of Pegu jars, or *martabans,*
has not prevented the Malay potters elsewhere from becoming pretty good at some ceramic specialty of their own.

A few years ago, Burmese jewelry was fashionable in Europe and America. But their textiles are not fashionable
abroad. The Burmese home-woven silks and cottons do not
have much of a foreign market because they have nothing
distinctive to recommend them. On the other hand, their
lacquer work, jewelry and pottery — also some of the carved
ivory and bronze — enjoy a foreign market because they
are exceptionally good, not as a matter of taste but as a
matter of workmanship. And so the Burmese, on their part,
let the Chinese and Indians make their slippers and much
of their furniture, because they are good at it; they continue
to make for themselves almost every other article of general use. And, despite the presence of so many foreign artisans in their midst, it is by no means a foregone conclu-

sion that the Burmese will not in time work up others of their many traditional crafts into export industries. The Government and the commercial organizations have hardly begun to look beyond the large cities for household arts that are intrinsically important and have export possibilities. Nevertheless, the main task in relation to some of these crafts, especially weaving, still is that of improving methods for domestic use, so as to make the people less dependent on those imported articles which, because of their shoddy quality, are too dear even at the low prices paid for them.

Generally speaking it is true, of course, that the most admirable crafts are those which use local materials. For that circumstance alone insures that skills are handed down from one generation to another and thus perfected in the course of time. The Moi women of Indo-China, for example, use many dyes for their cotton cloths, each of them carefully distilled from some local vegetable substance. When dyes are imported, such local arts are easily lost. In central Borneo, an elaborate preparation of the inner bark of certain trees is used to produce a serviceable textile fiber which, however, easily splits and therefore must be reinforced with threads made from palm fibers. This and other uses of locally available fibers would soon be forgotten, as in other parts of the world, if cheap imported cottons could easily be substituted. But the Moi who import dyes from China probably can give more time to the weaving of their usually rather coarse cloth; and the Dyak women of Borneo who buy cheap cottons from Chinese peddlers have merely changed their methods: instead of using palm fiber, they now use narrow strips of cotton cloth to fortify their bark cloth, and so probably get a better lasting fabric.

In short, the admiration which we feel for people who make ingenious uses of the materials close at hand must not become a shibboleth — as though it were a sin against the spirit of Art to take advantage of new materials or new methods. For instance, the best of the various fiber cloths of the Philippine Islands probably is not the famous *piña*, or pineapple, cloth, but the *husi*, a cloth made on the island of Panay of banana fiber blended with Chinese silk. And it should be remembered that the Philippine fiber cloths, so far from being altogether superseded by imported cotton cloths — as well they might have been after three hundred years and more — still provide three-fourths of the materials worn by the Filipinos and have begun to be exported as well. Not only this, but the Philippine fiber cloths, with and without admixture of cotton, provide the base for some of the most exquisite native embroidery.

The embroidery industry was introduced in the Philippines as one of the long chain of stop-overs in the perennial search of that industry for cheap labor — from Madeira to the Near East to southern China. But in the Philippines it did not kill the more refined craft, which is partly native and partly cultivated in the convents. On the contrary, the fact that the Filipinos already were good embroiderers in Spanish times made it possible for them to rise quickly above the low level of the tawdry export trade forced on them by the Syrian-American factors; and so this trade has wandered off in search of yet cheaper labor, while Philippine embroidery once more enjoys a high reputation. As three million dollars of American capital are invested in the industry, efforts will no doubt be made to help it survive any change in the tariff law.

Home Industry and Foreign Trade

Curiously enough, the combination of native and imported purposes and techniques was responsible for yet other developments of what once were home industries with only a local market. Because they know how to handle brittle leaf fibers and also how to weave bamboo and other reeds into building materials that will stand up for a long time, the Filipinos have become the world's experts in what may be called structural weaving. I have already mentioned furniture and hats. There has begun also a foreign trade in various kinds of mats, in pocketbooks and rope baskets, and many other articles designed for Occidental use. In a sense, the remarkable growth of the Philippine cordage industry — owing its origin to the needs of Spanish shipping, and its development to the good quality of its product — may be said also to have arisen from the humble home industries of the Filipinos, from the expertness which they have acquired in the handling of many different fibers. (Embroideries, in 1940, made up 4 per cent of Philippine exports, cordage 1.5 per cent.)

Although the need was not as urgent as in Netherlands India, the Philippine Government also has been searching for new opportunities to build up the home industries. It was not, however, so much with a view to exports — though these might come later — that the Bureau of Commerce a few years ago explored the possibilities. It found that if the competition of cheap Japanese imports of substitute articles could be overcome, perhaps by means of higher tariff rates, the home market for a great variety of articles was well worth cultivating. There was plenty of skilled labor in the villages, and abundant raw material, both widely distributed over the islands. I myself have no idea what some of these materials are which the Bureau mentions in one of its reports, so I will give the whole list: rattan, bamboo, coconut, nipa, wood, scrap iron, cotton, leather, clays, ticug, cassava, pandan, maguey, kapok, buri, hemp, abaca, shell, jusi and piña, nito, fruits, and fish. As regards the food products, some of my Filipino friends were financially interested in canning factories; but since fresh fruit is to be had all the year around in every part of the Islands, the only point in developing a fruit canning industry would be for export. There is certainly a potential market. With their own cane sugar, and with their variety of tropical fruit, the Filipino canners might repeat the success that has attended the canning and export of tropical fruits in Hawaii. But to create a market means advertising; and the industry cannot develop in a big way until there is capital enough to do this on a large scale.

The Philippine Government is more concerned with giving the agricultural workers something to do in their spare time and has started in a modest way to encourage producers' associations to improve and standardize the products of certain cottage industries, to provide marketing services, and to help obtain the necessary capital. The one thing most lacking is organizing talent and disinterested leadership. And that cannot be created overnight.

Much less thought has been given to the need for modern business organization than to the technical industrial requirements. There are those rather romantically inclined people who would preserve the native arts in all their purity, at all costs. They frown on the use of foreign dyes by the Javanese batik workers, of Chinese silk by the Moi or Dyak weaver, of Swiss yarns by the Filipino embroiderer, and so forth. They would keep the native workers, millions of them, isolated from the world of modern trade, themselves museum pieces of pre-industrial civilizations. They forget that the greatest developments in all the arts have resulted from contact between different cultures. One might even go so far as to say that it is only through such contact that art keeps alive.

It would be easy to spend many chapters on the deeper aspects of this theme. Suffice it to point out that at about the same time that American Indians learned to use factory-made beads in many artistic ways which would never have occurred to the bead manufacturers. Western decorators incorporated oriental lacquer work in artistic furniture the very purpose of which Asiatics would not have known. They tried to imitate the lacquer work itself, too, but did not achieve either the solidity or the variety and distinction of the prototypes introduced from the East. Lacquer work today is a good illustration of the industrial possibilities of a region rich in skills for which there are large potential markets, even without standardization, provided that a modern, perhaps co-operative, organization of the trade is brought about.

In Burma, two towns, Pagan and Laikha, already practically subsist on a lacquer industry which uses techniques somewhat different from those practiced elsewhere. It is a very old art. Its origin is just as utilitarian as is that of glass and of porcelain ware. It excels in rich polychrome decoration. In the lighter pieces, such as betel boxes and rice bowls, it retains its flexible character. The enlargement of the foreign market for the products of this native art has resulted in the birth of a new industry rather than the destruction of an old craft. Under the encouragement of a Cottage Industries Department, a good deal of lacquer work has in recent pre-war years been made for export; but good business sense and the natural inclination of the workers have combined to maintain the quality of the product. In fact, it would be truer to say that some of the cheap lacquer articles made in Burma for domestic sales, whose manufacture has not been influenced at all by the new trade requirements, have deteriorated in quality.

The Indo-Chinese lacquer work excels in large pieces, such as screens and chests. With effective promotion, it would have a large market in Europe and America, and this for two reasons. A solid traditional craftsmanship has been retained much better here than in some of the large Chinese producing centers. While some of the Annamite workers keep alive traditional designs, more or less Chinese

Two young Balinese engaged in beating out of buffalo leather the puppets for a shadow play.

A Balinese woodcarver at the court of the King of Karangasam.

(Above) *Indian mechanics on the Burma Road have taught many of the mountain people how to make simple repairs to trucks.*

(At left) *A custom tailor of sarongs (skirts) and kabayas (jackets) at Djokjakarta, Java. His only capital is his sewing machine. He also hires himself out, with his machine, to customers who prefer to have their clothes made in their own homes.*

in conception, others, educated in France or by French
teachers, have fully entered into the spirit of post-impres-
sionist European art. Some of their panels fairly glow with
the freshness of original design and color, rendered in a
most effective medium.

Two living currents flow from the humble loom and
potter's wheel, from the anvil and the dyeing vat. The village craftsman may become absorbed in modern industry,
or he may continue at his old task — but now with a much
larger potential market and not without being influenced
by contact with the world outside his own native community. I have listened to many arguments as to which of
these two developments is the more desirable — or the
more dangerous to the welfare of the people. The renaissance of the ancient Asiatic crafts is now seen by most of
those who have given serious thought to the matter as a
practical necessity. Mechanized industry does not fulfill the
purpose of making the rural worker's spare time productive. When it assigns to the native worker none but menial
functions, as is usually the case, it deprives him of every
opportunity for creative effort and undermines his self-
respect. The inner health of native society requires that at
least some of its members, but preferably many of them,
shall for long retain those useful forms of production which
satisfy both practical and aesthetic needs. Only so can a
gradual transition to modern industry evolve organically
from the old roots.

The post-war period of reconstruction will be especially
favorable to industrial developments from traditional
crafts. Not only may we all be poor, not only may we have
to husband our mastery of diverse skills along with all other
resources; but the very fact that elementary needs must
more and more be satisfied by means of mass production,
so as to reduce costs, makes us the more susceptible to the
value of originality and uniqueness in the less primary ar-

ticles of use. There is a trend in the direction of larger
appreciation for hand-made things of good design, to make
more bearable the standardized monotony of our tenements
and "victory" bungalows.

For these reasons, it is possible that in the post-war economy of Southeast Asia the old crafts of the people, enriched with new materials, facilitated with new implements, and organized for world-wide distribution, will play
a far more important role than could have been anticipated
by those economists who, when they think of international
trade, think only in terms of major commodities.

Imitators and Inventors

When an Oriental sets up in a Western occupation, be
it the opening of a beer restaurant or the manufacture of
brass bedsteads, he is liable to be dubbed a "mere imitator."
Despite the versatility of their talents and the variety of their
arts, native producers of objects also made in Occidental
factories, and native organizers of services on foreign models, are accused of lack of originality. Old people will remember that, at one time or other, every nation that has
entered modern industry has had to meet that charge. New
competition always is resented, especially when it is effective. The newcomer cannot be sure that the potential cus-
tomer will be receptive to new ideas; he starts out by of-
fering him the wares to which he is accustomed and which
until now he has obtained elsewhere. As Asiatic peoples
have come to compete in foreign markets, the old charge
assumed a semblance of truth from the fact that most of
them are exceedingly conservative in what they produce
for their own use. There is very little in the Japanese household, for example, that differs from what you would have
found there a century ago. So the idea gains ground that
"Orientals never invent anything, they just copy."

What happens is, however, that under the impact of a

technically more advanced civilization, an older and less advanced one first adopts and then adapts, before it is stimulated to develop something new from the new level of achievement. This is especially so in colonial dependencies where production with foreign capital and under foreign management is solely for the purpose of utilizing a supply of cheap labor and not for that of out-distancing the motherland in developing the industry. We have an interesting example of this in the Philippines. Some people have told me that they consider the native crafts of the Filipinos — textiles, wood carving, metal work, pottery — rather mediocre compared with those of other Malay peoples. They seemed to be surprised about this because, they thought, three hundred years of Spanish rule should have given the Filipinos a special advantage, a special stimulus to grow industrially and artistically on their old native foundations. But the effect of Spanish rule quite naturally was the opposite. So it was in Latin America where, likewise, it resulted in remarkably faithful reproductions of European art forms but not in the development of indigenous ones. Only with several generations of freedom from Spanish rule has that situation changed. The native Indian arts of Latin America have been revived in recent times and given rise to an important new export trade. Anyone visiting Peru or Bolivia shortly after its emancipation from the Spanish yoke may have said of the inhabitants, as a writer recently said of the Filipinos, that their art is merely imitative. The Filipinos, too, are beginning to revive their own native arts. The movement has, in fact, already gone far enough to predict a rich growth from the basis both of the more primitive indigenous arts and from that of the Arab-influenced Moro arts.

Indeed, as the French have shown by the influence of their two great art schools in Indo-China, it is only the oppressive imposition of foreign tastes that degrades native arts; a free association of traditional taste and dexterity with modern technical improvements introduced from without makes for progress and vitality. Some of the Indo-Chinese textiles, as well as the lacquer work already mentioned, are both traditional and modern, in that they combine both attributes in a seemingly effortless amalgamation.

The contra-position of art and industry is just as arbitrary as, in the last chapter, we have seen that of agriculture and industry to be. Industry is devoted to the production of articles of use; but, although we may not be aware of it, their usefulness often depends on the aesthetic as well as the functional adequacy of the design. The blowpipes made by almost primitive Borneo blacksmiths are works of art because, considering the limitation of their technical knowledge and that of the materials available to them, those men adapt the weapon they forge as perfectly as can be to its purpose. The same may be said about the Borneo Muruts' large cylindrical baskets, made from the bark of the sago tree — a watertight and weatherproof receptacle which fits the human back so comfortably that to this day Europeans prefer it for jungle trips to any contrivance made by a Western manufacturer of travel gear.

In short, the peoples of the tropics no less than those of milder climates contrived through the generations to provide themselves with precisely those articles which they needed most. In doing so, they developed and handed on special skills which now permit their descendants and heirs to learn rapidly how to make a thousand new things to meet a thousand new needs. Some of these incipient new industries are little more than doing with power-driven machines jobs that have been done less quickly by hand for generations.

For the future economic development of Southeast Asia it is a question of some consequence whether its inhabitants possess inventiveness and originality, or whether they will

always have to depend on foreign leadership. It is sometimes said that the climate militates against mental effort,
and that this is reason enough to believe that no new industrial processes and no other striking innovations will
originate in that region. When I showed them Filipino or
Javanese or Annamite plans for industrial developments,
some of the experts said: yes, they have good minds, some
of these people; but they don't have that combination of
qualities which leads from vision to realization; all the
adaptations necessary to fit Western methods of production
to a different climate, to different materials, and so forth,
will have to be made by white people. "And what about the
Japanese?" "Oh, yes, they are different — amazing how
quickly those little devils have learned all the ropes."

In the Philippines one is sometimes told that the Spaniards, obliged to repair and refit their ships in the Islands,
were responsible for the beginnings of the Filipino ship-
building industry (and also, as we have seen, of the rope
industry). But I have not been able to find any similarity
between a Spanish caravel and a Philippine *vinta* with its
brightly colored sails. Indeed, the latter, despite its Spanish
name, is of ancient local origin and could not easily be re-
produced in the heavy woods beloved by European ship-
wrights. Nor can the little schooners built on the beaches
of eastern Java be described as slavishly following some foreign model. Not only are they different in design, but they
are also worked on principles with which the Occidental
mariner would be unfamiliar.

So much has been written about Malay seamanship by
people who are good judges that I need not add my praise.
I have already mentioned in passing the successful competition of some of the native craft with up-to-date cargo liners
in European ownership. But it is precisely in the adaptation
of alien devices to their own needs that the peoples of Southeast Asia have shown the greatest ingenuity. Thus, for ex-

ample, the ancient Javanese, the Cham people of Cambodia, and other groups have adapted what originally may have been the same Hindu system of measuring time to the peculiarities of their own natural seasons and to the particular needs of their own agriculture. If you want to learn of a really clever method of calculating when to plant rice and when to harvest it under different conditions of altitude and exposure, each of the sixty clans of the supposedly "savage" Ifugaos has its own knot calendar and its own time-keeper, who is a person so revered that he may not engage in any work that might impair his health. This calendar provides for thirteen months of twenty-eight days, with one day a year left over as a very special holiday sacred to the dead — in other words, it is an accurate solar measurement.

Inventiveness is not limited to any racial stock. Just as our American Indians had their smoke system of telegraphy before the advent of the white man, so the native Malays have their drum systems. In the mountains of Java, the hours are struck on hollow tree-trunk drums so that, like church bells in Swiss valleys, they re-echo for miles around. And the sound is so distinct that the villagers instantly arouse themselves if, instead of the hourly chimes, the drum gives a fire alarm or some other signal of distress.

If the inhabitants of tropical Asia were lacking in inventiveness one would expect them to use everywhere the same primitive type of weapon or one imported from the neighboring civilization of either India or China. But actually there is at least as great a diversity of weapons in this region as in any region of similar size in Europe or America. Mention has already been made of the blowpipes used by certain groups in Borneo. There is not, I believe, a similar weapon in existence anywhere. It is particularly suited, travellers tell us, to jungle hunting, where a man cannot take a step without making a noise. The mountain tribes of Indo-China and Thailand, the Dyaks of Borneo, and many

tribes of the Malay Peninsula, on the other hand, seem to
have been especially successful in the distillation of vegetable poisons, used for various kinds of hunting. The precautions taken to prevent an accidental poisoning of the
brewmaster and his apprentices are interesting, too. The
Moi, by the way, can probably claim to be the inventors of
poison gas. The poison which they concoct from the bark
of the creeper *Strophantus giganteus* emits fumes so nox-
ious that, according to Baudesson, the operation takes place
a great distance from the village. The Moi, moreover, excel
in preparations for both offensive and defensive warfare.
Their feats with a deadly crossbow of their own construction are matched by the strength of the armor and shield of
buffalo hide with which they go into action. Not only this,
but they also have invented a fortification system of their
own. This consists of man-traps made of slender bamboo-
spears which look like reeds but rip up an approaching
enemy like razor blades. Trapping with spears, however, is
an art widely practiced among Malays. The Bilaans of
Mindanao have a contraption made of spears and saplings,
held together by vines, which are practically invisible but
are released with great force when an animal brushes
against the trigger.

Why tell us all this primitive stuff? the reader may ask
impatiently. What has it to do with the problems of building up an economic and political future for the Malay people when the war is over? Throughout my discussion of native industries and native arts, I have deliberately switched
back and forth between what is pertinent to the more advanced and the less advanced among the tropical Asiatics.
The reality of their civilization covers a wide range of differences; and we must understand these differences if we
do not wish to dismiss half of the reality from our thinking.
Who knows whether fifty years from now — and that is a
short time — the present achievements of the inland Mu-

ruts and Dusuns will not, in retrospect, appear to have
been more important for the future of Borneo than those
of the more sophisticated Coast Malays?

The Man people of northern Indo-China would, by
Western standards, certainly be adjudged rather primitive.
They are still in the squatter stage of "shifting cultivators."
Their agriculture, their houses, their diet, their costume —
all are very simple. In fact, the name by which they are
known is a nickname bestowed on them by the Chinese and
means Barbarians. But these same people, living for greater
safety on hillsides, are inventive in things that matter to
them. Some of their villages have a water supply which is
piped to each house through a common bamboo main from
a mountain spring. The individual connections are so ar-
ranged that water may trickle continuously into the bam-
boo-fenced vegetable gardens or that the flow can be
stopped by raising the pipe. How many American suburbs
have anything so sensible?

Decorative Design

At least brief reference must also be made to another
kind of invention, that of decorative design. It may be
asked whether the mentality of the Malay and related peoples does not preclude that openness to new impressions
and that adaptability which would be necessary if old traditions in design are to give way to new forms. Aesthetic and
technical problems, to be sure, are closely interrelated. An
artisan who is bound by the traditions in the ornamentation of a utensil is also likely to be bound by the traditional
view of what is useful and what is not. The betel-chewing
village elder who likes to have the people around him conform to the established standards of conduct and the established social customs is not likely to become enthusiastic
over a power-driven lathe that turns out spare parts for
bicycles; for the bicycle will take the younger people away

from his benevolent sway. But he may be childishly pleased with some new gadget that does not in his mind call forth any idea inimical to the old-established ways of the community, his livelihood or social status. I have seen alarm clocks and gramophones in the homes of extremely conservative village magistrates in the Philippines, and bottled drinks from a near-by soda factory on the table of a Javanese Moslem who was reputed to be an old warhorse in the defense of established customs. Such a man is not necessarily against every innovation. He can even appreciate the beauty of a Western-made umbrella, functionally so superior to his own.

It was probably a rather daring departure from orthodoxy which first made a Bali sculptor include the figure of a man on a bicycle among the panels of a temple wall. But when that bit of modern art attracted favorable attention, he did it again, and yet once more; until even those of his fellows who at first were a little shocked, told that the tourists admired this sort of thing, encouraged others to do likewise and even took credit, perhaps, for the liberal statement that "with the Balinese, art is a living force." Of course, art might be a living force among them even if they never touched a modern subject. It by no means follows that an art which remains traditional is therefore dead. And, indeed, the Western connoisseur is more likely to pick up a traditional piece as corresponding to modern Western taste than a piece made on purpose to throw tradition overboard.

Malay art has a remarkable affinity with modern Western art. Unlike the Chinese artist who follows an inner vision which is often choked by literary references, the Malay looks around him, and with such means as he knows renders what appeals to him. This is true of the relatively primitive tribes in the backwoods as it is of the children in Philippine schools. Some Javanese paintings recently exhibited in New

York include village scenes as they are today, plants that
grow today and may not have been known when this kind
of painting was first introduced from India. But the curious
perspective and the crowding of scenes in a limited space
— which is, of course, a practice common to artists in every
clime who have to be economic in their use of material —
are unmistakably Javanese.

Our own modern art is largely a return to art as the Malay
understands it and is a result of influences from the East in
the latter part of the nineteenth century. Not because the
Malay has become modern but because the European and
American artist has become simpler and more straightfor-
ward, is there that similarity which we find between many
Western and many Malay works of art today. This is true
both of the representative arts, especially in sculpture, and
of the decorative arts. In short, the Malay artist, after a
brief contact with Western art — if contact there was at
all — has arrived at a stage of feeling which we, starting
from similar primitive beginnings to his, have reached only
after the most devious circuit through the Renaissance and
the so-called Age of Enlightenment, which really was an age
of sophistication. There is no insuperable distance between
modern Malay and modern American in their feeling for
beauty or in their sense of fitness in design. One is poten-
tially as creative and as adaptive to new conditions and new
problems as is the other.

Again, the reader may ask impatiently, what has all this
to do with the Filipino's or the Thai's capacity for modern
industry? Suppose he is clever with his hands, a good artist,
quick to observe and to adapt himself to modern conditions
— could he build a bridge? Before I answer that question,
I want the reader to forget for a moment our inherited scientific knowledge and our enormously larger resources.
Both, it will be admitted, could be transmitted and shared.
The question is whether in the general social background

of the Asiatic there is anything that prevents him from ap-
preciating those qualities that make for good engineering.
Is there anything in our modern civilization that is indispensable, let us say, to the building of a bridge, which
the Malay or the Burmese does not and cannot possess? We
think in terms of steel and cement, of huge cranes and cop-
per cables. And we see the brown man, lightly clad, in his
tropical surroundings, with no building higher than two or
three stories even in the cities, untutored in many of the
things which we consider important, often childlike in his
attitude toward nature, old-fashioned in his social relationships. We can see no connection between that modern construction work and the Malay who stands on the threshold
of modern industry. How could he possibly fit into that
world of steel? And yet it was the Malay who taught us how
to build that suspension bridge. Its prototypes are not to be
found in ancient Europe but in the Malay jungle.

Part **II.**

THE NEW ERA

VII

TRADESMEN AND COLONISTS

THROUGHOUT the world, the arts flourish in centers of trade where ships or caravans meet to exchange the products of their homelands. And when the merchants of a culturally more advanced country establish their own colonies far from home, so as to be able to carry on their business more expeditiously, they often send home for artisans as well as accountants, for silversmiths as well as shipping clerks. For the native people of the place, too, such a settlement is a good place in which to ply a craft appreciated by the foreigners. Those who sneer at the curio trade should reflect that with it from Damascus spread the Christian faith and that the importation of artistic stimuli from its Byzantine colonies led to the cultural greatness of Venice. Without the fashioners of things of beauty in Mexico and Guatemala and other countries of Latin America, the birth of an era of good neighborliness in the Western Hemisphere would be more difficult.

When many carpenters and weavers, stone carvers and metal workers congregate in such a center, the traditional crafts of village and small town assume a new economic significance. Skills handed down become valuable trade secrets. Guilds form, and its members move close together, perhaps along both sides of a single street which now becomes the mart for their wares. Rules are made about the quality of the work and sometimes about minimum charges, so that the trade shall remain in good repute and there shall be no unfair competition. The merchant from far away no longer looks only for natural products for which to exchange his manufactures but also pays increasing attention to the products of the local trades. He may discover that there are many skilled people there who can manufacture things — say cotton cloth or cigarettes — at a lower cost than he can buy them for at home when the additional cost of shipping them is taken into account. So he sets up a shop or a factory and starts importing raw materials — cotton, perhaps, or tobacco, or metals — to be manufactured on the spot. In this way, he makes two profits, one as an importer and one as a manufacturer and employer of wage labor. After a while it may occur to him that he can substitute, at least partially, some local raw materials for those he has imported and — more important still — that he need not employ skilled workers but can use the much lower-paid services of laborers, whom he can train himself, and of women and children. And so he imports tools and machinery.

The Spaniards found out long ago that it was more profitable to make cigars in Manila and export them to Europe than to export merely the tobacco and have Spaniards make the cigars in Spain. They got their nuns to teach the village children lace making and embroidery; thus an industry was born, at first importing all materials but later getting many of them spun, dyed, and woven on the spot. But generally speaking the colonial governments were against the development of industries that might take the bread out of the mouths of people at home. No, they said to their merchants, employ as many people as you like in the colony to grow tobacco for you or coffee or tea or coconuts or fibers, or whatever you want, employ as many brown and yellow people as you like to dig for coal or tin or gold — but don't undersell the labor of your own compatriots.

The Chinese merchants had no such scruples. They did not have to play native wage-earners against Chinese; for there were people enough in their own home community in China who would come overseas and work for a mere pittance in their little sweatshops and dark, insanitary factories. In Burma, and to a lesser extent in Thailand and Malaya, Indian merchants played that same role of budding industrial entrepreneurs (as Polish immigrants at the beginning of the nineteenth century played it in Silesia, and Huguenot refugees, in the seventeenth century, played it in England). As a result, most of the cities in Southeast Asia have become centers of Oriental industry, combining the use of many skills with the precision of power-driven machinery. And this explains why these cities, some of them after centuries of occupation by Western powers, still look more Oriental than Occidental.

The growth of large cities set in the midst of an impoverished agrarian society obeys no inner law. They are magnets that lure both poor and rich: those who have lost their land and must look for employment, and those who are well enough off to choose their domicile with a view to the enjoyment of modern amenities. Especially those villagers, both wealthy and willing to take a chance, whose income comes from rent and is large enough to permit of a life of luxury are greatly attracted by the city with its many comforts and refinements. Such a landlord finds that he can collect his rents once or twice a year and, by squeezing just a little harder, make enough to live in the city. This is more likely to occur to him if his village is not too far from a city and if he is engaged in some trade that occasionally takes him there so that he knows his way about. In the Philippines and Thailand, the connection between wealth and political power has attracted to their respective capital cities many families of means, and with them, of course, more and more of those who cater to the needs of the wealthy.

The encroachments of foreign trade have broken up old-established native patterns of life by substituting a money economy, and finally wage labor, for an economy that used to be mainly one of self-sufficiency. Compared with that larger influence the urbanizing effect of foreign trade may be a matter of minor consequence. But the growth of cities introduces a new class distinction in the Oriental society, and this eventually becomes dangerous to the social health. An exaggerated aggregation of people in the port cities and capitals fosters a lack of realism in attitudes toward the national economy and toward the responsibility of the individual. The citizens lose the sense of their roots in the countryside. And we need not think in this connection only of the big port cities. Roads and railroads, steamship lanes and air routes branch out from them, distort the former routes of interior trade, create new subordinate centers of activity and of population at the crossroads of travel, and always take the thought of officialdom and of the influential classes away from the broad basis of the national life in the fields and the modest homes of the peasants.

Foreign Capital and Foreign Labor

Large-scale modern enterprises are planted in the midst of a jungle and draw there masses of people who, in the ordinary course of events, would never have gone there; and so another distortion of the traditional society takes place. Indigenous population is concentrated in areas with large immediate opportunities of employment. But these opportunities may not last and later may leave the artificially created communities stranded without means of livelihood. Or alien labor is imported and settled on the land without regard for the livelihood of the native people. In Indo-China we find many examples of the former kind of concentration, in British Malaya more of the latter.

In Netherlands India, the total value of exports in 1931

was only one-third of what it had been in 1929. Between
1935 and 1937 it doubled; that is, it rose to two-thirds of
what it had been in 1929. In 1939, it was down again to
less than one-half. Or take a single commodity — say, sugar.
In 1913, the average wholesale price was twelve and a half
guilders per hundred kilograms. In 1919, it was forty-three
guilders. In 1926 it was down again to nineteen guilders
and continued to go down, with minor fluctuations, until
in the early thirties you could buy a hundred kilograms for
less than six guilders — only the seventh part of what it
had been in 1919. Nor was sugar an exception. Pepper went
up from eighty-five dollars in 1913 to two hundred and
thirty in 1929. But if you started growing pepper that year,
you were disappointed by getting less than one-tenth as
much for your crop ten years later.

Now, the owners of estates that grow such crops as these
do not go on employing the same amount of labor through
good years and bad. There are violent fluctuations in employment, too; and the peasants who grew food for these
laborers find themselves without a market. The Javanese
laborer who worked on an estate to grow sugar or pepper or
kapok or coffee or tea or cocoa or coconuts, was politely
told to go home when, after 1926, the market broke. And
he did — there was nothing else he could do. Since he was
not called back the next year, or the year after that, or in
fact at any time in the next ten years, he decided that maybe
he had better learn how to grow more food on his own bit
of ground and not count any longer on earning money by
working for an estate. His government quite agreed that
it was wiser to do so and helped him make himself independent of foreign trade as far as he could. But, of course,
that does not suit the estate managers who like to have a
labor supply on hand to draw upon when prices seem to
be going up. They prefer to see people around who are not
too independent. Long before, the employers in British

Malaya had discovered — and others had come to agree
with them — that "Malays are lazy" and must be replaced
with imported wage-earners. The Javanese and the Filipinos were the only large indigenous labor groups that
worked on foreign-owned plantations when the great depression came.

Out of every ten people in British Malaya, just before
the war, four were Malay — both native and immigrant,
that is, Javanese — four were Chinese, and two were Indian. Of Europeans there were so few, they did not make
up even one per cent in the Straits Settlements where they
were thickest. If you count only those employed on foreign
estates, in mines, factories, public works, railways, and public employment of all sorts, only one out of every ten was
a Malay, three were Chinese, and six were Indian. There
were nine times as many Indians working on the estates
as Malays and almost four times as many as Chinese; but
in the mines there were not many more Indians than Malays, and the Chinese were roughly five times as many as
either.

Who are these Indians and these Chinese, and why are
they there? Both groups come from overcrowded regions
in their respective home countries, the Indians mostly from
Madras, and the Chinese mostly from the provinces of
Kwangtung and Fukien, the two southeastern coastal provinces of China. Both groups are employed because they are
extremely poor and will accordingly put up with very poor
labor conditions. They are extremely poor not only because
there are so many of them in the districts from which they
come but also because they have for a long time been land-
lord-ridden and debt-ridden. There are among them assisted laborers, those who come only if the employer advances the travel cost, and free laborers, those who come
on their own account and are glad to do so. In recent pre-
war years there has been a great increase of the latter class,

and this shows that the conditions of employment must have improved, since conditions in the homelands could hardly be any worse than they had been before.

On the surface all would seem well. Here is India, with its millions of poverty-stricken peasants, a reservoir of willing labor for the other parts of the British empire in southern Asia. Both Burma and Malaya are short of labor. But all is not well. Burma does not want the Indians. Malaya — or rather, the foreign-owned estate industry of Malaya — wants them very much but, since 1938, cannot get them. The labor turnover has been enormous: almost a million immigrants were brought in from Madras in ten years, but over half a million were shipped back. In bad years, more laborers were sent home than came in; but even in a boom year almost as many returned as arrived. In short, there was a sort of tug-of-war going on all the time between the Malayan planters and the Indian Government: the employers, as is the wont of their kind, want to have a large reserve of workers close at hand, "just in case. . . ." The Malayan Government is neutral, as long as the planters feed and house the waiting throngs, or provide them with the means of self-support. So, in 1938, the Indian Government — under pressure, it is said, from the Congress Party — decided this business was unworthy of a free and self-respecting people and asked the rubber estate managers to think things over. If they found that, perhaps after all, they could afford to treat the Madras men as human beings, perhaps they would come back.

I have simplified a situation which in reality is more complicated. The Malayan employers were able to point out, for example, that every year more Indians came over at their own expense and of their own accord, without having been signed on in advance. So, they concluded, "things can't be as bad as you say. Or why do those chaps fall over each other to get our jobs?"

One answer is that these Tamil peasants in southern India are extremely poor, some of them close to starvation most of the time. We know from our American experience that when that is the case, a socially-minded government must step in and protect such people against themselves as well as against others. You may remember how thousands of American families permitted and even desired their young children to work for wages because the parents never earned quite enough to keep them in clothes and shoes. We needed a federal law to make an end to the disgraceful exploitation of children; and we have not quite finished that job yet.

The Indian Government found itself in difficulty in Burma, too, but on somewhat different grounds. The Burmese Government in recent pre-war years became stronger and wanted to know by what rights these Indians thought they could come in there and work under conditions which no self-respecting Burman would accept. The Indian Government could only admit that the fact was as stated. The reason for an influx of laborers from Eastern India was that they would take jobs which the native people refused. In July 1941, the two governments signed an agreement greatly curtailing the right of Indians to enter Burma. But labor competition was only part of the trouble. The Burmese, who not so long ago had been affiliated against their will with the Indian Commonwealth, have always cherished a political antagonism against India. This was re-inforced by the strong social position which many Indians and descendants of Indians occupied in Burma. Indians own banks, rice mills, saw mills, and many small factories. Railway workers, postmen, seven out of every ten skilled workers in Rangoon are Indian. Over a million of Burma's sixteen million inhabitants speak an Indian language and, for that reason, are not considered by their Burman neighbors as having been wholly assimilated. But there are probably even more people of Indian descent who do speak Burmese in every-day life and who think of themselves as nationals of Burma and not of India. So, in this recent agreement the Burmese Government promised as a special concession to accord full citizen rights to those Indians who, as property owners or on other concrete grounds, could show that they had wholly identified themselves with the interests of Burma. The agreement to regulate Indian immigration and the status of Indian residents in Burma was signed, but the Indian nationalists were by no means satisfied. There are too many clauses in the document which reflect obliquely on the character of Indians and on the part they play in Burmese life — for example, that they are in the habit of marrying Burmese women and then leaving them. Mr. Gandhi said that public opinion in India had not been sufficiently consulted; or such an agreement, casting a slur upon Indians, would never have been signed.

And thereby hangs yet another tale. The Indians, both in Burma and in Malaya, and in fact wherever they have gone as immigrants, have played other roles besides those of respectable artisans and of indigent laborers who grab at every chance to earn a living. They have also gone as merchants, and above all as money-changers and money-lenders. Their unpopularity in this role led to riots in Burma in 1938 and 1939, in the course of which two hundred persons were killed and much property was destroyed. In Thailand too, it is primarily as a money-lender or a business man with rather sharp practices that the Indian immigrant is thought of by the man in the street, not as a laborer or a peasant. A few years ago, there were about a hundred thousand Indians in Thailand, and they were no more liked than the Chinese. Both were objects of popular attack when the Siamese decided to free themselves of foreign pressures of all sorts and run the country to their own liking. That was when they changed their country's name.

Of the hundred thousand Indians quite a large proportion probably had already left the country — some of them with a Thai boot at their back — some years before the Japanese army marched in. But from Burma there was a real exodus of Indian refugees right up to the last.

If Indian immigrants were conspicuous in Burma, Thailand, and Malaya, Chinese were practically everywhere in Southeast Asia. They had for generations poured from the two southern coastal states of China over the seas. Their junks had prodded into every bay and every river mouth. Their merchant adventurers had created little colonies which for many generations have intermingled with the indigenous peoples of Farther India and Malaysia, so that a yellow skin and slanting eyes today no longer signify, anywhere in the Asiatic tropics, more than possibly a remote Chinese element in a man's ancestry. The old cities of South China traded with India and with Arabia when the Roman Empire was still a rather isolated little affair huddled around the Mediterranean Sea. Their citizens, themselves the offspring of old and sturdy inland stocks, were the master race if ever there was one. To them flowed amber and ivory, ebony and rare hardwoods, powerful drugs and curious pelts, things good to eat and things good to smell, and the most beautiful women of Asia. But when European fleets came to capture the trade of Malaysia, the Chinese merchants, already installed in its principal ports, had no strong government to back them up. In fact, they had never had a government working in their interest: anyone wilful enough to go abroad lost the benign protection of the Son of Heaven and was no longer entitled to the respect of his countrymen.

Chinese Immigration

An entirely new chapter opened up when Chinese migration ceased to be motivated solely by the hazardous purposes of trade and became motivated also by the surer but smaller rewards of menial labor. Some of the migrants, though the sons of poor peasants, were descendants of the once proud merchant adventurers in the stone-built but ruined towns and cities of southern China. But far larger numbers now were recruited to help in building new empires, the colonial empires of European merchant princes. No such empires had ever been seen in the Orient. They rested upon the power of systematized knowledge. A handful of white men, equipped with that knowledge, were able not only to dominate proud and ancient peoples but also to tame nature. They appropriated what grew upon the soil and, more and more, the soil itself and what lay below it — a wealth never before appropriated to enhance the might of a conqueror.

From the native standpoint, the Chinese under these new regimes only added yet other roles to those which for centuries they had played among them. They were still the middlemen through whose efforts a peasant might convert his crops into cloth or hardware or any other desired commodity not made by local artisans. They still were the money-changers from whom it was possible at times to secure a loan, though at a high rate of interest. In the closed ranks of their shops in towns and cities, they still made many things which the natives themselves had never learned to fashion. But now, under the orders of the white masters, some of these same Chinese also came to compete in wage labor of all sorts, in fields and factories — wage labor equipped with the old-fashioned tools of the peasant and the new-fangled tools of mass production.

There were probably more than six million Chinese residents in Southeast Asia just before the war, about 1,700,000 of them in British Malaya, where they were two-fifths of the total population, 1,233,000 in Netherlands India, 117,-000 in the Philippines (far more if we include all those visibly of Chinese blood), 445,000 in Thailand, 326,000 in Indo-China (actually three or four million if we include all those of Chinese ancestry in the last-named two countries).

In Malaya, in the Philippines, in Thailand, everywhere the small Chinese business men penetrated to the farthest hinterland. They sold silk threads to almost primitive villagers in the jungles of Borneo. I once came across a little Chinese store on a road between two rubber estates in Malaya, successfully competing with the much larger stores kept on the estates themselves. Little more than cabins, these stores resemble the general stores of American villages in the variety of goods they have to offer. They purchase the small peasant's produce. They serve as inns for the weary. They are the news rooms of the neighborhood. Through them the local government broadcasts its decrees. Sometimes they are reported not to be too scrupulous in the means they use to get native peasants into their debt or to act as their brokers when they must sell their harvest in advance. Once, at the university in Manila, I read a score of essays by Philippine students enrolled in commercial courses, showing with much detail how impossible it is for the Filipino storekeeper to compete with the Chinese. Sometimes it was a story of a small Chinese clique that had got possession of all the milling facilities in a district so that all the rice had to pass through their hands. Then, again, there was the storekeeper who refused credit to any of the peasants who would not buy their supplies from him — at prices far above those current.

Whatever the particular practices, and however large or small may have been the proportion of Chinese traders who engaged in them, dislike of them, even acute enmity, has been rising in most of the region for many years. As a result, social ostracism and legal discriminations followed each other in close succession. When the war broke out, there was no longer an entirely free right of immigration for Chinese anywhere in Southeast Asia and this just when the chances of economic success had become somewhat brighter. The conditions of contract labor have been regulated in the interest of Chinese and other workers through international action, especially through the abolition, some years ago, of the so-called penal sanctions which enabled an employer virtually to enslave those immigrants who had contracted to serve him. The Chinese National Government has passed from an attitude of disapproval in the former imperial days through one of helpless concern to an attitude, at last, of open and active intervention in behalf of the welfare of the Chinese residents abroad.

Through their own energy and intelligence, ever larger numbers of the Chinese residents in Malaya have attained a social status far above that from which they started. Some of them have been knighted for generous contributions to public charity and education. In Netherlands India, several have received high honors from the Queen. In the Philippines, Chinese business men have served on important government commissions, both at home and abroad. In Thailand and Indo-China they have married into the native aristocracy. Many more have acquired if not wealth at least a modest competence. And yet, in the pre-war years the situation became steadily worse. The enormous fluctuations in the prices of those export commodities on which immigrant Chinese worked, in which they traded, or which they shipped, hit them with special severity. Millions of them were directly interested as wage-earners or as small entrepreneurs in the economic life of the countries where they lived. The world economic depression which began in the late 'twenties wiped out whole communities of overseas Chinese and sent hundreds of thousands of them home to China penniless.

So much for the Chinese in Southeast Asia. They have

for centuries fulfilled the function of connecting eastern Asia with the rest of the world. Without their industry and endurance the great tropical empires of Farther India and Malaysia could hardly have developed to their present state of productivity. And in the post-war years they will be among the principal carriers of modern knowledge and of democratic ideals into the very heart of this traditional seed-plot of despotic ambition.

Southeast Asia might serve as the scene for an intensive study of the relative potency of trade and of military force as means of subjection. Both the Hindu and the Chinese civilizations have left deep marks in the indigenous cultures. Their arts and their scriptures have become so intermingled with the native lore and the native traditions that a distinctive culture with Indonesian and Indo-Chinese features has emerged, with an inner life and a future of its own. Yet the names of the conquerors have almost been forgotten. At least, in as far as they are known, the wars of conquest do not make especially interesting reading. As one studies the history of the region one becomes convinced, rather, that the real triumphs were those of the old shipmasters, the real adventures those of the old traders and of the Hindu and Moslem and Buddhist missionaries who, often unarmed and unprotected, went everywhere into the interior and brought to the native people gospels of a better life — both here and in the world beyond.

Pilgrims of the Prophet

Two other peoples, each of them the exponent of a distinct cultural theory and fired with a religious message, have invaded the Asiatic tropics and emphasized with fire and sword the all-embracing universality of their love for mankind.

From the seventh century on, the Arab empire expanded southward and eastward and in time established itself all

An Arab-descended Hadji of East Java, orthodox in his religion, for he has made the pilgrimage to Mecca, but a successful business man and social organizer. After some years spent in Singapore, he came to Sumatra, built himself a large house, a cassava factory, a mosque, and a private school.

An old Javanese guru (religious teacher) and his grandson. The copy of the Koran which the boy holds up is made of a local bark paper the somewhat primitive manufacture of which, once widespread, is now practiced in only a few villages.

Modern-style hats and caps do not prevent these Malay boys in the heart of Malaya from enjoying a traditional game. Each participant tries to knock down, with a spinning top, as many pegs as possible.

A nationalist workers' demonstration in Burma. Although just before the war it became more difficult to secure permits, such parades, even with banners bearing anti-British slogans, still took place. (Many of the marchers are unaware of the meaning of the communist banner.)

across the Indian Ocean from Madagascar to Java. The zeal of the Arabs, like that of the Christian Crusaders, recognized no color differences. Indeed, they rather prided themselves on being without race prejudice and freely intermarried with the white people of Asia Minor and the Caucasus, the Negroes of Africa, the dark-skinned peoples of southern India, and the light-colored Malays. Nor did they hesitate to give their daughters in marriage to any of these.

Perhaps because of this universality in their human sympathies, the Arabs soon became enmeshed in ambitions of a more worldly sort than that of disseminating the word of the Prophet. At any rate, they were the first great exponents in Southeast Asia of that commercial imperialism which eventually merged with the rising nationalism of Europe and the Near East in movements of Western expansion. Where peaceful commerce was possible, they preferred it to conquest. For centuries they dominated the trade of the Indian Ocean, far into the Pacific as well as into the Mediterranean and Europe by way of the Red Sea.

I do not know whether Arab statesmen ever spoke of a co-prosperity sphere, but they certainly did not claim to belong to a superior breed divinely entrusted with the responsibility of leadership. Whoever embraced Islam was one of them. And so, identifying themselves with peoples of all sorts, the Arabs became absorbed in the trading communities of all the coasts and islands of the region. As in the case of the Chinese, the number of those now officially identified as Arabs or enumerated with other distinct groups as "Oriental aliens" bears no relation to the amount of Arab blood that is flowing through the population.

The original homeland of the Arab merchants, sailors, and missionaries who had sailed east and settled among the Indians and the Malays — never in overwhelming numbers — became the spiritual homeland for millions con-

verted to the faith. But just because of the deep respect of
every Moslem for the birthplace of the Prophet, those who
in later times came from Arabia to settle in Southeast Asia
remained somewhat aloof from the rest, as a chosen people,
and enjoyed a reputation for piety and wisdom which they
took care not to lose for themselves and their families. Two
of the present sultanates under the Netherlands flag are
dynasties of Arab origin. In the small ports of Celebes almost pure Arab minorities survive.

Pilgrimages to Mecca, in which thousands of Malays take
part — in some years more than fifty thousand from Netherlands India alone — have kept alive that special prestige
of the Arabs. They still are regarded as cultural links between Near East and Far East although their monopoly of
ocean commerce has long gone and soon even their survival
as a separate national minority group may cease — unless
they achieve some new recognized function in the predominantly Malay Moslem community. The pilgrimages to
Mecca are used by the Netherlands Indian Government as
a fairly accurate barometer of prosperity. Between good
years and bad years it may vary by more than a thousand
per cent. In this connection an interesting common concern has developed between the Netherlands Indian and
the Hedjaz Governments. The great literary lights revered
among the Arabs have, in a surprising number of instances,
been physicians, and pious Moslems consider themselves to
have a kind of hereditary interest in matters of health. To
this interest the Netherlands Indian Government was able
to appeal diplomatically at times when the conditions under
which pilgrims to Mecca travelled and were housed at their
destination became especially bad — and they have always
been notorious. In the years just before the war an arrangement existed under which a representative of the Netherlands Indians Government shared in the sanitary control.

In early times, the Arab fleets were probably more instrumental than were the caravans over the ancient "silk route" of Central Asia in linking Occident and Orient. For only the most precious stuffs can be loaded on camel back in central or northern China, by degrees find their way to the Near East and Europe, and still repay their owners for the tremendous cost of so long an overland transportation. But more bulky goods still pay their way, despite long distances, when loaded on ships. The Arabs' ability to make themselves at home in the port cities of Malaysia equalled that of the Chinese. Indeed, some of those cities owe their origin to small Arab trading centers. Perhaps even the Biblical myrrh and frankincense could be traced to this old connection.

They did far better than did the Chinese in converting people to their own beliefs and ideas. The reason is that they did not start out by regarding themselves as altogether superior people but were eager to share their religious enthusiasm and all the good things that flow to those who obey Heaven's commands. Arab colonies still form the centers of pious Mohammedan communities in Celebes, Java, and elsewhere. There are eighty or ninety thousand Arabs in all Netherlands India, about one-half of them in Java. These are small numbers which do not indicate the influence of the group. That influence derives not only from their piety but also from a tolerance that attracts and binds. Like the Catholic missions in the Philippines and in Indo-China (to a lesser extent also in Netherlands India), the Moslem institutions won over people by not disturbing them too much in their accepted beliefs but trying, rather, to combine these beliefs in a unifying monotheistic philosophy. Even when they had conquered the great Hindu empires of Sumatra, Malaya, and Java, the Mohammedan Indians and Arabs did not destroy the old shrines — except the more important ones that were really symbols of political power. Many of the old Hindu legends and plays are as popular as ever, and these include rites and allusions that go even farther back to ancient animistic beliefs and practices.

As middlemen and money-lenders, the Arabs are probably no better liked today than are the Chinese. But many of them are clever artisans. In business affairs they sometimes have a special knowledge which other people find indispensable. Most of them come from the arid Hadramaut coast of southern Arabia and, as long as they can make a living of sorts elsewhere, do not intend to go home. Their numbers are not large enough anywhere in Southeast Asia to excite fear or political suspicion. But it is quite possible that, when this war is over, Islam may find itself in a strengthened position, and its various branches may recombine politically to form a more influential power group than has supported the faith in the past. Some Netherlands Indian officials seem to detect a trend in the direction of such political re-orientation in the spread of Mohammedan mystic fraternities, *tarekats,* which have shown a combination of religiously emotional and nationalist leanings.

Advance Guards of Aggression

Yet another group in Malaysia, a relative newcomer, has combined enthusiasm for a religious idea with commercial shrewdness and willingness to employ force, when needed, in the propagation of its ideas: the Japanese. Perhaps it will be their fate, like that of the Arabs, to vanish from the records of history with a brief note here and there about the continuance of a certain prestige, about their mystic exaltation, their fanatical belief in a fine ethical creed lost in the mazes of mythology, and their brief hour of glory as a great imperial power.

Before the first world war few people in Southeast Asia gave thought to the Japanese, though the latter were already beginning to compete successfully in a number of trades. Even after the beginning, in 1931, of the anti-Japanese boycott by the Chinese, who then had almost a monopoly in most lines of retail business, the Japanese did not retaliate by setting up many stores of their own. Instead, they organized an immense wholesale organization and, as far as possible, broke down the boycott through native retailers. When necessary, they bought themselves into partnerships with them. This was not especially difficult; for the natives who were trying to run a business had no love for the Chinese.

Like the Europeans, the Japanese had no really serious objection to the quasi-monopoly which the Chinese — or here and there the Indians — had acquired of the retail trade of the region until it turned against them. Like the Europeans, they had larger fish to fry. "Strictly wholesale" might have been painted on the window panes of the many corporations which they formed, sometimes under names not in the least suggestive of Japanese ownership, to forward Japanese import business. The dominant commercial interest of Japan in Southeast Asia did not include any desire to help large numbers of poor Japanese to work out their own salvation individually by peddling a few lengths of cloth in the Malay villages or by setting up as innkeepers and rice merchants. The Japanese have always been averse to emigration as an individual venture. When, like the Chinese, they lifted the age-old ban on emigration, it was only to make possible a concerted movement of Japanese settlers; and such a movement always was directed to lands where a colony of nationals might help to open up new sources of food or raw materials urgently needed to improve the Japanese economy. The acquisition of dependencies did not begin until 1875, with the modest gain of a few islands from Russia, and further augmented during the following year. Formosa, taken from China in 1895, gave more scope for the transplantation of Japanese farmers, but noth-

ing came of it. After forty years of occupation, Japanese
nationals form less than six per cent of the population even
in this strategically important island commanding the
northern approaches to the South China Sea. Later, nothing much came of large schemes to settle Japanese farmers
in Korea and in Manchuria.

Japanese emigration to the countries of Southeast Asia
was, like European and American migration to that region,
for purposes of trade. It was never large because obviously
it was much cheaper to employ native and Chinese wage-
earners on the spot than to send Japanese ones; and only
the more responsible positions were filled with compatriots.
Thus the Japanese concessions of iron mines in Malaya
were worked with Chinese immigrant labor. One device
which the Japanese used wherever they could was that with
which we are familiar in California: the purchase of partnerships or stocks in native companies, even when this
meant an evasion of those laws which had been framed precisely to prevent the permeation of trade and industry with
foreign capital. In this way, Japanese interests managed to
dominate the whole ocean fishing industry of the western
Pacific, and this without appreciably adding to the number
of Japanese residents on foreign shores. In the Philippines,
four out of every five deep-sea fishing boats before the war
were operated by Japanese, despite a law passed in 1932
prohibiting foreign ownership of commercial fishing vessels. Sometimes there is a genuine Filipino majority in the
fishing company; but the Philippine Government — like
most other governments in the region — was too busy trying to appease the Japanese to make an issue of every instance in which the Filipinos registered as stockholders and
officers were suspected of being merely dummies for a Japanese wholesale concern.

It was the same thing with many other kinds of enterprise
which, under the Philippine constitution of 1935, were re-

served for corporations with at least a sixty per cent Philippine ownership. The Japanese only did, of course, what Europeans had done a century earlier; that is, they put themselves by guile if they could, by force if need be, in possession of those raw materials which they desired. The Japanese came rather late. They were willing to invest their own money in mines and saw-mills and land concessions; but in the meantime laws had been framed to prevent them from doing so. What were they to do? There was nothing in their ethics to prohibit their use of whatever loopholes they might discover. Sometimes a Japanese store served the purpose of camouflage: it was for the purpose of giving an ostensible reason for the presence of a group of Japanese men who really owned some land held near-by in the name of natives. The store was a blind for a much larger enterprise, a plantation.

The Japanese colony in the province of Davao, Mindanao, about which so much has been written, was an exception to the usual kind of Japanese enterprise. Here the object was a large increase in the supply of hemp of which Davao is the center of supply. In the market, the Japanese were in competition with American bidders and could not get nearly enough. So they decided to grow some of their own. Later on, purely military purposes may have outweighted financial ones, but the legitimate origin of the Davao colony can hardly be disputed. It goes back to 1904, when there can have been no thought of military conquest. If there was an idea of building up a strong military foothold it was eventually given up; for when the campaign for the conquest of Southeast Asia did take shape, Davao played no very important part in the Japanese strategy.

In the other countries of the region, Japanese residents played an even less conspicuous role. In Indo-China there were not enough of them to be separately counted in the census. But here, as in Thailand and probably elsewhere, everybody knew that many Japanese tradesmen, photographers, students, members of over-staffed commercial and travel bureaus, sportsmen and tourists really were military spies — everybody knew — and laughed about it.

In Saigon I heard complaints about the competition of Japanese goods smuggled in from Singapore, which was a free port. But I doubt that Japanese business men of repute had a hand in this. The rumor may have been no more than an attempt to explain the singularly low prices at which Japanese manufactures could be bought. Nobody did anything about this, either.

In Thailand, the only conspicuous Japanese were some technical experts in silk and cotton growing and a few teachers of embroidery. But a large proportion of the country's imports were from Japan. In Burma, Japanese buyers managed to secure for their country a large part of the cotton crop but did not try to form Japanese colonies to grow cotton. In British Malaya, curiously enough, the Japanese seem to have seen no opening for participation on a large scale in the growing of rubber, although they must have had great need for that product. Nor did they share to any large extent in the ownership of the other major estate industries. The British have, of course, long followed a policy of "Malaya for the Malays," but this has not prevented them from peopling the peninsula with Chinese and Indians or from giving the Japanese important mining concessions. It must therefore be assumed that the Japanese saw no particular advantage in settling many of their subjects in this hospitable land, or they could certainly have pressed for that right. People with whom I talked about this in Singapore all seemed to think that the Japanese could not stand the climate. But they did not need to grow their own rubber since the market was free. And that was true also of tin.

Japanese goods, especially silk fabrics, were handled almost exclusively by Indian and Arab dealers, though the number of Japanese stores in Singapore and other Malayan cities had increased somewhat. The only Japanese store I saw in Johore was a photographic studio.

In Netherlands India, Japanese are officially regarded as Europeans, nominally because, unlike other Orientals, they are monogamists, but really because their activities and social status were not in the least like those of Chinese or Indians but rather like those of European residents: they were engaged in wholesale trade and in the professions, wore European clothes, stayed at European hotels, and did all the sights like other foreign tourists. Pretexts were not wanting for surveying all the coasts, climbing all the mountains, and taking photographs of all the landmarks.

VIII

IMPACT OF THE WEST

YET one more alien race came after the treasure of tropical Asia. Their ships, too, drifted toward its white beaches and the green spell of its forests, lured by wondrous tales of spices and precious woods and ivory and gems. They, too, came as merchants and colonists, as before them had come the Arabs — who told those tales — the Indians, and the Chinese, as after them were to come the Japanese.

No one knows how many Portuguese, first Occidentals systematically to explore these seas, there are in Southeast Asia today, not even in what remains of their own former empire, the eastern part of Timor. On Celebes, once a Portuguese stronghold, there were in recent years only a few hundred Europeans, not counting the garrison, out of a total population of four million. But this does not mean that the Portuguese have disappeared from the scene. Both their blood and traces of their cultural legacy are quite evident. Both in Celebes and in the environs of Malacca in British Malaya you may come across people who look in no way different from their neighbors but who carry high-sounding Portuguese names and, if encouraged, will tell you of their illustrious ancestors. Christians for many generations, these quasi-Portuguese often have a better education than others and are employed in secondary positions in the army or in the civil service.

The Spaniards, dispossessed of their Asiatic empire only

a generation ago, have retained their identity to a much greater extent. Between four and five thousand Philippine citizens are supposed to be of almost pure Spanish strain, and there are also several hundred thousand Filipinos of mixed Spanish and Malay blood, spread throughout the islands. Like the Normans in England, those families of the conquering race which possessed themselves of large landed estates have survived longest. Only one industry of importance, cigar-making, has remained to some extent in Spanish hands, and this because much of the capital is still owned in Spain.

How many Hollanders have settled and become part of the permanent population of Netherlands India, I do not know. In the first place, the census statistics are made up on political rather than ethnic lines, and secondly no distinction is made — or could easily be made — between permanent residents and transients. The number of Netherlands "immigrants" in the last two decades was second only to that of Chinese — but a long way second. The rigid trusteeship assumed by the Government over the native interest in the soil had discouraged European immigration, so that the 1930 census enumerated only 200,000 Netherlanders in a total of only 240,000 "European" residents. Most of these Netherlanders have Malay blood in their veins. These mixed bloods range through the whole colonial hierarchy — from the disinherited Indonesian proletariat to the alien upper crust. In Holland itself one per cent of the population is said to have a Malay strain.

The number of Frenchmen and Britishers permanently resident in the East Asiatic tropics is too small to be counted. Even with the transients, armed forces and all, their total number before the war came to only 18,000 in British Malaya, 43,000 in Indo-China, and much smaller numbers elsewhere. In the Philippines, Americans numbered not quite nine thousand before the war, with only a few hundred of each of various European nationalities.

A good deal has been written about that rather picturesque group, the American army pensioners of the Spanish War who refused to go home and managed to live fairly comfortably with their Filipino wives and children — usually not too far from a post office to receive their pension, which they eked out with the proceeds of an occasional fishing expedition and of a few banana or coconut trees in their yards. Obviously, there are not many of them left. Their children have not found it difficult to accept the rights and duties of Philippine citizenship. They never were as badly off as the several thousand children of American soldiers left with deserted and unwedded Filipinas, on whose behalf the late Bishop Brent and General Leonard Wood often pleaded with the charitably disposed. These Americans also seem to have by now become fully absorbed in the Filipino population.

Colonial society in Southeast Asia is sometimes described as a pyramid at the bottom of which are the natives, above them Chinese and Arabs and Indians as a middle class, and Europeans at the top — numerically a mere pin-point, but controlling all the rest. Actually, the situation is much more complicated. I would place at the bottom the wage-slaves who may be native or immigrant, quite a step above them the independent peasants, however poor they may be. Most of the so-called "merchants" are little better off than the peasantry, being small storekeepers or holders of market stalls or even peddlers who travel up and down the countryside. They hardly constitute what we would call a middle class. It is true that the more prosperous merchants, clerks and overseers, and civil servants, professionals of all sorts are often immigrants or sons of immigrants; but natives everywhere increasingly offer these a stiff competition as they, too, enjoy better chances of education and better social connections.

As for the top, we should think, first, of the princes, like the Sultan of Sulu — the only monarch who rules under the Stars and Stripes. They certainly must be ranked high even if they no longer exercise as much political power as in the past. As a matter of fact, several of these princes, with a good European education and part owners of some of the largest enterprises, are more powerful today than their predecessors were a hundred years ago. Below them is the indigenous aristocracy with roots often deep in the past but likewise sometimes surprisingly modern in their grasp of political and economic issues. Europeans, it is true, own the most important enterprises and occupy the highest posts in all the governments except the two republics, Thailand and the Philippines. But the Occidental owners of those enterprises do not reside in the colonies.

In the dependencies, the European managers of mines and estates are well paid and, because of the magnitude of their responsibilities, often politically influential. The European public officials also may be powerful beyond the limits of their immediate responsibilities. But always — and we are too liable to forget this — there is also a rich and influential native social group which, however few of its members may attain to high offices, must be reckoned with politically because of its influence with the masses.

In recent decades there has been a change in the European personnel, both public and private, which it is important to know about, especially if you have read fiction or books of reminiscence that feature the old-time magistrate or plantation manager. Both officials and business executives have become more professional and less despotic in their outlook. They may have fine homes and treat themselves well; but their expenditures are not nowadays intended so much for purposes of ostentation — to show the natives what superior beings they are — as for comfort and efficiency. No doubt some of them could live more simply.

But has not that been true, in the pre-rationing days, of a good many of us at home, too?

Since in this as in any truthful book that touches upon the fruits of Western imperialism there will be statements that criticize existing or recent colonial regimes, I want to say here that I have nowhere found a finer type of men than among the British, Dutch, French, and American officials in Southeast Asia. Think of half a dozen men in our own government who, in your opinion, are doing their jobs conscientiously, are well equipped for them, invariably place the public interest before their personal convenience, are considerate in their contacts with the public, industrious to a fault, and of wide culture. Their combined portrait gives you the average high-ranking colonial "bureaucrat" of Southeast Asia. I also have had occasion to admire the Occidental military officers whom I met in that region; not one of them was a blood-thirsty militarist. Many of these officials, military and civil, have made valuable contributions to scientific knowledge. One Hollander whom I came to know, a horticulturist, and not high-salaried by American standards, paid out of his own pocket for the publication of an interesting scientific report when, during the financial crisis, the appropriations for his department had been cut. A British bureau head in Singapore I found spending all his spare time in befriending the unfortunate. In Saigon I met, during an exceptionally hot spell, a French official who was a scholar of international reputation and who could easily, had he wished to do so, have had himself transferred to a climatically more pleasant center. These men, I discovered, were not exceptions, though I also met other officials who seemed lazy, self-indulgent, and incompetent. There is an occasional tyrant in every bureaucracy; but sometimes a seemingly despotic decision results from timidity rather than from self-assertion. I saw an example of this when I took up with a colonial official a frequent criticism, of which he was well aware, that he did not promote native civil servants to the degree to which their competency and their attention to duty entitled them — in their own opinion and that of their sympathizers. I found that this higher-up was so jealous for the reputation of the native staff that he preferred to be charged with prejudice rather than risk making appointments that might add to the uncertainty still prevalent in European circles concerning the stability and honesty of those native groups that were clamoring for greater recognition.

In the European business community also, the social climate has changed. Heavy drinking, gambling for large stakes, the irresponsibility of men far from the restraining influence of family and set, have given way to the manners — if not all the refinements — of European country life. This is largely a question of investment: with the enormous sums which a large foreign-owned enterprise often represents nowadays, a high-class staff cannot be allowed to dissipate its usefulness to the company. Better homes are provided, better transportation, a more active social life.

Partly because of these improved conveniences, perhaps partly causing them, more European women have joined their husbands in the Asiatic colonies. Their presence has had both a favorable and an unfavorable consequence — from the standpoint of the other population groups. It has ended a good deal of informal social intercourse between Occidentals and Orientals. Naturally, white women are more prejudiced than are white men against meeting Orientals on equal terms. But even if this were not so, the more elaborate homes maintained since the coming of white women widen the gulf between Occidental and Oriental modes of living. On the other hand, the presence of well-bred European women has made for a more lively concern, I was told, in the welfare of both the natives and the immigrant Oriental labor forces. Women accustomed to pay

attention to the practical side of problems often see at once
how an obvious ill can be corrected where men, and especially college men, shrug their shoulders and discourse on
the inevitability of maladjustments in a complex organization. They may point out how unnecessary is the inhuman
"coolie line" type of housing which permits no family life
whatever and gives the workers the dreariest of imaginable
environments in which to vegetate between one work period and another. They may be able to show how, at no
great additional cost to the company, the legal requirements of provision for first aid, clinic facilities, hospital
beds, medical service generally, might be met pleasantly
and attractively rather than grudgingly and quite inade-
quately. Under the influence of such women, even the di-
rectors may learn that it pays to secure the good-will of
the workers, that fear and resentment are dangerous com-
bustibles to have around in any compound. Naturally fond
of children, such women will sometimes be impatient with
the schools provided for the children of workers — schools
which may meet the legal requirements and yet be farcical
as instruments of popular education when held in damp
and dark sheds, without proper equipment, by teachers who
have had no training for their posts. So, on the whole, the
trend toward a more paternalistic policy of management
has been re-inforced by the introduction of at least a little
maternalistic concern, as well.

This does not mean that race prejudice, snobbery, and
selfish group discrimination have ceased to be powerful
factors in the colonial society of Southeast Asia. Both Filipinos and Malayans have told me that social discrimination among Occidentals against natives is on the increase.
But I suspect that this only seems so because there is more
reaction to it on the part of race- and class-conscious members of the subject group. "Oppression psychosis" in the
days before the war was a contagious disease.

White Man's Prestige

When people said that the Japanese, through their victories over European powers in Southeast Asia, ended the feeling of the white man's superiority, they talked through their hats. That feeling, if ever it did exist widely, disappeared long ago. You can make it difficult for the intelligent Malayan or Annamite to secure a higher education, you can keep him out of important jobs and train him to obedience, but you cannot easily implant in him a sense of inferiority. He sees the white man's fumbling, his frequent lack of self-control, his dependence on physical comforts, and other far from super-human qualities. The whole idea that white men could maintain their prestige by wearing white linen suits and kicking other people around has probably been a mistake from the start. Only the rifles in white men's hands and the priceless fruit of their inventiveness which they were able to hand out gave them their position of power. When they arrogated to themselves superior wisdom, the Orientals outwardly agreed with them but never doubted that in time they themselves could master all the tricks.

If you had happened to be in Manila or Batavia or Singapore or Rangoon in the years just before the war, the social discriminations against Orientals in white circles would probably have struck you as more or less inevitable in some circumstances and preposterous in others. Where there are legal bars against the employment of members of one group or another — as, for instance, in most of the armies and navies — it would be rather artificial for officers in their private lives to cultivate a social equality that is taken out of their individual judgment in their vocational life. On the other hand, most of the discriminations against natives or Orientals in general are merely customs without anything to justify them.

There was in recent years more social contact between people of the different racial groups than there used to be, and more of it on a level of equality. This is not difficult to explain. I have already referred to the European's changed attitude toward his job. Nowadays, a young man who expects to spend several years in Tonkin or Java or Borneo or Burma will almost certainly learn something of the local language. In fact, his employer, whether private or public, will probably insist on it. His predecessor, thirty years ago, went around with an interpreter or used the so-called Coastal Malay language which is a simplified and sterile medium of intercourse between superior and inferior, very much as pidgin-English used to be until, quite recently, it was subjected to a process of refinement. The main reason, however, is that there are more natives and more immigrant Orientals who are the young European's intellectual equals than was the case a generation ago. Despite all the educational set-backs and prohibitions, many thousands of them speak a European language fluently and, what is more, have almost the same attitude as the educated European toward most matters of common interest.

The only subjects on which it is sometimes a little difficult for a European and an Oriental to converse are those that have to do with Oriental society, Oriental customs and beliefs, and the like. On such matters the one is prone to be ignorant but inquisitive and the other antagonistic. Not that the Oriental is ashamed of his cultural background, but he sees no point in dragging out "those old superstitions" which, to his mind, are of no importance in these days. He wonders what the Occidental would think if he, the Oriental, were continually trying to shift the conversation to questions on medieval torture chambers, ridiculous cults, or the social customs of Coney Island. When it comes to discussions of the essential differences between Oriental and Occidental society or mentality, the interested white person will easily hold his ground, for his Oriental friend will probably not be able to grasp what it is all about, never having had an opportunity to scrutinize the occult Oriental talents which he is alleged to be carrying in his own mind. Therefore he would rather discuss with you the latest motion picture, some political personality, some peculiarity of language — in fact anything that involves some tangible difference or difficulty of understanding that might be cleared up in friendly confabulation. It often came as a shock to me when a Filipino or Javanese acquaintance in some little backwater of a small town would interrupt a conversation about local matters to ask me whether I had read such and such a book by H. G. Wells or whether it was true that a man cannot be punished in America for killing a colored person.

English colonial society differs from French, Dutch, and American in that it represents a more unified class. Not so long ago those who went out to the colonies belonged, in the main, to the public-school set (in the English sense where it means the opposite) or tried to behave as though they did. And although there are now greater social distances between officials, planters and traders, these people, as Englishmen, still feel superior to anyone else, whether Occidental or Oriental.

In Indo-China I was told that European society had sufficiently changed in character to make a difference in its relations with the native people. Since the World War too many people of a crude type had come out to make a fortune; and as they were ostentatious and vulgar they were tending to lower the esteem in which French officials and business men had been held. I do not know how much truth there is in this charge. However, on the positive side it was evident to me that the officials and the French people with old-established connections in the colony were sensitive to the finer shades of considerateness in their relations with the Annamites and other natives.

Some people now go around saying that the white man's time in Eastern Asia is over, that after this war his every position of special privilege will be gone, and the various colonial peoples will, on a world-wide wave of democracy, gain the right to run their own lives, economically and politically. To me it seems that several different propositions are jumbled together in such a statement. Without going into matters that have no place in this chapter, it may, first of all, be agreed that a strong push will probably open much wider for the natives those doors of vocational and political opportunity which now creak as their hinges all too slowly turn. The heavy hand of foreign rule will become, much more quickly than in recent decades, the helping hand of foreign partnership. "Preparation for full self-government" will be a program rather than a pious phrase. Here and there — certainly in the Philippines, perhaps soon in Netherlands India or in Burma — the white man's privileges will disappear altogether. But that does not mean that the white residents will go home or that foreign financial interests in the region's trade, production, and development will suddenly be withdrawn. Capital cannot be created out of thin air; and even the more advanced indigenous groups often still have to learn how by saving they may finance their own economic security and progress. Where there is foreign capital there will also be a certain amount of foreign control.

But the Occidental interest in Southeast Asia is changing. Already, in Netherlands India, it is no longer true that white men never dirty their hands with manual work. There, thousands of Hollanders and sons of mixed marriages, who legally rank as Europeans, are engaged in it. They are represented in every income group, from three hundred guilders a year up. In the British colonies, exceptional Europeans have established themselves to experiment with dairy farming and to engage in a variety of manual trades. In the Philippines, many of the White Russian and Jewish refugees belong to the working and small shop-keeping class rather than the owning class. Some white Americans, too, had before the coming of the Japanese established themselves in small shops and were competing successfully with Orientals. There were among them auto repair workers and skilled mechanics in other metal trades. They were employed as clerks, editors, teachers, craftsmen, skippers, machinists, inventors, horticulturists, mining engineers, and a hundred other vocations, all without benefit of a vocational monopoly.

Mixed Blood

Mixed marriages are not often successful — as we measure success. The reason is social and not biological. (There is no dearth of children sound in body and mind.) The gulf between the societies of husband and wife, of father and mother, is often too wide for one generation to span. The sense of mutuality attained in intimate personal relations is not matched by a similar sense in the surrounding community. On the contrary, the members of such mixed families may be made to feel from both sides that they do not quite belong. This is, in fact, usually the case; and the unhappiness in their external relations may interfere with absolute cordiality and mutual devotion within the family.

It must not be imagined, however, that marriages between Occidentals and Orientals are any more fraught with danger than those between any people with rather different upbringing. The motion picture called "The Tuttles of Tahiti" portrays happy interracial family life at the bottom of society. For an example of such wedded bliss near the top, I offer the following. In one of the Outer Provinces of Netherlands India everybody knows the head of a technical school, a jovial Netherlander who has done more for the district where he lives than any other five men combined. His wife is a Malay and highly respected by everyone. She is not a "princess" either, or daughter of a chief, as a romantic writer might make her out to be; she is of humble peasant origin. Her husband fell in love with her when she was still quite young, made it possible for her to go to a middle school and a teacher-training college. She knows a little Dutch but not enough to speak it fluently. They live in a European house, but she never wears any but native dress. Their children are going through the European branch of the dual school system with a view to a college education in Holland for all three of them. But they are brought up in an atmosphere of intense concern for the welfare of the native people. The home is a center of discussion of industrial and educational plans to improve the social and economic life of the district, a very museum of native handiwork and humming with the gaiety of people who know where they are going and get satisfaction from their labors. I am sure there are many more such homes.

At one time, the Dutch Government with its Puritan traditions actually encouraged marriage between its colonials and native women and frowned upon irregular unions. I do not see how, in view of all the evidence, this policy can be said to have been anything but successful. The only reason why doubt has been thrown on its desirability more recently is purely political: the fact that the mixed bloods quite naturally become strong supporters of movements of liberation. There has never been any difficulty on the ground of religion. The children of such marriages have been considered little Hollanders by birth and have been given all the privileges of education and protection which European children born in the Indies enjoy. They were accustomed to the climate from birth and therefore less prone to its ill effects than other Europeans.

In the earlier years, these mixed bloods were missionaries for European ideas and strong upholders of colonial rule. They were everything an imperial government could wish for in the way of an intermediate group ready to facilitate the relations between the rulers and the ruled. Only with the rise of nationalism did this happy picture fade. The mixed bloods now became problem children. With better hygienic and housing facilities, more European women had come to live in Indonesia, and they would not associate with half-bloods or recognize the native wives of some of their husbands' colleagues. Perhaps the rise of racialist theories in Europe also had something to do with the change in the prevailing attitude. The leading families of Amsterdam felt a little embarrassed when they had to invite to their parties relatives with Malay features. It required an enthusiastic American tourist traffic before the good people of the Netherlands woke up to the fact that the cultural heritage of Island India and the beauty of its people was something to be proud of. Until that happened, the fashion was to look down upon those of their countrymen who had permitted themselves to be "dragged down" to the level of the "natives" (pronounced with scorn). The law could not be changed, but life had become more difficult for Hollanders with Javanese grandparents. Even now, officials with native wives are debarred from promotion. The great rubber and coffee corporations show a preference for colonial employees with wives at home awaiting their return.

Of late, a new handicap to the children of mixed marriages has arisen from the disinclination of race-conscious nationalist groups to recognize Eurasians as equally interested with them in the building of an independent native state. These political groups are not large, and their discrimination against the half-bloods, while understandable, has little justification in fact; for the Eurasians more than

anybody else are concerned in getting rid of European rule
with all the limitations it places on their own professional
and political advancement. They are in the forefront, at
least, of the negative side of a movement the positive, asser-
tive racialism of which they cannot, of course, fully share.

Often the mixed bloods occupy technical key positions
in the social structure, a fact obscured by their lack of execu-
tive power. For instance, many of them in Burma before
the war filled those railway and public service positions
which, half-way between manual labor and profession, neither Englishmen nor Burmans could or would take up in
sufficient numbers. They were extremely loyal to the Government — more British than the British themselves — but
at the same time constantly complained about their inability to get promotion to jobs of real importance. For
them, "dominion status" would mean an opening of vocational opportunities now firmly barred by race prejudice.

Sometimes the position of the half-Europeans is described as "tragic." This is an exaggerated view of a situation that is already passing. Dutch, British, French and
American attitudes toward racial intermarriage and toward
the Eurasian differ in many respects; but throughout the
region too many of the latter have broken through vocational and social taboos to permit a pessimistic outlook as
regards the future. Certainly, no one can say that the mixed
blood in Thailand or the Philippines is a tragic figure. Perhaps, the description is meant to apply to those who, although partly of European blood, have never worn shoes
or spoken a European language, yet think of themselves as
members of the ruling race. The several half-caste members
of the Volksraad — the popular legislative assembly of the
Indies — sit with their Javanese colleagues, make no such
pretensions, and are not unhappy at all. In the Philippines,
Bishop Brent used to say that the politicians were mostly of
Spanish-Filipino blood, and that one could not really tell

much about the political capacity of the racially pure Filipinos until more of them had had a chance of a good education.

In some parts of the Philippines, the daughters of American fathers and Filipina mothers have a high price in the
marriage market because they are exceptionally pretty and
resemble the aristocratic Spanish girls. In white circles they
are regarded as Filipinas — and kept at a distance; but since
they usually come from modest homes, they are quite content to marry into a good Filipino family.

We must remember that throughout Southeast Asia, and
especially in the coastal areas, we confront historically cosmopolitan communities in which the melting pot has been
simmering for centuries. Chinese immigrants of the second
generation more often married native than Chinese women,
simply because there were not enough of the latter around,
also for the practical reason that a native woman can be
a great help to her husband in his business. Even in a Mohammedan neighborhood, a typical street crowd tends to
be racially mixed. In Batavia, people who had lived there
all their lives could not tell me by looking at them the racial
origin of the people walking around the market. Englishmen in Malaya never seem to be able to get over their surprise at the complete harmony that reigns between Malays
and Chinese and Indians and Javanese.

Against the influences which accentuate the major ethnic
divisions, consider the inevitable tendency of the different
native groups gradually to grow together. Though they
are biologically as different from each other as are the various peoples of Europe, the ever-increasing contacts between them must result in intermarriage and gradual assimilation. In Java itself, little more than half the people
are Javanese. On the other hand, the Javanese have spread
out over several islands and there, with others of the more
civilized Malay groups, have formed at least a thin upper

crust. Because of their superior economic position, the men
of this native upper class secure women of the other groups.
This is, in fact, an "old native custom," as the great anthropologist Walter William Skeat pointed out long ago: the
more advanced Malay groups on the mainland, too, in their
customary law recognize marriages with women of more
primitive groups but place a strong taboo on marriages of
their own women with men of the despised groups.

As in the Occident, so in the Orient, too, cultural rather
than racial distinctions determine the rate of intermarriage.
Thus, the Annamites, who are far more advanced than the
other major groups in Indo-China, rarely intermarry with
Cambodians, though they have settled in large numbers
among them to benefit from Cambodia's rich rice lands.
The Cambodians, on their part, seem to have considerable
racial pride and are stricter in refusing their daughters to
Occidentals than are Annamites of a comparable social
status. Cambodians and Tonkinese have few points of contact; but from what I heard, there is no acute dislike between them like that between Cambodians and Annamites.

Abolition of the Hindu caste system has made for racial
intermingling, some of it in quite recent times. So little of
the Hindu physiognomy and gait appears among the people of Bali today because the few high-caste women of Indian descent could marry only into their own caste, while
its male members were free to marry women of the lower
castes. Thus the original blood of the conquering upper
stratum of society has grown thin. And since the new nobility, when it did take native wives, most likely took them
from the old proto-Malay aristocracy, this group, though
small, had a better chance of survival.

So also in the Philippines the intermixture of strains is
far more complex than one could assume from an enumera-
tion, say, of the languages spoken. Hindu and Armenian,
Japanese and Arab elements have entered into these strains

during four centuries and more of active trade relations. The Spanish ship crews were made up not only of Iberian but also of Moorish and diverse European stocks. This explains why the Tagalogs look different from the Ilocanos and other groups with a lesser content of Spanish but a correspondingly larger content of Chinese blood. According to H. Otley Beyer, the well-known American ethnologist at the University of the Philippines, there are today in the Philippines no less than forty-three distinct ethnic groups, speaking eighty-seven languages and dialects. Yet basically they are all Malays. Now they are growing together into a single people through the large increase in mobility and through their political unity. The present war, I have been told, has gone far to remove what clannishness there still was among politicians and among students. The latter, when I was in Manila in 1936, still flocked together in the dormitories according to whether they were Pampanguenos, Visayans, or Ilocanos.

Both the last war and the present one have produced an enormous increase in international marriages — some successful and some otherwise. Far more numerous and socially significant, however, are those war-time marriages that effect an internal mingling of ethnic strains in the various nations. I am not referring to the ravages of conquering alien troops or the gentle amorous exploits of national troops when encamped amidst an admiring rural population, but to the more continuing influence of mobilizing the civilian populations of whole districts and provinces. There has not, in modern time, been as much general movement of population in the Malay world as the present war has produced. It is difficult to estimate its racial and cultural consequences, or those of the incipient movement of population re-settlement which, begun just before the war, will undoubtedly take on much larger proportions as the war continues.

Throughout Southeast Asia population movements took place in pre-war years that tended to interrupt the isolation of separate cultures and separate ethnic identities. There has always in this region been much more mixture of peoples than is shown by their degree of cultural assimilation, although this also is clearly recognizable. But their separation has been overcome by no influence as much as that of modern means of travel. Technical backwardness, political oppression, and the inertia always associated with extreme poverty long prevented them from meeting as pioneers in the exploitation of the virgin soils that were waiting for their use. With modern transportation and with the need of large-scale enterprises for concentrated labor forces, the old melting pot of Southeast Asia has started simmering again. Will it this time produce a more homogeneous society? Or will international jealousies and imperialistic rivalries again place their barriers between the peoples of the East Asiatic tropics?

IX

NEW WANTS

In his Monterey speech on April 20, 1943, President Roosevelt said: "We know that the day of the exploitation of the resources and the people of one country for the benefit of any group in another country is definitely over." That is not, as some newspaper writers have intimated, a declaration aimed at the European empires, now our comrades in the war for freedom. For each of them — if one may accept the leaders of Fighting France as spokesmen for the French — has already declared much the same thing. (Chiang Kai-shek gave forcible expression to it on behalf of China in his war anniversary speech of July 7, 1943.) Each of them can look back upon steps already taken to reduce that exploitation. Nevertheless, much remains to be done; for with the business men and the officials who administer Western economic enterprise in the colonies there go the silent shadows of the anonymous shareholder, the rentier, the speculator, the industrialist and working-man and consumer who profit from the cheapness of tropical raw materials — all the millions of beneficiaries of sweated colored labor. The impact of their often wholly unconscious greed has not yet been entirely removed and cannot be entirely removed as long as the livelihood of the colonial peoples depends so largely on foreign private capital.

The one short sentence in a presidential speech brings

us up sharply before the core of the colonial problem and
the central problem, too, of the external relations of countries which, though politically independent or on the way
to independence, are economically bound by the same system. Conditions of labor have much improved — especially
in Western-owned enterprises — but the ills of unfreedom
and exploitation live on. Not only this, but the effects of
former oppression continue to dominate the economic
landscape. Physically, some of the lack of vitality and sus-
ceptibility to disease which we find in tropical countries is
undoubtedly a result of bad living conditions suffered for
generations. Mentally, some of the opposition to change,
some of the lack of enterprise that has been noted by so
many observers, comes from the hopelessness of enslaved
peoples; such attitudes permeate the social outlook and are
handed on from generation to generation. Illiterate population groups have long memories. A new labor policy or
a new trend in colonial administration, which would go far
to wipe out old wrongs in a people kept intellectually active
by many interests outside those of home and job, takes much
longer to elicit a changed response in the backward hinter-
lands of civilization.

It also takes time, as we well know in the United States,
to wipe out the prejudices nurtured in the dominant social
group by contacts with a socially inferior group. The ration-
alizations by which injustice has been supported for so long
continue to falsify attitudes and beliefs even when a sincere
effort is under way to modify the relations between the two
groups.

Freedom from Want

For the average American who has had no direct contact
with the Orient there is an essential likeness in all Asiatics.
He thinks of all those in Eastern Asia, at any rate, as belonging to the "yellow race," a race quite differently con-

stituted from his own. For example, Asiatics "can live on a handful of rice." The Asiatics, on their part, see themselves confronted by a race which arrogates to itself the right to exploit the labor of others. Some of them have been so cowed that they accept the white man's estimate of his own superior worth. Others, with a lurking pride in their own by no means contemptible historic past, have come to doubt whether white civilization can survive at all unless supported by colored labor. If these attitudes should prevail there would be no meeting ground between East and West. Efforts at co-operation for common ends would continually go to wreck on misunderstandings and mutual suspicions. We must face the truth, and the truth is not palatable.

White men have hypnotized themselves into believing that, in terms of their own standards of living, the Orientals — and especially the inhabitants of the East Asiatic tropics — are as well off as Occidental workers who receive several times their pay. Let us look at the argument. From the standpoint of international trade it is obviously nonsense. No matter where it is spent, twenty-five cents in our American currency is just "two bits" and no more. You can change it for a half a peso in Manila or for a fraction of a Singapore dollar, or for its equivalent in any of the other currencies of Southeast Asia and it still grows no larger in what it will buy. For many articles prices may be different from those paid in America, but not because your half dollar is more in Manila and in Singapore than it is in New York and San Francisco. Apart from the charge for brokerage, it will remain the same, no matter how many times you change it back and forth.

We are not going to let ourselves be deceived, then, by the conspiracy among colonial writers who play up that peso or that Singapore dollar or that florin in Java as though, "judged by local conditions," it were pretty adequate pay for a job which in Europe or America would cost several times as much. For the "local conditions" are precisely those which the Western wage-earner refuses to accept and refuses to compete against if he can possibly help it. But the writer whose business it is to display colonial economics in a favorable light grows almost lyrical over the generosity of an employer who pays half a peso a day to large numbers of laborers. He plays up that half-peso, or whatever it is, as though it were a sort of ideal standard wage which, once attained, should satisfy any native worker.

Apart from the fact that the great majority of field workers do not get even as much as that quarter of a dollar a day, it does not represent a "living wage," as any arbitration court in a civilized country would interpret that term. It does not permit the wage-earner to live with his family in health and reasonable comfort. It buys only the most monotonous kind of diet, and this lacking in nutritive value. With such a wage he cannot provide for his family even the minimum of decent clothing or more than a single room to live in. It does not enable him to make any provision for his old age, to take out insurance, to pay anything for his own education or that of members of his family.

If anyone were to dispute these points, it would still be true that a laborer earning no more than the "standard" wage in any country of Southeast Asia would go through life entirely cut off from the modern civilization which science and invention have made possible and which he, if he is employed in a modern enterprise, helps to support. When a Philippine or a Malayan or a Netherlands Indian employer can prove that his workers receive the equivalent of an American quarter dollar a day, he still is far from proving that they receive a "fair" wage. Even an individualist who believes that inequalities in reward are inevitable as long as there are inequalities in the value of men's efforts, will admit that there must be something wrong with a sys-

tem under which only the stockholders and the white employees of large economic enterprises can enjoy some of
those things which Occidentals usually consider essential
for a worthwhile existence — say, three meals a day, a
change of decent clothes, a clean bed and a reasonable
amount of other furniture, reading matter and writing
utensils — and the knowledge to use them — medicines, a
dwelling proof against rain and insects, opportunity for at
least short travel and for communication with friends, a
little equipment for recreation and for a hobby, ability to
make modest contributions to charity and other public purposes. I will stop there. One can't enumerate all such
niceties as table linen, ice water, an occasional bit of finery
for wife or daughter, or such varying necessities as baby
carriages, surgical appliances, and sewers. The point I am
trying to make is that it is sheer hypocrisy to say that a
workman in a warm climate does not need even the equiva-
lents for those things which a workman in our own climate
needs for physical and mental efficiency.

But then we are told that, even though the native cannot with his wage buy the same degree of physical and
mental efficiency as the Occidental, he is happier in his
native civilization. An enthusiast of the simple life — for
others — may even add that the native is happy in proportion to his lack of contact with Western life and his
ignorance of its paraphernalia. There might be something
in this — though I doubt it, as everybody must who knows
of the perils and fears of primitive life — yet those who
use that argument do not in the least intend that the carriers of Occidental civilization should move out and leave
the natives a free field. Nor do they wish to spare the native
contact with modern forms of production and modern tools.

Of course, living conditions must vary with climate and
local environment. But the white man does not cut out of
his life all the refinements to which he has become accus-

tomed as soon as he settles in the tropics. On the contrary, with the aid of cheap colonial labor, he adds to the refinements and the complexity of his standard of living. And just because he depends so much on the low cost of native labor for the maintenance of his own standards, he often decrees that members of the native races shall not enjoy the instrumentalities of modern living.

For the Asiatic the impact of the West has nevertheless meant a considerable change in *standards* of living, though sometimes with no commensurable change in *planes* of living: schools and health officers, and not least the example of the Occidental's own way of life, have given large numbers of native people new tastes which they are unable to gratify. In a more or less homogeneous society, such as that of most European countries, the introduction of new wants makes for progress: seeing others enjoy some new comfort or convenience, the average person will be stimulated to earn more so that he too may enjoy it. In our country, the plane of living in the countryside has risen as, with better, cheaper, and quicker facilities of travel, the agriculturists came more often in contact with the life of cities and it became feasible for them to participate more fully in the advantages previously enjoyed only by city dwellers. But this gain was possible only because the rural folk had the opportunity of earning more by applying greater ingenuity, efficiency, and organization to their productive efforts. An expanding industry provided them with expanding markets.

When these or similar conditions are not present, the example of higher living standards set by outsiders has the effect, not of creating the incentive for higher production and hence a higher purchasing power, but rather a false and socially injurious imitation. A Filipino writer complained to me a few years ago about the influence of American efforts to improve Philippine homes, clothes, diet, and recreations without providing any solid economic foundation with which to sustain additional expenditures. He was referring more especially, of course, to city people and to the educated classes. Americans sometimes smile about the superficiality of the Filipino worker's adoption of Western tastes, his love for showy clothes and jewelry: the framed enlarged photographs, the fountain pens, the ornamental brasses, the silken hangings. But is not all this very natural? The Filipino factory worker, clerk, or servant, still paid as though he lived in a small nipa hut, on the produce of a tropical garden and on intermittent wage labor, cannot appreciate the real character of the "higher" culture to which he aspires.

The wealthy and educated Filipino is not so naive, and indeed often is completely assimilated if not to American then to Spanish tastes and ideas, including sports and literary enjoyments. Even he, with greater insight into modern Western living standards, often is tempted to indulge in additions to his own which he cannot really afford; and that temptation arises out of that totality of social relations between white man and brown which produces in the latter a sense of inferiority unless he can, at least in externals, raise his status to that of the former.

The Luxury of Good Health

Even the genuine demand for education and for modern sanitation may be injurious when these are luxuries which economic discrimination in business or public service do not permit the sensitized Filipino to enjoy. President Quezon in a speech before the National Assembly in 1938 pointed out that, with all the "progress" recorded in the reports of government departments, a majority of Filipinos still were not in a position economically to send all their children to school or to let those who went finish primary instruction.

Much the same may be said about the changing living standards of Javanese, Annamites, Thai, and others. The incongruities in their incipient assimilation to world civilization spring to the eye. But always there is a deeper and more widespread demand for things of real worth, and especially for those ingredients of modern — no longer exclusively Occidental — culture which individuals cannot buy for themselves but which only organized social activity can provide. Because he lives in a tropical country, with its many hazards to health and life, the Malay is more in need of costly public improvements than the dweller in a temperate climate. We can be happy in a rude cottage in the Rocky Mountains, because in our climate it is easy for the individual to provide himself with the essentials of a healthy outdoor life. We need more food and more clothing than the Filipino, perhaps a greater variety of implements to meet the demands of our changing seasons. But it is not true therefore that the dweller in the tropics can live that more cheaply. His needs are different but just as great. Trails are more quickly overgrown, so that roads are essential to communication even in sparsely settled districts. Water putrefies more quickly, insects are more numerous and more poisonous; therefore disinfectants and antidotes and drugs of many kinds are an elementary need. In his climate he needs more soap, a more appetizing diet, more protection against storms and floods. The heat and the damp quickly spoil food, clothing, furniture, and the dwelling itself. Wood rots, metal rusts; a green moss covers everything untouched for a few days. So he needs preservatives of several sorts and great care in the selection of materials for his articles of daily use.

New Ideas of the Good Life

Personal cleanliness is so much a matter of health and comfort in a tropical country that one expects the standards in this respect to be exceptionally high. This, however, is by no means true for all tropical peoples. That it is true for the Malays has a number of special reasons: the abundance of fresh water in the areas of their densest settlement, the influence of Islam, and — only in the last place — that of the Occidental rulers. For even among the mountain people of Borneo, whom Western civilization has hardly reached at all, Lumholtz tells us, the women take baths three times a day and the men at least once, in the evening. The habit of building a house on stilts, observable in many parts of the region, seems to have always had cleanliness as well as protection for its motive. Houses are, whenever possible, built near a stream. The bathing and laundering habits of the Javanese have been observed by every traveller and often described in books. But those of the Thai and the Burmans are not inferior. Nor will you see a Filipino, unless he just happens to come from work, in any but a clean shirt. No matter how poor, the Malay peasant will not take any soiled object with him into his living room. (Shoes, of course, are not worn.)

The part which cleanliness plays in the standard of living of the Asiatic tropics illustrates the truism that quantitative measurements cannot determine the relative superiority of one standard of living over another. Environment and tradition so transmute the basically like values of the various branches of the human family that comparisons up and down a single scale make little sense. In some respects — not only in that of personal cleanliness but also in that of hospitality and generosity — the average standard of living among the Malays is probably higher than it is among most Occidental peoples. But one dare hardly mention this, because some one will immediately jump to the conclusion that differences in planes of living are not measurable at all; and so we are back again at the nefarious sophistry about the great enjoyment of life by the millions of colonials who have insufficient food, no clothes, houses that do not really shelter, and hardly any of the amenities which we consider indispensable.

When we see every evidence of primary poverty among the masses of a population, surely we cannot escape an honest evaluation and an honest search for causes. Not only is there something obviously wrong with the way in which the dependent and semi-dependent peoples of Southeast Asia live, as shown by the high incidence of disease and mortality; but there are also obvious things that can be done about it.

To remedy the grave deficiencies in their planes of living still remains primarily an Occidental responsibility — not so much because their continuation into this era of potential plenty is in large part a result of foreign exploitation but because the Occident has the remedies that fit the ills. Except for a small elite, the colonial peoples do not and cannot yet fully grasp what centuries of European expansion have done for them, and done to them. They cannot know enough to demand that kind of assimilation to the higher living standards of the West which, objectively considered, is best for them. The simple peasant and laborer is most attracted by those material traits of our culture which glitter or perform mechanical marvels. He reaches for our matches, lamps, tools, bicycles, if he can get them. Articles of Western clothing may lend distinction, but even more so does the possession of clocks and victrolas, anything made of shining metal, of colored glass, or of some such previously unknown or rarely seen substance as celluloid or rubber.

Christian missions and governments may have been instrumental in making the sewing-machine ubiquitous. The Malay's own sense of values accounts for the bicycle. A newspaper man (Walter B. Harris in *East for Pleasure*, 1929) tells of the experience of a Dutch Protestant Mission official who visited the churches in his outlying district in the Moluccas:

> "He addressed the local native schoolboys on the subject of salvation which, he explained, was the highest object a Christian could attain in this life. At the end of his address he asked the boys — 'Tell me, what is the highest attainment a good Christian can hope for in this life?' With one voice they replied, 'A bicycle, Sir.' "

This reminds me of the story which the China Relief Association has been sending around about a ten-year-old boy in Manila who used the money which he had saved for a bicycle to buy bread (literally, from a local baker) to aid the starving in China. The bread was sold to school children in Manila, and the proceeds were sent to China. An American woman who heard of the affair gave the boy a bicycle, to reward him for an unselfishness which, perhaps, only those can appreciate who know the glory which possession of a bicycle confers on any boy in the Philippines. Some months later, the boy wrote a letter of thanks to the donor, saying he was now earning money for relief in China by renting out his bicycle to other boys.

This story happens to be a good symbol of assimilation between the cultural standards of East and West. Its prerequisite is an economic level somewhat above that of the great majority of the people. Its dynamic is a high common purpose. Its means is an instrument of increased mobility.

The reader may think that too much has been made in the preceding pages of the West's influence on the material living standards of the East as represented by the Southeast Asiatic countries under the economic domination of the West. After all, our civilization is not to be measured only by our comforts and conveniences. What about individual freedom and the sense of personal responsibility?

Those Occidentals who have lived in the Asiatic tropics may even go so far as to say that a higher wage level will not bridge the essential difference in attitude between East and West: that difference, they may contend, lies precisely in the fact that the workers of Java, of the Philippines, of Tonkin, or of Thailand will not exert themselves when they do have the chance of raising their purchasing power by a more continuous effort. Give the brown laborer a higher wage and he will only work that much less. Make it possible for him to earn in three days what formerly it took him six to earn, and he will be off on the fourth day to watch a ball game, to fly a kite, to gad about, or simply to sit in a shady spot and smoke.

We must admit the truth, not because so many people testify to it but because it is psychologically sound. A higher wage offer does not in itself provide the incentive by which a people long exploited and outwitted may be raised to higher levels — even of material enjoyments. But, first of all, what is the first consideration to which in the given circumstances they must be expected to devote an addition to the regular income? If *you* had to work strenuously in a tropical climate without being physically very fit, what would you buy with the surplus of your earnings after the most urgent living costs have been met? Additional leisure, of course. These laborers do not, for the most part, have such a suitable diet as you would provide yourself with, they do not know how to keep free from parasites, never have had time enough to recuperate from their physical ills.

A higher wage, it is true, is not enough in such a situation to raise the plane of living. But there are examples enough among the modern enterprises carried on with foreign capital in Southeast Asia to show that the payment of a higher wage is indispensable for a transition from leisurely and inefficient ways of doing things to reasonably well-regulated modern ways. Under the new impetus of the

Atlantic Charter higher earnings for the workers will come from a fairer distribution between prices, profits, and wages; but this will not be enough. The general level of remuneration for colored labor — yellow as well as brown — is so low that only a real increase in productivity can raise it to the point where it will change the outlook of the workers. And with the rise of wages other influences must go. The worker's physical and mental fitness involves charges on industry as inescapable as does the supply of effective tools. I have seen some of the machinery that has gone into sugar centrals and other agricultural industries in the Philippines: it was either the best that money could buy or at least (I am no judge in such matters) reasonably up to date. But few of these industries as yet supply their workers with weather- and insect-proof houses, with adequate bathing and laundering facilities, with cool and distilled drinking water. Few as yet have made medical care and prophylaxis both freely accessible to the workers and members of their families and also attractive and educational, evoking a sense of partnership in the common concern of management and labor in better health.

English estate managers, more so than French or Dutch, believe in athletics and take an active leadership in them, often making up teams that play each other and so creating a good deal of playful *esprit de corps*. As long as they do not use such activities to take their workers' minds away from real grievances that ought to be corrected, the organization of such recreational facilities by the managerial staff is justified by its results. From what I have seen and what others have told me in Malaya, Netherlands India, and the Philippines, there is by no means too much of this kind of paternalism; or it is not sufficiently carried from relatively superficial relations between management and labor to the larger concerns they share — or should share.

Large estates far from cities often still rely on very in-

adequate provision for the health and welfare of their workers and then express surprise, sometimes, that these do not
"stick." Sometimes they try to hold their workers with the
aid of such incentives as bonuses or presents on holidays
but are dismayed to find that the peasant-workers do not
respond as wage-earners in Europe or America would.
Nothing in his experience has given the native worker the
feeling that it behooves him to work regularly if he can.
On the other hand, he cannot but be aware of the incon-
gruity between a show of paternal benevolence on the part
of management or of the authorities and the seeming
lack of consideration for him in matters of fundamental
importance to him. Interference with his freedom often
arises from the management's sincere concern for the welfare of the estate community; but he cannot understand
that. As a result, there is much dissatisfaction which on rare
occasions even expresses itself in destruction of property
and rioting. Native workers with almost no previous experience other than voluntary discipline do not like to be
pushed around by the plant police. They are sometimes sullen because they know of their employer's influence with
the local courts and do not expect to get justice there.

I am under the impression that in these respects there
is more tension in British Malaya than in Netherlands
India. The Dutch seem to have been more successful in applying paternalistic methods of management without need-
lessly offending the self-respect of the native workers. Americans in the Philippines at first were inclined to adopt the
rather impatient and unsympathetic ideas then current
among British plantation managers. But they soon learned
that Filipino workers could not be coerced, and that even
an occasional football game did not make up for the hatred
which any show of brutality engendered among the men.
The more successful American concerns today employ
managers or managerial assistants who speak the language

A crew lined up to report for afternoon work on a Sumatra rubber plantation. Their assignment is to treat the scars left in the trees after the collection of the latex.

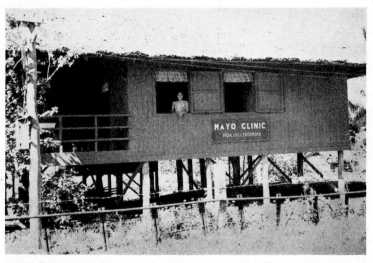

This clinic, with the nurse in the window, stands on a coconut and sugar plantation on the east coast of Negros, P. I. The Filipina who owns this plantation was educated in the United States.

The beginning of heavy industry in British Malaya. This foundry in Singapore, the largest in the colony, worked on a twenty-four hour schedule just before the war. Most of the laborers are Chinese.

of the workers and try to explain measures devised to improve health and efficiency, instead of harshly enforcing regulations that are meaningless to them. In Indo-China, problems of labor relations have not been studied with the same practical thoroughness. Large-scale foreign enterprises there are not as important as they are in Malaya and the two island archipelagos.

Labor under Duress

Let us now proceed to the more serious forms of unfreedom which are not matters of individual judgment but of public policy and even international legislation.

Corvée, or performance of labor for the state in lieu of tax payments, is still quite common everywhere in Asia. Glowing tributes have been paid to the Chinese and Burmese natives who did such valuable services in repairing the Burma Road during the Japanese attacks so as to insure a continued movement of supplies. But it is to be feared that much of the labor performed by these hundreds of thousands of men and women was neither a patriotic gift nor even a service contracted for and paid for in cash, but rather forced labor — and this arbitrarily imposed above that normally exacted for local and regional purposes. I am not sure, as a matter of fact, whether in any of the dependencies of Southeast Asia compulsory labor services in any one year are always strictly kept within legally required limits. Rather one gets the impression from various reports that it is always possible for local officials to impose extra services when these are needed. It may be that these are charged, like advance payments of taxes, against future obligations; but there seems to be no money compensation.

In Netherlands India, groups of men and women engaged in road-mending may more frequently be seen than elsewhere, this because there are more roads and these kept in better repair. To judge from the dense traffic on such roads, especially in Java, it must be supposed that the villagers benefit considerably from their exertion even though individual labor may not be paid for. In Indo-China, according to a report made by the Labor Inspection Service in 1939, "forced labor is in principle prohibited and has only been retained as a transitional measure in some outlying areas without means of communication, where no wage-paid labor whatever is available." In Thailand, likewise, it is a common excuse for compulsory labor services that free labor is not obtainable. This explanation is more likely to be true in the undeveloped hinterland than in the populated districts of estate and intensive farming where in normal times most of the road-making and other public works take place.

The hiring out of convicts, a system abandoned in most civilized countries, still seems to be in force in some parts of the region. A former British magistrate in North Borneo mentions this practice quite naively in his memoirs. He even commends it as giving an educational experience to felons who have committed crimes of some severity, while he does not consider it desirable treatment for petty thieves, who are less likely, indeed, to make good servants. But the system goes back before the time of foreign rule. Thailand used to have an especially odorous reputation for its treatment of crime: a whole village sometimes was rounded up to pay with forced labor for the alleged offense of a villager who could not be found. Only since the constitutional reforms has that country introduced an administration of criminal justice which substitutes reform schools and agricultural colonies for the former penal methods. Perhaps just because its modernization of the penal system is so recent, Thailand is rather ahead of the class in that respect — at least on paper. A rather dubious kind of penology must have been common in all the dependencies under "indirect rule," since the Orient is far more cruel in such matters than the Occident. Yet I have come across no accounts of *recent* instances that would indicate a widespread use of imprisonment as a means of securing labor services.

Serfdom continues among the descendants of rebels and criminals who, as in Cambodia, have served their noble masters for so long that they have acquired a more or less recognized status as craftsmen — similar to that of Greek slaves in Rome — and may even be settled in separate villages under a discipline not so strenuous as to make their lives intolerable. In one such case, enfranchisement under French law has been realized in name only. Actually the former serfs, the Khas, find it difficult to live as freemen and so continue in bond to their former masters — under the thin legal disguise that they are paying off debts.

The German Nazi government has raised to a new high level of public policy that mixture of public justice, of private interest, and of personal vengeance which masquerades as punishment for crime, as rounding up of hostages, and as compulsory labor service under military necessity. We no longer can speak of such practices as distinctively Oriental — if, indeed, they ever were. The colonial governments of Southeast Asia that adopted indirect rule have had considerable trouble with them in the past. Acknowledging the rule of native law and custom in the local authorities' criminal jurisprudence and in their treatment of native crimes and misdemeanors, they could nevertheless not altogether wash their hands of some responsibility for practices so cruel as to be repulsive to Western thinking. Today, native and Western concepts of justice seem to have become much more similar — except on one point, and that is the unacknowledged survival of caste attitudes in native thought. For example, the Poso tribes of Central Celebes — who came under effective Netherlands jurisdiction only in 1905 and who still are allowed considerable

freedom in the interpretation of their own *adat* or customary law — could not, a few years ago, be persuaded to
mete out equal treatment to members of different classes.
For them the status of slave and of freeman, at least, still
was a reality, even though they were no longer allowed to
sell slaves.

In the Philippines, the feudal peonage which existed at
the time of the Spanish conquest has never been quite eradi-
cated. It survives not only in the disguise of enslavement
for debt, but there are also still extant, though legally un-
recognized, hereditary relations of serfdom. These continue
either because the conditions are not too onerous or because
the members of the subjugated groups are too weak and
ignorant to effect their emancipation, and other population groups are too indifferent to do anything about the
matter. Among the Moros, slave raids into the forested hinterland of Mindanao still occurred within living memory.
The possession of female slaves was still common a decade
ago and presumably has not quite died out. The women
were, however, in recent times taken less often in raids than
in payment of debt, and they do not by any means always
serve purposes of concubinage or prostitution. Some of
these women may be seen hard at work around the homes
of prosperous Moros, doing the heavy work, living in hov-
els, and enjoying none of the usual amenities of household
servants.

In Laos, whole Moi tribes are practically enslaved to
their Laotian neighbors. Similar continuing relations between the descendants of ruling and subjugated groups
exist among others of the mountain peoples in Farther
India. Some have bought their freedom by retiring to bare
rocks, thousands of feet above sea level.

Furthermore, there survive in many parts of the region
conditions of peonage, pure and simple. The worker with
his family is part of the livestock of a given piece of land.

Although the owner cannot sell him, and other mutual obligations are settled by custom, the worker can neither rid himself of his overlord nor move off to lease another farm. This system exists in many outlying parts of Eastern Asia, even where it is not recognized in law. It is disguised by the fact that customary law does not make the clear distinctions between rent, tax, and obligatory labor services to which we are accustomed in the modern world. It resembles in that respect the feudal flavor which pervaded rural social relations in England right up to the first World War: a tenant farmer who displeased his landlord or failed to render any one of numerous services demanded of him, and of members of his family, could be sent off without compensation for the improvements he had made and, though nominally a free man, could not obtain another farm or even a small house. It was: obey or starve. Such a man is bound to the soil. But the relationship between the man who owns and the man who works the land in many parts of Southeast Asia is even more medieval than that. If the sharecropper absconds and is caught he can be punished and sent back to his employer and virtual owner. If he belongs to a tribe subjected by heredity to another, a Western judge would have even greater difficulty in disentangling his individual rights and responsibilities from those socially recognized as his according to general custom. In short, many types of partial unfreedom occur even under regimes that would not tolerate slavery. Nobody could say how many peons there are in the various countries of Southeast Asia. There can be no doubt, however, that their number is diminishing in proportion to the penetration of modern law and modern economy. It is disappearing, as serfdom disappeared from the English manor, because the owner can do better for himself with free labor.

Mention has already been made of what is usually called slavery for debt. As distinct from peonage, it is common in all parts of the region. But like peonage it is a survival under alien rule and not a consequence of Western conquest. In this chapter, devoted to the impact of the West, it may serve to illustrate the incompleteness of colonial rule. Pre-occupied with its own purposes and problems this has nowhere penetrated into the shady hinterland of native custom with its own heavy heritage of ancient wrongs.

X

CONFLICT OF OLD AND YOUNG

THE FIRST effect of the modern world's impact upon the tradition-steeped societies of the Asiatic tropics is discontent. If this were the only outcome of his new contacts the peasant might be better off under a system of rigid isolation. There are some people who think so. But discontent is only the reverse side of ambition and of hope. The Asiatic peasant's hopes and ambitions are usually modest enough to be realizable in a generation or two. Why put a stop to them? Just because some oversophisticated Occidentals like to watch the "native peoples" of the tropics in the unspoiled purity of their traditional culture? It is altogether too late to think of reconstructing a wall between races and cultures. The "unsurmountable barrier" between East and West is melting away. The "unchanging East" is changing so fast that Occidentals returning to it after an absence of thirty or forty years hardly recognize it. The young Malay of today emphatically does not feel or think or act or talk as his grandfather did. (One is tempted to add: "nor did his grandfather"! For that gentleman has been atrociously misrepresented in our literature.) He is as remote from the jungle head-hunter as the young American Indian soldier who sells war stamps from the steps of the Public Library is from the Red Man of Fenimore Cooper's tales. He is not likely to "run amuck," and you need not be afraid of his *kris,* if he does carry one.

Among the organized workers, tenant farmers on large estates, public employees, you will find few who chew betel — though in the villages there are still many people with teeth blackened by this unaesthetic habit. You may travel through large parts of Southeast Asia without once being accosted by a beggar. You may have dealings with a hundred officials not one of whom is hinting for a bribe. You may stay in scores of hostelries without coming across a servant who cringes. You may even meet Burmans who do not laugh and Javanese storekeepers who are not solemn. In short, the reader is advised to disregard at least one-half of all the generalizations about the peoples of this region which he may have read — including perhaps some of those to be found in this book. As everywhere in the world, climate and habitat, occupations, the state of civilization attained, inherited beliefs, traditions, customs — all have left their mark — but no more. They do not cut off one ethnic group from another to such an extent that they cannot assimilate.

Our writers have overstressed the unusual in describing the costume, ornamentation, marriage customs, and etiquette of this tribe or that, in order to make it more interesting. And these distinctions *are* significant. But the poor, half-starving peasant or laborer does not have time to live up to his reputation for "the unending patience of the East," nor has every indigenous noble the means to "bedeck himself with Oriental splendor." The latter as likely as not is puzzled how to fit the never-ending new demands of the modern economy into his accustomed and tradition-hallowed way of life. The former is a simple soul who responds as best he can to the more elementary demands of society upon him and tries to make a living. The one fundamental fact to remember is that vast numbers of people in our region are chronically underfed, suffer from permanent ailments, and are without the slightest security for the morrow. They are the tenants of nature's most prolific garden; but its fruits are not for them.

Among a certain class of writers it has become fashionable to emphasize the "inner conflicts" of the natives who are more advanced in civilization rather than the "unspoiled happiness" of the more primitive. Self-indulgence, passion, crime are the recurring themes. We are treated to dissertations about the "hot blood" of the tropics and given to understand that the indigenous man lives altogether for women, game-cocks, opium, and a cruel persecution of his enemies.

Actually, the Burman or Thai or Indonesian or Ilocano whom you are likely to meet — one of the great majority — does not conform to a type in all respects any more than you do. He may be conservative in some things, experimental in others, cautious on one occasion, daring on another. "A real Malay, didn't I tell you?" my English host exclaims as the smiling houseboy sweeps the dust from the porch and then, with a broom of somewhat different shape, sweeps it back again from the yard onto the porch. A real Malay, yes, because that boy did, as best he could, what he had been told to do; and he had never quite grasped the purpose of so much sweeping and cleaning. But his opposite will be a "real Malay," too. I remember a conversation between a Filipino foreman-contractor and his American boss in which the former refused to try out a suggested new plan for work assignment to his crew, simply on the ground that it had never been done that way. This same person carried a fountain pen and stylo, a cheap American watch, read a newspaper in English, drove an American car, and sent his children both to the village school and to a Protestant Sunday school. The Javanese with whom, through an interpreter, you talk about the management of the labor cooperative society will be able to explain an elaborate credit arrangement and yet be wholly and unquestionably ortho-

dox in the observation of his religious duties as a Mohammedan, including both his daily prayers and an elaborate
schedule of fasts and holidays.

In a time of change, there is, of course, a much greater
distance between the attitudes of youth and age than is
usually the case. The "inner conflict" of the individual may
be nothing more than the tension between a pull to the
ideas current in the older set and a pull to those current
in the younger one. The conflict is mainly external: between those who prefer to dwell in the past and those, the
great majority, who have made a partial adjustment to the
demands of the present.

Old Folks Shake Their Heads

Anyone who has lived in the Orient, whether in China
or in Japan or in any part of Southeast Asia, has at one
time or another met a member of that older indigenous
generation which is puzzled and chagrined by the changes
going on around it. I have met many such. One I remember well: an elderly Filipino bookseller in the old walled
city of Manila. He spoke English with difficulty, and I did
not understand all of his fluent Spanish, but I got the gist
of his remarks. I expressed some disappointment at finding
his stock of books so largely theological and jurisprudential,
because I had hoped to discover some literature, not too
difficult to read, about the Chinese community in Spanish
times. He did not share this interest. For him, Manila had
ceased to be a civilized place since trade and industry, and
with them much of the social leadership, had fallen so
largely into the hands of people grown rich through trade
and industry — people without good family connections
and without land. "They are only interested in money,"
he said, "and they do not care how they get it. They have
no respect for the Church even when they call themselves
Christians. In the old days people would take off their hat

when they met an *illustrado*. Today a judge of the Supreme Court can walk the length of the Escolta without even being recognized."

"But are you not all living better?" I asked. "I have heard much about the slums of Manila, but I find these old streets clean and in good repair. There are none of the skin diseases among the children which one sees in all Chinese cities, nor old people in rags." He admitted that few people went hungry, and that the sick were well provided for. What filled him with anger, apparently, was the materialism of the age. And back of it there were other tendencies in the city of which he disapproved but which I could not fully grasp. He did mention the unending sale of lottery tickets on the streets, high food prices, strikes among cigar workers, and — evidently no less a weight on his mind — the lack of respect toward him, an elderly intellectual, on the part of the law students who frequented his shop. And he blamed it all on the Chinese (and probably the Americans whom he was too polite to mention specifically).

In the same way, European residents in Java who spoke the language and dialect of their locality told me of the pessimism that prevailed among those Mohammedan storekeepers and artisans who had made the pilgrimage to Mecca and were called Hadjis. These men used to be treated with great reverence. Now the younger people will not even listen to them and their sayings from the Koran. Time was when everybody sat in silence while a Hadji told a story from the life of the Prophet or from the classics — a story with a moral. Time was when the patriarchs who had seen the holy city were called upon by others less fortunate to express themselves on the fairness of a business deal or the punishment suitable for the misdemeanor of a wayward child. Now nobody consults these old boys; and they, too, blame their loss of prestige on the foreigners and on the new ideas set afloat in the minds of youth. Their criticism of the Chinese merchants of the city — I happened to be especially interested in that subject at the time — was different from that of high government officials. Moslem shopkeepers, whether Arabs or Javanese, are not hostile to the Chinese national government — of which they know very little. (The Netherlands Indian officials at that time complained bitterly in private about the political pressure exerted by that government on the Chinese communities in the Indies through its consular representatives and, sometimes, special emissaries.) But they do not like to see their Chinese neighbors so prosperous because they are infidels. This is not just a matter of difference in religious faith, as when Catholics and Protestants fight it out in Holland or in America; but the two groups have conflicting attitudes on social matters. The Moslems say that these wealthy Chinese, by their example, lead the Javanese boys and girls astray. But what about the Europeans, I asked a friend, an editor.

"Nobody cares," he asserted, "what the Europeans do and how they live; they belong to a different world, are a law unto themselves. What they do and what they say is simply incomprehensible to the local people who do not associate with them in any way. But these Chinese are in small businesses and trades like the Javanese themselves, and the Indians and Arabs."

"Do not," I asked, "the Chinese keep themselves as apart from the rest as do the Europeans?"

"They do in a way," he continued, "but they are always visible. Everybody knows how they live, what they eat, how they do business, amuse themselves, and bring up their children."

The Moslem storekeepers dislike the lack of dignity among their Chinese neighbors and rivals. These do not keep up appearances or old-established class distinctions. There is not among them that respect of youth for age, of women for men, of servants for masters, which these Moslems like to instil in their youth. With their modern schools and with their newspapers, they say, the Chinese are tearing down the walls of social stability. From other conversations, too, I gathered that in the minds of these Javanese elders, much as in that of the Manila bookseller, personal and impersonal grievances are fused: they see their established position and their security waning; and the doings of the minority group offer the most obvious and respectable explanation.

Both in the Philippines and in Java, I have heard the Chinese referred to as "the Jews of Southeast Asia." A study of their unpopularity, especially in the older native groups that come in close contact with them, would throw considerable light on the nature of anti-Semitism. As in Europe, and to a lesser extent in America, the foundations of social security for those groups, usually orthodox and fundamentalist in their religious beliefs, have been crumbling for some time. And the main cause is everywhere the same: peoples which for many centuries have developed their distinctive ways of life in relative isolation have been thrown together, have been made unsure that the old ways are the best. They see people get on in the world whose tastes and morals, from the standpoint of their own traditions, are appalling. The kind of status and authority which the perplexed and horrified older men — and women — seek to retain can survive only as long as their own kind of society remains intact. If it can no longer be protected by isolation, it can survive only by being reinforced with wealth and political influence.

If one could get close to the more primitive communities in the different countries of Southeast Asia a similar state of resentment and fear for the future would probably present itself. But the situation would not be quite the same everywhere. Away from the coast there are no conspicuous

minority groups on which to blame the changes that undermine the established authority of the elders and of the native chiefs. Nevertheless, the breath of the new era is felt
even in communities remote from the marts of commerce
and the contact of races. Travelers who speak the native
languages sometimes mention that there is a good deal of
dissatisfaction among the headmen and among the old people generally with the ways of youth. This happens especially when the young people have gone to work for foreign masters and have either failed to return or else have
come back but refused to lay their earnings, as is their duty,
at the feet of their elders.

It is a hopeless task to retain the old customs intact when
generation after generation mobility increases and men
come and go with the growing and waning opportunities
of employment elsewhere. I made exactly the same observation in Chinese villages from which many of the young
men had gone abroad. In the early stages of such a labor
migration movement, the young men who return quietly
slip back into the old routine; except for an odd piece of
clothing, the possession of some gadget, or a few slang expressions, one would hardly know they had ever been
abroad. But if there is a continuance over many years of
such export of labor, whether seasonal or for a contract
duration of several years, a gradual change in social relations takes place. The prestige and status of different families in the community are affected by the uneven change in
their economic condition. Old men and the nobility — if
there is one — still rule as of yore and receive the deference
which is their due. But money also speaks, and its voice
grows louder with the years just as that of the *nouveaux
riches* does everywhere. There will be nothing more, at
first, than a little unacknowledged consultation of those
who yield economic power. Then there will be attempts to
imitate their style of living, perhaps to adopt their views

The manufactures of three continents are sold in the main shopping street of Bangkok, by Thai, Indian, and Chinese vendors.

An Indian brass shop in Singapore.

Wedding of the son of a local Batak ruler in Sumatra. The bride's and the bridegroom's formal clothes are equally "correct."

Not all Buddhist priests in Farther India are reactionaries. This kindly Thai monk is known for his generosity to persons of other races and creeds and for the humanism of his teaching.

on marriage, house-building, or some other matter. Not the least reward of success is the homage of the less successful.

But money does not always flow into the backward community when some of its sons work away from home. Even when it does not, the contact with the outer world may become socially disturbing. If the head of the family is very autocratic the young man may not return at all under the paternal roof, except as a visitor. The more stubborn the community as a whole is in its adherence to the traditions, the more likely is it to lose some of its most able and hardworking members. The isolation of such a village remains more or less unbroken. New-fangled ideas as to how its fields should be cultivated, how its business should be conducted, how the holidays should be observed, or how the daughters should be given in marriage, may have been rejected. But the stability of the village society has become undermined just the same: the example of the unruly son who prefers to live his own life will be followed by others. More and more the younger generation will learn that, on the big estate, in the big city, or in the new farm settlement near the big mine, one can quite safely live a freer sort of life than at home.

This breaking up of old tribal communities is still exceptional, but other effects of contact with the modern world are ubiquitous. The older generation does not like to be rushed. There may be a clock in the house of the village elder, but he does not allow it to tyrannize over him. The younger people always are in such a hurry (even when to the Westerner they seem provokingly dilatory). I am not sure whether, comparing age group with age group, the Burmans or the Indonesians really are so much more leisurely than we are. I was sometimes bored by the length of their musical or theatrical performances. But how many Malays could sit through "Parsifal" with equanimity? A

Dutch-speaking custodian of one of the ancient monuments in Java tried to explain to me the beautiful ceremonies that at one time had taken place in the lovely setting before us; and I gathered (though I did not understand all he said) that he regretted the old days when the ritual formalities prescribed by tradition or precedent for stated occasions were performed without abridgement.

In the early days of American rule in the Philippines, an immense amount of time was consumed, to hear old-timers talk, with the efforts of magistrates to make sure that their decisions were sufficiently in conformity with custom to be understood and to have the desired effect. Among the Ifugaos native law, among the Moros Mohammedan law, was drawn upon to give the judgments a semblance of conformity with eternal justice. The Netherlands-Indian Administration has gone even further in efforts to make everything new acceptable to the natives by its appeal to native law and the sanction of many precedents. From some of the accounts of Netherlands-Indian jurisprudence one can only conclude that a large part of the Government's revenue and personnel is invested in a legal apparatus so complex in its adaptation to ethnic, tribal, and even local variations in custom as to leave very little uniformity — and little money or energy for other branches of government. Today this patient effort bears fruit in the loyalty of the vast majority of the Indonesians.

In these ways, the transition from beliefs and ideas deeply rooted in a more primitive past to those in harmony with the demands of the modern age can be smoothed, though it can never be quick. Above all, it is difficult for people to abandon once and for all their belief in magic when so much in their life from early childhood has been governed by trust in its efficacy. Some years ago we had an Indian student live with us. He took part in the housework, and we were astonished to learn how in his childhood every

smallest item of the daily routine was linked to religious belief with an appropriate saying, song, quotation from the
classics, tale, or gesture. One need not be in Southeast Asia
long to be struck by something of the same sort as soon as
one gets below the surface of polite intercourse between
strangers. Whether he be Buddhist, Mohammedan, Christian, or of none of the great institutionalized faiths, your
native friend will recognize a significance and inner cohesion in everyday sights, actions, occurrences which the Occidental is wont to brush aside as of no importance whatever. I once discussed with a Filipino the almost ferocious
tenacity with which the *tao* (peasant) clings to his *bolo*
(knife) — almost as though it were a talisman without the
feel of which he would be helpless. His answer indicated
that he, an educated man, also retained something of a religious awe for an object fashioned by human hands. He
said:

"The bolo gives a man his strength. Without it he
could not face the dangers that lurk in the cane field
or around his house at night. With it he is a man, without it a child. But the knife has no power when the
man who carries it does not trust it. Once I was, with
some of my friends, in a brawl. . . . No matter what
it was about. An angry crowd attacked us. My comrades stood their ground. I heard their shouts and saw
the knives in their hands. But my own knife felt like
a leaf; it had no strength at all. *I* knew that anger is
a terrible thing. *My* bolo gave me no confidence,
though I knew it was sharp. When that crowd moved
upon us, I trusted the speed of my legs."

This statement, it has occurred to me since, indicates not
only the sudden burst, in a crisis, upon the mind of even
an educated person of a very old magical belief, but also
the inescapable breakdown of that faith under the influence
of a modern education. A new medicine will be tried on

the recommendation of a friend even when nothing is known about the principle of its effectiveness. No one hesitates to adopt — if he can afford to do so — some improved tool, some new mechanism that works. No one hesitates to surround himself with the pretty artifacts of a strange culture even when he has no notion of their significance. There, among the inessentials, the gate is wide open to cultural influences. We ourselves show this trait when we fill our homes with Oriental works of art but are insensible to the aesthetic principles of their design.

Women Demand Their Rights

The position of women in our Western civilization is something that no Asiatic finds it easy to grasp. He accepts the evidence of his eyes, as he accepts many others of our peculiarities. In Asiatic society, woman's inferior status is unmodified by an attitude which we could recognize as chivalry. Even in the Philippines, during the three centuries of Spanish and nominally Christian rule, women had no authority outside the home, were expected to obey their husbands without question, and would rarely think of pursuing a profession. Yet in the ordinary farming communities they enjoyed many rights under ancient customary law; and their authority in the home corresponded to their economic contributions as breadwinners quite as much as to their social contributions as mothers. Dr. Encarnación Alzona, a well-known woman historian and suffragist, in one of her many writings contrasts the place of women in native society with "the artificialities which Spanish culture introduced into our life." She adds:

> "The modern Filipino women who are demanding
> civil and political rights are in fact asking for no more
> than the restoration of their ancient rights and free-
> dom which had been taken away from them by an
> alien rule of more than three centuries."

You get a rather different picture from those writers who
have described in detail the position of women in the non-
Christian societies of the Philippines. Most of them stress
the fact that women are loaded down with work to such an
extent as almost to make them slaves. Nor can the subjection of women in Christian Filipino society fairly be attributed to the Church, since their status actually is higher
than in the Moslem societies of Malaysia. The contradiction is explained when we look closely at the everyday life
of Filipino women rather than the formal rights accorded
to them (although these go far under the new Constitution).

Generally speaking, when a peasant in Southeast Asia
gets drawn into the money economy of modern commercial
farming, the function of the wife as primarily concerned
with household and secondarily employed as a sort of auxiliary labor force tends to remain unchanged. But in the
Philippines the woman tends to have control of the family's finances. Although she herself often is an inveterate
gambler, she endeavors to keep her husband's and her own
little flings with fortune in reasonable bounds. Plantation
managers say that a successful Filipino household usually
is one in which the woman keeps the reins tight. Since
American education got under way, the vocational opportunities for women in the Philippines have, of course, increased enormously; and it may be added that the Filipinas
have taken to new callings in industry, trade, and the professions like ducks to water. Nor have I noticed that Filipina nurses and teachers are more timid in their relations
with male colleagues and superiors than are American ones
— especially if comparison is made with the etiquette in
American Catholic circles.

In short, the changed position of women is considered
by many observers the outstanding example of assimilation
of Western traits in the Philippines. Compared with the

inferior position still assigned to women in most Asiatic societies, and especially in those dominated by Islam, it is revolutionary. One can hardly think of an important social or political concern in the Islands in recent years that has not been intelligently shared by women and received the benefit of women's effort. This is something very different from merely reaffirming the importance of the contributions which women make to the social good by being good providers and by keeping up high moral standards. One interesting sidelight is that the opposition to female suffrage in the Philippines did not come so much from old-fashioned women horrified at the thought of getting into an unseemly brawl of politics, as from men who were afraid that the women's vote would too much strengthen the power of the Church. Whether it has done so, I do not know. But in any case only conservative and property-minded candidates, men or women, could be elected in the greater part of the Philippines.

The change in the status of women that has come in the Philippines with the long exposure to Western example and Christian teaching is only one of many striking effects of change in social attitudes and social organization. Some recent writers stress the claims which the large family still has on the household. These claims, they say, represent a universal trait in Oriental society and indicate that culturally it still is very distant from that of the Occident. As soon as a man gets ahead a little, a swarm of impecunious relatives descends upon him and eats him back to his previous social level. Actually, this remnant from the pre-commercial agrarian way of life is far less evident in the Philippines today than it is in some of the neighboring countries. Indeed, old-fashioned Filipinos are alarmed at the speed with which the ties that used to hold the large family together are breaking. Many young couples, now often married without parental consent, go off somewhere to build up an existence of their own, without benefit of aunts and cousins.

How the individual feels toward his family and toward the community at large marks him more than anything else as either belonging or not belonging to the otherwise rather vague category, modern society. Throughout the Orient, loyalty to the family has always been the most important social bond. Nepotism in public affairs is universal. In Indo-China or Thailand or Malaya, a native official who failed to fill with relatives any minor posts which he had at his disposal would be looked upon as unfilial or crazy — at any rate, of dubious morality. This is not because Orientals naturally think differently from Occidentals in such matters, but because ties of blood have for uncounted generations been the only social protection for the individual. I do not believe that the teaching of the Spanish Friars in the Philippines has in itself made much difference. On the contrary, it seems to have reinforced the economic interdependence of the large family, both as a matter of social virtue and as a practical means of keeping down the cost of charitable relief. But the introduction of a money economy, with its new demands on the industry and thrift of the individual, undoubtedly has made the old familial form of mutual insurance impracticable. You do not find the Annamite or Thai or Malayan wage-earner of the second or third generation sharing his possessions with relatives who neither delve nor spin. Many employers who find their native workers unwilling to exert themselves beyond the degree required to earn a given sum explain this on the ground that it is unlikely that the individual worker and his immediate dependents will enjoy the additional income when there is a larger family in the offing. But this seems to be a passing symptom: a transitory and false adjustment to a change in basic economic relations.

There is, as a matter of fact, a good deal of variety in the degree of family cohesion in different parts of Southeast

Asia. A fairly independent status for women usually goes together with a loosening of obligations to the larger family. Among the Man in northern Indo-China, for instance, the individual households are more on a level of equality than they are among the Thai. The greater esteem in which they hold women is emphasized by one observer as the explanation. He says that the husbands share more of the work and that the wives sit down with their husbands at meals. A similar relative independence has been noted among the Miao; they pay much less attention to the graves and shrines of their ancestors than do their neighbors who have come more strongly under Chinese influence. Among the Miao, too, a widow succeeds her husband as head of the family.

In Burma, both the status of women and family life generally deviate from those of their neighbors, none of whom are Buddhists. But they also deviate considerably from those of Indian Buddhists. Perhaps some older religious beliefs, less rigid in the subordination of the individual to the supposed needs of social survival, continue under the crust of the official creed. Or it may be that land and climate have been kinder to the Burmese peasants than to the Indian during the many formative centuries before foreign imperialism broke in upon them both. The happy temperament of the Burman, which has already been mentioned, may be both a cause and a result of social relations not quite so rigidly organized for survival of the group.

When I read what people have said about Burmese civilization in recent pre-war years (very different from what is said about them since the British withdrawal), I am reminded of what travellers used to say about Russia in Tzarist days, what Goethe wrote about the Italian people at the time of our Revolution, and what has been said time and again in similar circumstances: there is a natural democracy at the bottom of society, which stands out in sharp relief just because there is no political organization to express it. In all these instances — one might almost speak of a special social pattern — we find the counterpoint between want and a gay irresponsibility; between oppression and unlimited mutuality; between political immaturity and a high regard for personal freedom. With that kind of nonpolitical social democracy there always goes a relatively high degree of independence, especially, for women. In Burma, their marriage age is unusually high; their household work is not made burdensome by an undue insistence on speed and productivity; they are not expected to have an intolerably fast succession of babies; they have an equal right with their husbands in whatever property there may be; they can inherit; they play with their children, go where they wish, need pay no heed to the mother-in-law or to a privileged "first wife." In fact, they behave and are treated very much like human beings.

Although there are these contrasts between various parts of Southeast Asia in the matter of family life, dissatisfaction with the coercive social disciplines of the past is stirring everywhere. For example, long before there was a widespread aspiration to nationhood among the Javanese, there was already an organized feminist movement — inevitable outcome of the Dutch-language branch of the school system which could not but inoculate boys and girls alike with the virus of European social thinking. Today, the theme of sex equality goes through the whole nationalist movement from its most conservative to its most radical branch.

There were in Netherlands India a few years ago three distinct branches of the feminist movement: the Moslem, the nationalist, and the radical suffragist. The programs of the three groups differed not only from each other but also from those of comparable organizations in the Occident. For instance, equality in educational opportunity has still to be sought as a rather distant goal. The non-Moslem organizations combat polygamy, and this is perhaps their strongest plank. However, all of them try to improve the status of married women and to raise the marriage age. Success even in the milder of their joint proposals would upset time-honored arrangements in the relation between the sexes and between daughters and parents.

A Netherlands official once said to me about the organized feminists in the Indies: "If these harpies ever get their way, there won't be much left either of the *adat* (the customary native law) or of our indirect rule. Whatever is based on tradition, they are sure to be against." Most of the European officials, however, have a friendly feeling toward the feminist movement which they consider helpful in almost every kind of campaign for social betterment. More especially, they appreciate the help given by organizations of educated women in efforts to secure changes in the marriage law so as to make the position of married women less hazardous and to make it more difficult for men to escape responsibility for the upbringing of their children. The leaders of all three branches of the feminist movement are aggressive in the pursuit of their respective immediate objects, and show the influence of their contacts with feminists in other parts of the world. Many of them are teachers.

In Singapore I watched on one occasion some simple country people in a government office apply for licenses of one kind or another. There were four of them, and they were accompanied by two young men who did all the talking for them. The older villagers were evidently uncomfortable in the strange surroundings, but the young men were self-possessed. They, too, wore sarongs and velvet fezes, and spoke in the Malay language. But their whole demeanor was one of self-identification with the modern office and of apology for the older men's ignorance. As I myself was waiting, I was able to watch the little party through the whole procedure — starting with the difficulty which at least one of the older men seemed to have in negotiating a short flight of stairs, and culminating in a smile of relief when the business was accomplished. The two young men did not so much seem ashamed of the older ones as they seemed to belong to a different class. Their behavior toward the elders was courteous with a shade of condescension. I asked a question about them when I had occasion to go to the counter and was told that the two young men were sons of the leader of the group, a man of some standing in his district.

This little picture must suffice to epitomize what this chapter has been about: the change of social attitudes in Southeast Asia. Thus far, this change expresses itself mainly as an incipient conflict between youth and age — which no program, not even a closing of all the schools, can suppress, since it emanates from shifts in basic economic conditions and relations.

XI

FIRES OF DISCONTENT

IN AUGUST 1942, the Federal Bureau of Investigation arrested a Filipino, Mimo D. Guzman, who had been going about the United States for some years trying to organize a "Pacific Movement of the Eastern World." He had taken Japanese money to spread his gospel of the brotherhood of all colored peoples. Years ago, I met other Filipinos who thought it was up to their nation to bring together all the peoples of Malay and kindred races in Southeast Asia. Not all of them were charlatans. They pointed out to me that the native inhabitants of that region were confronting a solidly organized colonial capitalism, functionally united in spite of national differences; that only by a similar unity could the native peoples of colonial Asia save themselves from perpetual "serfdom."

When the Japanese began their propaganda to organize the colored races against the white, I knew that they would fail because, among the various brands of madness which I have encountered in the course of many years' acquaintance with Asiatic rebels, I had never met the particular lunacy which Major Takahashi and other Japanese propagandists have tried to put over. The idea of unity among all colored peoples against the white race might take root, perhaps, in Central Africa, or even in India, but certainly not in a region where the white man was a late-comer among the many "master races" that swept over sea and land. Most of the native peoples of Southeast Asia have been, or consider themselves to have been, oppressed at one time or other by Asiatic tyrants, no whit less cruel than those who have come a longer way. Moreover, the fate of Formosa, at the northern end of the South China Sea, and of Korea, has not remained unknown, nor have the millions of Chinese residents failed to inform their fellow citizens of the Japanese doings in Manchuria and in China itself. Even ten years ago, the Japanese already were the most feared of all nations among the people of Malaysia — certainly not one with which one would make common cause against imperialism.

Is there, then, no racial basis for the many so-called "nationalist" movements that have sprung up in Southeast Asia? Yes, some of these movements, not the most important, may be said to be racial in inception. But only a few sophisticated persons with a modern education could be racialists; for the different branches of the indigenous stocks have no sense of kinship. In the course of centuries, the stocks have been disjoined and exposed to many different historical experiences. Each branch had to adapt itself to the requirements of a geographical environment that could not fail to put its stamp on habits of living, on natural selection, and so eventually on physical characteristics as well. They were further drawn apart by different opportunities for intermarriage with other racial groups. And they forgot their common ancestry. The large number of idioms spoken even within some of the individual political units of the region testifies to their long lack of contact. On a single island, such as Luzon, Java, or Celebes, the tribes have gone their separate ways for so long that a sense of kinship if it exists at all today can only be a result of recent propaganda.

The word "racial," where it is mentioned in relation to Malaysian movements, must always be understood to have about the same connotation as it has among American Negroes: it expresses a concept that is ninety-nine per cent social and cultural and only one per cent biological. It took a long campaign on the part of a small, purposeful colored intelligentsia to produce a feeling among American Negroes that they had anything in common with Africans. There has never been even that much "race-consciousness" among the peoples with a large or small infusion of Malay or of Indian blood. Increased mobility and intercourse, not kinship or intermarriage, are responsible for the growing similarity of outlook in the Philippines and Indonesia.

In short, a movement of emancipation based on color is not necessarily one based on racial identity, actual or imagined. Among Indonesians, there is often no consciousness of kinship with the people of the next village if these happen to have a different religion and a different *adat*. The educated Malayan of Kuala Lumpur has no feeling of special affinity with some primitive tribe in the mountains comparable with his feeling for Chinese and others of his own class. The Batak would not willingly subject himself to Javanese rule; and the Javanese would not think of treating the Batak as an equal. The Moro certainly does not identify himself with the Christian Filipino. The Ambonese looks down upon the Sundanese, the Annamite upon the Laotian, the Thai upon the Cham, and so it goes. When any of these people talk about race equality it always is about that of their own group with the whites. This alone lends a quasi-racial color to the many motives which animate Malaysian movements of liberation or defiance. I have already mentioned the clannishness of Filipino students from different provinces. There is a similar separatism among high-school students in Netherlands India (which has almost no university students). But they are united in their anger over any teaching, any piece of literature, any speech, or any event that seems to them to belittle the contributions of the Indonesian people to the progress of their country and to exaggerate the contributions of Occidentals.

What gives a sense of unity to fellow-countrymen with different origins is not, then, consciousness of similarity in looks or of common blood. It is only beginning to be patriotism in the Western sense, and this more in the self-governing countries than in the dependencies. It always is a negative union of protest and defense — like that of the United Nations against the Axis. But what brings such diverse groups together is not necessarily a common antagonism to Western imperialism. Not long ago, Thai, Malayans, Javanese, and Filipinos of the student and middle classes shared a furious dislike for the Chinese because the latter seemed to monopolize the positions and functions in society to which they themselves aspired. At present, all — except perhaps the Thai — not only are but know and feel themselves to be united in a fight for freedom from the Japanese yoke. A strong undercurrent of anti-imperialism is always there, but it is not inherently anti-Occidental.

Growing Class Consciousness

As among the American Negroes, so in Southeast Asia an artificially produced race-consciousness — animated by a desire for strength through numbers — is gradually developing. This is a socially useful assertion of mental health despite its occasional exaggerations of pride, since it counteracts that "oppression psychosis" which may so easily undermine the sanity of subject peoples. The cultural achievements of the immediate group gain in significance when they are looked upon as contributions to a larger cause shared by many peoples. Thus the United Nations were able, in dark days, to keep up their morale by persuading themselves that they were all fighting for democracy. In Southeast Asia, native and colonial authorities have in re-

cent pre-war times seen the value of pride in cultural attainment and helped spontaneous movements to express themselves. Old music and plays were re-introduced. Pre-Islamic
lores were retold and given new interpretations to make
them more timely. Old customs were revived, old rites and
ceremonies re-instated. Among the well-to-do it became
fashionable to revert to native costume and to reproduce
with modern means and in new applications native forms
of decoration. Rulers whose homes used to be filled with
expensive European junk began to collect the finer products of indigenous art. Schools were set up to revive dying
crafts.

This cultural nativist movement was strongest in the dependencies with indirect rule, where native customs had
been honored even by the alien rulers. With all its diversity
it had a delightfully democratic flavor, just as the revival
of folk festivals and folk costume in Europe after the last
war. There is a meeting point, and so also a growing feeling
of solidarity and equal worth, between those who take pleasure in returning to the ancient roots of their native culture,
and those who, still rather close to vulgar and primitive
beginnings, use this reviving interest of the upper classes
to advance themselves a little in social position and self-
respect.

All this is quite recent in Southeast Asia — about as recent as in China. Even two decades ago, people of Malay
and Chinese descent alike regarded it as a mark of distinction to wear foreign-style clothes. Now Filipinos again display with pleasure their much more colorful home-made
shirts, and American schoolboys imitate both their use of
cheerful fabrics and their sensible habit of wearing the
shirt outside the trousers in hot weather. Malayans and
Javanese in good circumstances no longer are ashamed to
appear barefoot. Fezzes are to be seen on the heads of young
men whose fathers wore hats.

The outward appearances of class difference are naturally strongest when those who can afford it go in for the accoutrement of a foreign culture. When I was young, large parts of European and American society still were under the impression that female apparel had to be from Paris and male apparel from London to stamp the wearer as a cosmopolitan. The *nouveau riche* could not always buy his way into society; but on the other hand, a household that did not have English knives, French glass, Oriental rugs, and at least reproductions of Italian art, hardly "belonged." So in eastern Asia, some Western possessions and the rudiments of a Western education were passports to a society which did not care how far it travelled from the paths of the multitude. And as in our Western countries so in Asia, too, even a superficial nativist renaissance, a return to the enjoyment of native and local things, tended to have more important cultural consequences, including an incipient rapprochement between diverse classes.

This has not yet gone far by any means, but it has now reached the stage, for example, where native games — kite contests, sword play, and *chin-lon* (a ball game, variations of which are also known under other names, that is played with every part of the body except the hands) — have been revived and are played along with modern Western games in some of the best schools; where an Annamite whose father knew all about Jeanne d'Arc but with an indulgent smile denied all knowledge of the vulgar sagas about native heroes eagerly informs himself about the native lore and perhaps helps to give it new literary form; where educated Javanese whose ancestors would never have thought of such a thing travel all over Indonesia so as to get to know it; where schools under private auspices and always considered orthodox in religion and reactionary in social matters, combine modern programs of study with a cultivation of the native heritage.

Whether this incipient cultural renaissance will assume greater speed, as the false prestige of Occidental civilization drops away and only its genuine claims remain, is problematical. But it is likely, if we go by historical analogies. Latin was the intellectual and legal language of continental Europe for centuries but very quickly fell into disuse toward the end of the seventeenth century when the political influence of southern Europe waned. French was spoken by preference in the European courts and in polite society but disappeared soon after the French Revolution.

In Southeast Asia, it may be thought, matters of this sort affect only a small fragment of the population. Nevertheless, in all such cases there is a wide reverberation of changing tastes. While possession of objects of the Western material culture was a sign of distinction, even those who could not afford a Western article of apparel would display some small Western-style object, made locally or in Japan. Even those who individually express no such preferences at all, that is, the great majority, were by the example of their betters led to an appreciation of Western contributions which otherwise they might have refused. When the Sultan rides past in his automobile and the small local official on his bicycle, the new road which at first may have seemed an entirely unnecessary product of compulsory native labor assumes a new significance. For many millions of people the increased mobility, with just a little provision for the public health that did not exist in the past — both created by public enterprise — are just about the only share they have in their country's modernization, at least the only tangible share. But note the wider effects of even this limited experience. In the self-contained community, what always has been is right and proper. Tradition reigns supreme. Mobility makes for individualism, materialism, dissatisfaction with existing conditons.

The opening up of a colonial country through Western

technical means also opens up new mental horizons. Different kinds of people are brought together while people of the same kind are dispersed and thrown on their individual resources. Where the physical road-making is paralleled by programs of educational development, two new kinds of personal experience re-inforce each other: the man of the people learns that one can understand and be on good terms with people of a different tribe who speak a different idiom if one takes the trouble to learn some common tongue. Hundreds of thousands of people learn — with surprise — that the sanctity of customs and laws which for their own people has always been absolute is, after all, only relative; that there are many tenable beliefs, many ways of doing things.

Once faith in the conventions is disturbed, there is danger that a shallow cynicism will take its place. The farmer or laborer observes that money will buy most of the things men desire — when they are away from the pressure which public opinion exerts upon them at home. With money one can even buy a reputation and self-confidence. By paying no attention to the old religious duties and family obligations, one gains time, and that is profitable, too.

Thus an ever-growing number of people become alienated from their home soil and, finding that it is possible to live in disregard of *some* traditions and laws, lose their respect for *all* tradition and native law.

Occasionally a colonial government has unwittingly magnified this tendency by undermining the authority of the native village notabilities. The village chiefs not long ago were still clothed with the authority of their religious and judicial functions; but when the government tried to make its views prevail even in matters of detail, the native administrators lost status, and their functions suffered. It is true, there would in any case have been a decline in popular respect for the native authorities because of the new mobility, individualization, and school-learning; but the tendency was aggravated by progressive policies which required a correspondingly modern administration.

There is, further, the cumulative influence of growing literacy. Netherlands India has a censorship on books in the native languages. But it locked the stable after the horse had escaped. The demand for literature of which the authorities do not approve is insatiable. Therefore, in order to keep down commercial publishing as much as possible, the Government carries on a large publishing program of its own. Inexpensive booklets and almanacs are distributed in large quantities at a very low price. Public libraries have been set up in thousands of communities. Without effective competition, this attempt to diffuse innocuous literature was bound to be quantitatively successful. But the popular choices within the range of the Government's publications have disappointed some of the educators. Despite an abundance of fairy tales and native legends, people will read European history and novels dealing with social life in Europe. The hunger for information on the Occident ranges from brain-trusts to brothels.

This avidity for news of the modern world also throws light on the appearance of so many "fancy religions" as part of the general picture of popular discontent — not only in Netherlands India but throughout the region. Branching out from theosophy as, perhaps, the main fount of inspiration, there are many new cults which are trying to combine at least three elements: mysticism, a re-interpretation of native lore so as to bring it into line with a more spiritual concept of divinity, and a practical and up-to-date teaching of modern Occidental subjects, with emphasis on humanitarian ethics. The Netherlands Indian Government has tried to disinfect one such educational movement by gaining control of its schools through subsidies; but the offer was refused. Some of the missionary bodies seem to have met the obvious demand half-way: they have, according to one well-informed witness, actually increased devotion to Christianity in their communities by bringing their own religious teaching into some relation with the upwelling enthusiasm for native culture. The combination of religious teaching with the teaching of practical skills and Occidental subjects of interest to the students — history, literature, the arts, elementary social science, and so forth — is, of course, an old story for the mission schools.

Nowhere, probably, are there better opportunities for studying the part played by new cults in a national awakening than in the Philippines. Some of them have been set up by charlatans, but others are quite spontaneous in origin. Taken altogether, these cults with their appeal to the emotions and with their diffusion of half-knowledge, half-fiction, represent a real danger to social stability — a danger, however, which is not so great that popular education and freedom of the press cannot avert it.

In Indo-China a new faith made its appearance in 1927, which subsequently became known as Caodaism and has given the authorities a good deal of trouble. It is Buddhist in its tolerance for the most diverse credal elements, some of which are borrowed from Confucianism, some from Taoism, and some from Christianity. Freemasonry also is represented in its symbolism, and hypnotism was at first a favorite means of evoking a mood of response. The Government prohibited this dangerous practice and also succeeded in obstructing the diffusion of the cult in the northern provinces; but among the extremely poor rice farmers of the south it spread like wildfire. Government officials never quite lost their suspicion that sedition was being preached under its cover.

In Burma, the Buddhist order, the Poongees (or *hpongyis*), has for many years fulfilled the functions of a secret revolutionary society operating under a religious cloak.

This order has long been a thorn in the flesh of the British authorities since on several occasions it fomented movements of overt civil disobedience. In 1942, the Poongees lifted their time-honored saffron robes sufficiently to permit a glimpse of their cloven hoofs. They were often an organized "Fifth Column" which betrayed the position of airfields to the invading Japanese, engaged in espionage in behalf of the enemy, laid traps for retreating British and Indian troops (the Indians are the hereditary national "enemy number one"), and as guerillas fought the Chinese. According to a British missionary, writing in December 1941, not all the monks of the order are involved in this treason. "Many, especially the older ones, are fearful that if things go on there will be no Buddhism left in ten years."

However much our sympathies may be with the authorities and with the orthodox believers, Buddhism actually is taking on new life wherever it associates itself with nationalism. The same has proved true of Mohammedanism in the British colonies and in Netherlands India. Without becoming seditious, the two principal religious movements, the *Sarekat Islam* and the *Muhammadiyya*, with their hundreds of schools, are engaged in a spiritual assault on Occidental supremacy (or were so engaged just before the war). To fulfill the functions of leadership, such movements can remain somewhat orthodox in their religious teaching but not in their social teaching. Unlike the Poongees of Burma who seem definitely to have deteriorated, the great popular Mohammedan movements of Malaysia are shot through with reform tendencies. Moslem scholars are busy, for example, on the difficult task of reconciling with the essentially humanistic teaching of the Koran the principles of nationalism, and with accepted Moslem practice the advocacy of monogamy as being actually derived from the teaching of the Prophet. A similar movement is the revival of ancient folk rites among the Christian Bataks, the most sophisticated of Sumatra's native populations. Some of these rites, used solely for their emotional emphasis on the native culture, are said to be almost idolatrous.

Such association of a wistful retrospective cultural nativism with practical modern reform programs is not, perhaps, as surprising as it may seem at first glance. The Gothic revival connected with German nationalism a century ago was similar. England had something of the sort in the social creed and literary tastes promoted by William Morris. In the United States, there have been repeated outcries in church circles against the revival of Indian dances which appeared to them idolatrous; but the continued performance of these dances appeared to other friends of the American Indians a necessary part of that cultural revival which has done so much to raise both the spirit of that racial minority and its prestige among white Americans. In China, we have perhaps the best illustration today of the potency of such recombination of traditional and modern teaching. Its neo-Confucianism, combined with the New Life Movement, certainly is evident in the first great national uprising which China has experienced for many centuries.

Visionaries and Practical Reformers

I have only briefly alluded to the appearance of practical reform programs within the composite picture of typical nativist movements in Southeast Asia. That trend, however, needs another word of explanation. It represents the most promising of the various forces at work. For it expresses constructively and creatively the thought that a higher level cannot be reached without effort and sacrifice. Old evils inherent in the traditional social system must be removed. Hence, with the clamor for an expanded school program there go campaigns against serfdom, gambling and improvidence, against the unaesthetic though not otherwise injurious betel-chewing, against opium-smoking, against social irresponsibility generally. The more thoughtful natives realize that Western individualism is no substitute for the loosening bonds of the old community. Something else must take their place. So, throughout the region we see the formation of new societies devoted either to social reform in general or to some particular reform. Some of these bodies try to secure a wide participation. The *Pasundan,* a Sundanese society, moderate in its political demands, endeavors to prepare for national freedom by lifting up the masses. The *Persatuan Bangsa Indonesia,* or Union of Indonesian Peoples, founded in 1923 by a Javanese doctor educated in Hamburg, has a program resembling that of the Servants of India, the organization that has done more than any other to invigorate the nationalist movement of that country with demonstrations proving that the people can solve their own social problems. In Indo-China, underground communist organizations have absorbed many of the educated reformers of a decade or two ago; but others, and with them many of the younger men, are active independently and engaged, among other things, in campaigns for mass education in the villages and for other non-revolutionary immediate reforms.

A word should be said here in refutation of a libel against all middle-class rebels and reformers in Southeast Asia, a libel which, unfortunately, has been spread by writers who have neither first-hand knowledge nor insight enough to allow for the bias of the employers' and official circles where the libel originated. It is neither true nor even psychologically possible that these men are motivated solely, as it is said, by personal grievances because they have been denied access to position and influence. Here and there, a young fellow of good family who naturally would associate as much as possible with Occidentals may, after some shocking experience of discrimination against himself, have identified himself with the struggling masses of his compatriots.

There is nothing unusual in such an awakening to injustice. But this does not mean that such men compensate for an inferiority complex or that they are mere busybodies, disgruntled and desirous of gaining distinction in an unusual way. No one who has met any of the leaders in nativist movements, whether moderate or radical, will make that mistake. Some of them have sacrificed remunerative professions, some have suffered obloquy and estrangement from their families, some have gone to prison. All of them are idealists.

The major discontents among the natives of Southeast Asia spring from primary economic causes. How do they fit into this complex revolutionary pattern? Some may say that these causes explain everything, and that the matters just discussed are merely on the fringe of what is essentially a revolt of slaves. But that, I believe, would be too simple an explanation. Actually, the resentment against oppressive working and living conditions, while widespread, still smoulders and rarely bursts into a flame as incandescent as the political and cultural attacks on Occidental supremacy. At least, that resentment, wherever it occurs, goes on smouldering until a spark of spiritual defiance sets it aflame.

It is amazing what men will bear — and not only Orientals — as long as their faith in the social system of which they are part remains unshaken. It is equally amazing how quickly conditions no worse than those borne with fortitude by many generations — even conditions considerably better than those tolerated half a century ago — are felt to be intolerable when men have caught a glimpse of a possible alternative for which they can work and fight. Few economists believe that, unless other social changes are carefully contrived to increase the productivity of labor, political independence will improve the lot of the native peoples. But millions do believe it. They see things, as simple people do, in personal terms: get rid of the alien rulers who treat

us as inferiors, who drain the country of its wealth, who
prevent us from rising to the full stature of our ability —
and all will be well. Taxation, the sale by the government
of land previously held in common, compulsory labor services, foreign competition with home products in the domestic market — any one of a number of immediate irrita-
tions may become the cause of a violent agitation when
conditions are ripe.

Back of it all is the new-born consciousness of poverty —
the sense of injury and also the sense that there is no need
for so much suffering. There are many degrees of this social
self-consciousness, and that is a good thing for the colonial
authorities, since it is the distance between the most moderate and the most aggressive nativist groups that prevents
the movement from coalescing. Different degrees of radi-
calism cannot be identified with different classes. In Java,
for example, there is a class of very poor workers whose
view on the national situation is as extreme as that of a
communist-influenced intelligentsia which knows all the
causes and all the answers. Nationalist representation in
the Volksraad has been unified to some extent; yet the support for any aggressive program is not solidly anchored but
diffused.

The degree of inner unity in the nativist movements is
not determined by uniformity of social status; but no more
is it by common religious faith, by absorption of identical
concepts from foreign ideologies, or even by an approximately equal strength of social dissatisfaction and revolutionary ardor among the participant groups. That unity
grows, rather, with the logic of events. It grows in spite of
the diversity of the sources and of the interests involved,
in spite of the wide range of intensity of feeling. The Javanese estate worker may not be conscious of having anything
in common with the Dyak peasant. He may have very imperfect knowledge of what the half-caste post-office clerk or

the Ambonese Christian teacher is complaining about. But all four face the same foe — if not in objective reality at least in their imagination. They find themselves allied, not because they have diagnosed their troubles and traced them to a single cause, but because all their discontents happen to be focussed on the same point, their exploitation by an upper class. Not all of them identify this class with the imperial foreign rule. Some are too far from the source of the power that oppresses them to recognize it. Others who do may be aware that many national governments behave toward some classes of their subjects much as colonial governments do. Some remember the corruption that used to be rampant among their native rulers and, while feeling close to their fellows in a class struggle throughout the world, do not identify it in particular with one racial group or another.

The nativist movements of tropical Asia grow out of specific local conditions, though the causes that produce these conditions and that produce the reactions to them may be national and international. It is conceivable that if the present war had not intervened many of these fragmentary movements might have become absorbed in inclusive international Pan-Asiatic, Pan-Islamic, Pan-Malay, Communist, or anti-Occidental movements. But nothing of the sort has occurred. Movements of protest must have reached a considerable degree of maturity before they can become genuinely international. Almost automatically, the nativist movements of Southeast Asia have grown separately into nationalist movements.

The Japanese war of aggression has only accentuated this political orientation. Thus far, at least, it has strengthened neither the Japanese-inspired desire for a "Greater Far Eastern Co-prosperity Sphere" nor a sense of racial or regional unity against Japan. The fact that Indonesians of all tribes and all classes are fighting for their Queen welds them to-

gether and makes them more national in their feeling. The
Filipinos have become more attached in their loyalty to
both their own country and the United States. Malayans
and Burmese have, on the whole, stood with the British —
though with a lack of valor in the case of the great majority
that speaks louder than a volume of criticism of British
colonial policy. Indo-Chinese patriots are standing aside,
doubtless ready to use the failure of the French to protect them in claims to nationhood after the war. Thai, now
as before, are solely concerned with their own welfare and
independence.

And yet, the growth of so many separate nativist-nation-
alist movements is a historical accident that does not necessarily betoken their continued separateness after the war.
The so-called "nationalism" of the campaigns of liberation
in Southeast Asia is only a step, a short step, toward a far
different principle of their eventual organization. Behind
the outward division of the peoples into so many nation-
conscious groups there are vast areas of common experience, common interest, common desire, which no manipu-
lation of political boundaries and constitutions at the peace
table can indefinitely hold apart.

Part III.

FREEDOM AND WELFARE

XII

BIRTH OF NATIONS

THE LARGER popular movements in Southeast Asia, as we have reviewed them all too sketchily, may be compared with the eddies on the surface of a lake. Underneath are swift currents — economic, political, and cultural. But the visible pattern is slow-moving and incomprehensible. In its whorl several streams may be discerned. They come from different sources and run at different speeds. The curling flow may be conceived as one movement or as a series of interrelated movements. We are justified in thinking of them as "nationalism" or as a number of separate recurring protests against oppression. The people of this region may be visualized as an army in the global struggle for human freedom; but one may also think of them as so many different divisions, each carrying on its own little war. Again, one may place in the focus of attention the ripples of unrest produced by change within Oriental society itself or see the whole as a phase in the titanic contest between progress and reaction that divides the whole world.

We cannot now measure the relative strength of the nationalist surge and of local disturbances. These forces of political and economic conflict are expressions of something still deeper; everywhere new social, even religious aspirations vie with age-old fears and superstitions. New contacts between cultures that have developed in isolation now take something from the experience and the wisdom

of each people and make it the possession of all. New
knowledge cannot be suppressed, however dangerous it may
be to the established institutions. The Thai, the Indonesians, the Annamites, the Malayans, the Filipinos — even the
Laos, the Kachin, the Dyak, the Moro — are strangers no
more to the emancipating stream of new information that
flows through Oriental society. Analogies with the changes
which the Renaissance brought to Occidental society five
centuries ago are relevant and useful — but dangerous if
carried too far. We must never forget that the society we
deal with in Southeast Asia is still essentially an Oriental
one and one considerably influenced by a tropical environment. Such terms as nationalism, racialism, nativism, or
liberalism, industrial revolution, even bolshevism, here
have different connotations. In all the region there is no
"nation" and no "class" in the sense in which the social
scientist usually understands these divisions. In none of the
countries, for example, do all, or a large majority, of the
people speak the same tongue and have the same historic
traditions — a rather elastic term, by the way. The languages of this region are interrelated, yet distant enough
from each other for an almost complete lack of intercourse
except in the coastal regions and, of course, through the
educated classes and those engaged in trade and communication.

The Language Problem

Upon the many languages and dialects in all of the politically connected areas there are superimposed one or
more official languages, but even these are not taught in all
the schools. The Filipinos have had to throw away one such
official and supposedly common language, Spanish, as no
longer serving the purpose of more than a small minority,
and are on the point — against the advice of some of their
own scholars and educators — of throwing English into

the discard, too, so as to put Tagalog, a native language, in its place. There are many objections to this course, but from the standpoint of the Filipino ruling class the choice is logical. Similar elevations to official status of one of several native idioms have had to be made by many European nations before they could become united.

Since nationalism, as a movement, precedes the birth of a nation, a common language can take root only where the pre-national government permits it to do so. Otherwise we would have to define nationalism as a product of a nation already in control of the means of its own solidification and perpetuation. Now, colonial governments, especially those which manage to rule through partial recognition of native law and native dynasties, have no desire to see their authority challenged by having too many indigenous people share with them the use of an Occidental language in which "dangerous thoughts" are openly discussed. They solve the practical problem of making themselves understood by the people through the expedient of recognizing as an official means of communication a native idiom — one not too difficult to learn — along with their own alien language.

As a result, in some countries the language most commonly taught in the schools is one which is not that of a large majority of the people or even historically part of its culture. An interesting example is the language history of the Indies under Netherlands rule. First, after assuming control over parts of the archipelago now united under its flag, the Government had to extirpate the Portuguese language from its dominant role. But the effort to substitute Dutch for it failed, so that the colonial government made a virtue of a necessity and deliberately reserved the teaching of Dutch, and hence its use, for members of the privileged upper class. This policy coincided with the logic of indirect rule which also was adopted after failure of the initial attempts, in the seventeenth century and early in the eighteenth, to subject the diverse peoples of the new empire to a more unified form of control. The limitation of Dutch language teaching in the Indies also served to obscure the weakness of the Netherlands in competition with Great Britain in world trade.

Almost surreptitiously, Malay became the second official language, instead of Javanese which is spoken by six times as many subjects. One reason given for this choice is that the Javanese language is especially difficult to learn, but the same might be said of literary Malay which few Occidentals fully master. Another reason sometimes heard is that the Hollanders did not easily abandon the hope that eventually the Malay Peninsula and perhaps other neighboring territories might some day be combined with the islands under their rule. But there was no need for official encouragement: low Malay — *laag-maleisch* — is the common language of many groups dispersed over an immense area. Malay was and is the medium of trade for the coasts and islands in both the Pacific and the Indian oceans. This "trade Malay" is related to most of the languages of the hemisphere. As Wilhelm von Humboldt first pointed out a hundred and fifty years ago, the Indonesian and Polynesian languages are of common origin; a single language family rules from Formosa to New Zealand, from the Easter Islands to Madagascar.

From the standpoint of nation-building, an official language which is not that of the politically and economically dominant group, the Javanese, has advantages as well as drawbacks. It would certainly have taken a long time before some of the important minorities, some of them Christian and educationally more advanced, would have accepted the cultural dominance of the Javanese in a united Indonesia. Then there are large population groups, like the Chinese, which are descended from immigrants and still have contacts with their home country, groups which must

play an important role in a future Indonesian nation because of their international affiliations; and such groups
obviously are already somewhat familiar with an idiom so
largely used in the inter-regional and international trade.

The Malay language is officially recognized, along with
English, in British Malaya. Only a minority of the population are Malays; and these are not to be compared in influence on the colony's affairs with the wealthy and educated
Chinese. But the majority of the natives are Malays and
understand the standard Peninsula-Sumatran Malay dialect
even though their own local dialects differ from it in varying degrees. It is difficult to imagine that Malay will ever
take the place of English in Singapore — but stranger things
have happened. I have heard Europeans in Malaya say that
they have learned the vulgar form of Malay, sufficient for all
their purposes, in two months; but such a statement only
betrays how little interest such men have in the country
where they live and in the mentality of those around them.
An educated Malayan may converse with a foreigner in the
language of the market place and the dockyard; for conversation with his equals he has a language which in syntax
and flexibility is comparable with other media that have for
many centuries served moral philosophy, jurisprudence,
and poetry. Again, the situation is by no means unusual.
Almost anywhere in the illiterate world, the majority of
the native population know at best a few words outside
those in their own dialect; and this has a restricted use
when the landscape is broken up by sea or mountain.

In Burma, most advanced, perhaps, on the way toward
nationhood, Tibeto-Chinese, deutero-Malay and proto-
Malay languages, with many dialects and local variations,
are spoken. On the extreme southern coast one can get away
with only a knowledge of low — or trade — Malay; but it
is the regular idiom of only a small minority. Burmese is,
along with English, an official language. It is spoken as the

main language, in sixteen dialects, by almost ten out of the
sixteen million people. Several more millions speak a little
Burmese as a secondary language.

Thai, the official language of Thailand, has the advantage
that its different dialects are not too distinct. The absorption of other ethnic groups at different times within the
country's borders has produced no special problems since
these groups usually were less advanced in culture than the
Burmans and, anyhow, treated as subject peoples. There is
also a vulgar variation of the Thai language, which contains only a few hundred words, some of them of alien
origin. In the more elaborate form in which it is spoken
in educated circles, the Thai language has even more borrowed words — almost as much as has the Japanese — and
this is a sign of considerable cultural activity and change.
The puppet government will experience difficulty, however, in trying to make itself understood even by the upper
classes in the four northern states of Malaya which the Japanese Prime Minister presented to it in July, 1943.

The Government of Indo-China has until quite recently
stuck to the idea that French might become the only language of importance there. This was partly on political and
economic grounds: as the bureaucracy saw it, nothing
would so strongly chain the colony to France as a growing
community of culture. To the native people this desire for
the dominance of French was made palatable by associat-
ing with its advocacy the assurance that thus, and thus
alone, could racial discrimination be eliminated and educational opportunities be shared by Occidentals and Orientals alike. In certain Annamite circles, such assurances were
received with acclaim. They were eager to become recognized as carriers of French civilization. In favor of French
are the difficulty of the Annamese tongue and the enormous
variety of other native languages. Nevertheless, Annamese
has to some extent become a language of inter-communica-

tion, at least in three of the most populous provinces; and a romanized simplified version of it has been adopted for mass education. Its use is less widespread than that of Malay in Netherlands India or Burmese and Thai in their respective countries. This is only another way of saying that Indo-China is less advanced on the road toward national unity than are these other countries. Since the turn of the century, the building up of an Annamese literature has made some progress; but since the intelligentsia continues to look to France, and the rest of the population remains in extreme want and ignorance, there was no well-knit cultural nationalism from which a political unity might have been forged to arrest the Japanese encroachments.

The relation of language to nationalism in Southeast Asia is different from what it was in Europe during a comparable period of political development. When in the nineteenth century the height of national consciousness was reached on that continent, revivals of native cultures were necessary to independence because the ruling class was engulfed by the cultures of the more powerful states from which the people tried to break loose. But the cultivation of native poetry and song, folklore and history, did not mean that these people cut themselves off from the main currents of European civilization. In colonial Asia, on the other hand, even an incomplete cultural isolation would do just that, because there those currents have penetrated much less deeply, and the groups acquainted with European languages are both too small and too unrepresentative socially to be eligible alone for popular leadership.

This difference is significant for the nativist movement also in its supra-national, regional aspects. Pan-Germanic and Pan-Slavic movements originated with groups that were thoroughly versed in the dominant cultures of Western Europe but tried to get away from them. To attain to equality with the large powers it was necessary to strengthen the cohesion of those gathered together under the new racial or cultural banner. This meant that their common stock of speech, literature, and customs had to be freed as much as possible of the accretions. But in Southeast Asia no strong nativist union is thinkable that does not use to the fullest extent all the instrumentalities of modern civilization. And although that civilization is no longer limited to a few countries in Western Europe, the key to it is through European languages and ideologies. It is for this reason that access to education in a European language and to the teaching of European subjects has been so strongly stressed by insurgent native youth. Schools that keep locked the doors to the world of today and its inner workings cannot aid emancipation but only perpetuate subjection. To explain the insistent clamor for European schools with motives of commercial interest, with a superficial desire for equality, or with mere vanity, is to overlook the main issue.

It is true, there are dangers in an unlimited admission of the colonial people to Western knowledge — and not only from the standpoint of the colonial powers. A real mastery of the foreign language and of subjects but little related to the immediate realities of native life cannot be attained simply through an elementary education given in that foreign language. Only those who can afford a higher education will achieve that mastery. And they, instead of placing it at the service of their fellows, may use it only for their own advancement and through it may become alienated from their countrymen. However, we may pause at this point and ponder the fact that this has not to any large extent taken place in the Philippines where elementary schools are conducted in English and until recent years largely by American teachers. Fluency in the use of the foreign language there does not mean at all identification with American rather than Filipino interests. One often hears of English-speaking Malayans or Burmese that they are "more English than the English themselves" and of French-speaking Annamites that they are "better Frenchmen than the French." But I have never heard it said of any class of Filipinos that they are better Americans than our own citizens — not even in fun. The explanation is that where only the upper classes absorb something of the foreign culture they are liable to absorb with it the attitude of the dominant ruling class toward workers and peasants. But Americans from the start undertook to prepare the Filipinos for self-government; and whatever snobbishness there may be among individual Americans, it cannot be said that closer association with American civilization dampens the ardor for democracy. On the contrary, respect for the rights of even the most humble was one of the things which many of the sons and daughters of the well-to-do *caciques* (landlords) heard for the first time expounded in the American school.

The more affluent classes certainly will dominate the scene as the peoples of tropical Asia move toward larger instalments of self-government. With the language and educational situation as it is today, the only alternative to imperial rule is native class rule. This is neither in the interest of the people nor of the metropolitan powers. It can be averted only by making the knowledge which is necessary for a gradual rise to self-government available to the masses. The Philippine educational system may not be the best for that purpose since it does not actually, because of the cost involved, reach its objective. But there are possible combinations of elementary with advanced types of education, which without overstressing the importance of literacy in a European language nevertheless give the greater part of the population a grounding in the essentials of modern civilization. From the standpoint of the colonial authorities entrusted with the duties of trusteeship in a period of transition, it is important that the different stages of entry into the modern world do not become merely stepping stones to privilege for a favored few — with the probability of violent and destructive social upheavals later on. From the standpoint of the nativists, a wider access to modern civilization has the advantage that every forward step in civic participation will also be a forward step toward better mutual understanding between the different ethnic groups that make up the population. Moreover, only through the instrumentalities of modern civilization, as necessarily related in its early stages to an alien language and alien thinking, can the many separate peoples of the region eventually form a powerful regional society, comparable with that, say, of the Near East.

Nativism and Political Unity

Perhaps all this is not nationalism at all. It is possible to argue that in the years before the war the swelling opposition to imperial rule assumed the cloak of nationalism only as a temporary means of social advance and unification. In Europe we identify nationalist movements with ethnic separatism. Even small minorities there often become "nationalities," and some of them in recent history have been strong enough to create self-governing states which, even in the matter of cultural identity, have barely enough cohesion for national continuity. But in Southeast Asia the presumably nationalist movements include diverse, and sometimes sharply different, ethnic elements. The reason is that these movements develop within the frame of political units that are arbitrary configurations and derive from the rivalry of imperial powers and not at all from the logic of the racial, cultural, or economic history of the region.

Within living memory, territories have been swapped, annexed, provided with new forms of government, combined and divided, without so much as "by your leave" as far as the populations were concerned. Socially and eco-

nomically, British Malaya and Thailand overlap; so do
Indo-China and Thailand. The recent grab of French and
British territory by Thailand's war-time rulers may be of
little historic consequence since new exchanges of territory
will probably take place when the Axis powers have been
defeated and peace has been restored; or it may permanently alienate some millions of people from their previous
allegiance. The peculiar combination of possessions and
protectorates that make up British Malaya and British Borneo looks more like an accidental accumulation of territories rather than "empire building" — the more so when we
remember that the strategy which made the little island of
Singapore seem worth a trade with the Netherlands for
other territory much richer in resources did not, after all,
work out in the moment of crisis. British imperialists, in
fact, often point out that it was not a consistent policy of
aggrandizement but an accident of historic missions which
produced the peculiar configuration of the empire. Under
the American and Philippine flags we have the Sulu Archipelago, with its Mohammedan ruler, a possession which
with just as much fitness might have fallen to either Britain
or the Netherlands. And until very recently there were in
every country of the region groups which, so far from asso-
ciating themselves with the nationalist movement, vigor-
ously opposed it because of their fear of the dominant native group.

One might go on enumerating obvious anomalies. The
people of Timor still are subject to Portugal which can do
nothing for them, being itself practically a dependency.
The Malays of British Malaya, descended from those in
Sumatra, were separated from their kind by the battle of
Waterloo. Javanese laborers, forced by their poverty to go
away from home to work on contract, hardly seem to care
whether they are sent to Dutch Sumatra or to British
Malaya.

In short, among all these diverse peoples, with their diverse degrees of attachment to their own country, nationalism does not seem to make much sense. At any rate, it can hardly be the sole guide to post-war political reconstruction in Southeast Asia. But something else does make sense. That something has been so well said in a *New York Times* editorial of March 1, 1942, that I state it in the words of that newspaper:

"Should we expect a Filipino, a Malay, a Chinese, a Burmese, an East Indian, to die for South Bend, Ind., or Nottingham, England? Of course we should not. If he risks his life it will be for something near home, for a freedom that will make itself felt in his little street, within the four walls of his small house. The Filipinos have had assurance of that freedom — they fight magnificently. The Chinese war has been an epic of heroism — the Chinese hope to conquer freedom for themselves. The Javanese are militant — they have been promised freedom. The Burmese, the Malays and the East Indians have not been sure — they wait for a promise that has been long in coming, though it is clearly on the way.

"This, simply stated, is the problem and the hope of Asia. The dross of imperialism is being burned away in the heat of this war. The French Revolution of 1789, which Hitler hoped to kill at long last in Europe, has reached the Far East. It is a revolution that has been turned, by the majestic tide of history, against the Axis Powers. It is one that the Western civilization, surviving in Great Britain, the Dominions, the United States and the governments in exile, must accept because of the exigencies of war, and can accept because it is consistent with their own democratic faith.

"Difficulties lie in the way of any transition from dependence to independence. But the days when any people can be governed without that people's consent will end with the victory of the United Nations."

The goal here sketched can be achieved either within or without the framework of a national state. President Quezon and representatives of Free Thailand take a broad international attitude toward post-war problems of political adjustment because they are already in a position to look upon national independence for their own people as achieved. In some of their speeches they plead for the application of the United Nations' democratic principles to all the peoples of Southeast Asia and for the relinquishment of the old colonial system in every part of the region. They demand that the principles of the Atlantic Charter and the Four Freedoms should be applied fully and concretely to the social, political, and economic relations of Southeast Asia.

The task is primarily one for the peoples of the region themselves. The question is, will the spectacle of an India divided against itself be repeated? Will lack of political experience on the part of the masses bring to the posts of leadership in the different camps men who never can be expected to represent more than a small minority? Will the arbitrary division of the region between imperial powers and a few free states have to be continued as the basic pattern of nation-building — because no other political division is practically possible?

It is clear that the existing boundaries respect neither geographical nor ethnic entities. Do they fulfill useful economic functions? Perhaps they do if one accepts the traditional colonial concept. When that is abandoned, it is clear enough that almost any economic activity of advantage to the native people is hindered by the lack of any kind of machinery for their political co-operation. If the life of small states is economically unstable in Europe, that of the dependencies in the Pacific has proved even more precarious.

Suggestions are sometimes made for a closer political as-

sociation in Southeast Asia between neighboring countries
which have similar products. This obviously will be in the
main for the benefit of investors and producers who would
benefit from a more unified control of production and
prices. But in themselves the diverse opportunities of a
more effective international collaboration for economic
ends can hardly be considered reason enough to justify far-
reaching political changes.

Moreover, it is by no means sure that questions of economic interest, especially those concerning foreign trade,
will dominate or seriously influence the future political
configuration of the region. That might be the case if the
colonial orientation were to remain essentially intact. But
it is precisely the change from the old colonialism to a new
type of relationship between the technically more advanced
and the more backward parts of the world that will express
itself in the post-war political reconstruction. The great
majority of the people of Southeast Asia who are to be
gradually introduced into a democratic world order have
little experience in economic thinking and none in imperial thinking. Indeed, a fervent nationalism, as we know
from the recent history of Central Europe, may disregard
material interests and exaggerate the importance to national strength of cultural homogeneity. It must be supposed, therefore, that to the extent to which the indigenous
peoples are drawn into the formulation of policies, non-
economic motives will have great weight. Nations are not
born in the counting house nor federal unions in the stock-
market.

The main question still is whether the peoples of the
colonial and near-colonial regions of the world will have
any say at all on the issues of post-war reconstruction. As
far as Southeast Asia is concerned, only a few of them have
even the beginnings of representative government. Nevertheless, if a sharing of trusteeship between the stronger

XII. Birth of Nations

powers should develop and if the gradual preparation of
the dependent peoples for self-determination should become a major international policy, all regulations of boundaries and all new agreements for economic collaboration
would of necessity assume a forward-looking character. The
material interests of the masses without political power
may not at once prevail to the extent indicated in President
Roosevelt's remark, but some of the human realities of the
region certainly would be taken into consideration. These
realities involve economic and cultural patterns that overlap any political map which could be drawn.

The social cross-sections of tropical Asia — the religious
affiliation, for example — do not show up as much during
the war as they do in normal times. All we can see now from
the sparse news received are evidences of patriotism and of
loyalty to the cause of the United Nations in most parts of
the region, and the contrary in but a few. These, however,
are passing phenomena. Even the tragedy of the Japanese
occupation with all the brutality of its destruction and req-
uisitioning may soon be forgotten if the old class struggles
of the colonial era are allowed to return. Patriotism, as a
matter of fact, is a term to be used with discretion when
applied to peoples only just emerging to political consciousness and trained to obedience. It implies a mentality that
does not yet exist where the relation of a people to its government is still so largely a passive one.

Indeed, even the concept of nation-building in a largely
colonial region may strike some of my readers as odd. Why
should these masses of poor and tradition-minded brown
and yellow people, now tied as subjects to alien metropolitan powers, have to go through a national phase at all
in a world that is tending more and more to vast empires,
commonwealths, and federations of states? Perhaps one-
tenth of the population of Southeast Asia, moreover, are
immigrants or descendants of immigrants with ties to In-

dia or China, countries which are becoming stronger and
more self-conscious politically. Other millions feel drawn
to the foreign centers of their religious faith, or feel a special kinship with persons of their faith, irrespective of their
race and nationality. Will the man who takes pride in the
advance of his mother country or the man whose heart
aches for a glimpse of his holy city be classed as a second-
rate citizen in the country of which he is a national? Or will
the coming civilization of the region be a pluralistic one, in
law as well as in culture, with room for many degrees of
affection for the place where a man happens to live?

There is not in Southeast Asia a single country where the
sense of nationhood is strong enough to dominate all those
other pulls on men's interests and emotions that constitute
their social universe. There are beginning to appear economic classes more conscious of that which separates them
from others in their own community than of that which
separates them from members of their class in some other
country. The pounding, equalizing force of large-scale modern enterprise has created a proletariat before there was a
nation. "Importations" of labor, reducing millions to a
status little different from that of a work animal, have
driven wedges into the older group-consciousness that was
based on kinship.

Once anything like a popular franchise has been achieved,
there will not in this kind of society be a middle class strong
enough to stay in the saddle without the support of farmers and laborers. In the Philippines, in Thailand, and in
Burma, it is true, movements of political liberation have
been carried by a native middle class; but its strength in
every case has come from popular demands for reforms in
the interest of land-hungry peasants and sweated laborers.
When they dissociate themselves from the dynamic source
of strength, politicians and political independence movements are short-lived. In Indo-China, for instance, the rev-

olutionary groups were strong when they attacked not only foreign imperial rule but also the incompetent and corrupt officials of their own race and nationality. When they curbed their zeal in this respect, the movement disintegrated.

Before discussing at greater length the political future of Southeast Asia, let us once more review very briefly some of the main ingredients. The region as a whole is drawn together by a degree of kinship which does not suffice to create a consciousness of racial unity but is pronounced enough to preclude the appearance of serious antagonisms on the ground of race. Even the large immigrant populations — against which there has been much feeling because of the injurious economic role which some of their numbers have played — are to a high degree assimilated. A tropical climate and the living conditions which it so largely determines make for similarity in basic psychological tendencies. Hence there are also similarities in historical experience, and these have been increased by the rise and fall of empires that have spread over large parts of the region. Like forms of oppression have created like outbursts of revolt and like forms of adjustment of manners and morals. In contrast, the present joint task of deliverance from the Japanese domination finds by far the largest numbers of all ethnic groups in the region consciously allied with each other and with their respective metropolitan mother countries among the United Nations.

A certain unity of character and of outlook may therefore be claimed for all the peoples of Southeast Asia. But much stronger thus far are those ties which are neither regional nor national but bind particular groups and classes together in the pursuit of common ideals and common interests. It would be an exaggeration to say that a single, inclusive new nation, composed of all or most of the peoples of the region, is in the making. But it is possible that, without going through all the stages of a maturing nationalism, these people will enter the comity of nations with new types of regional adjustment, corresponding on the one hand to their more recent experience of a more or less benevolent imperial affiliation, and, on the other, to their common stakes in a more secure and prosperous regional *Lebens-raum.*

Human bonds that did not exist a century ago, causes that were not even dreamed of, stresses and strains created by top-heavy administrations and controls — all have contributed toward the formation of a type of society in Southeast Asia for which there are no true analogies. No one knows of what heights of cultural achievement that society may be capable when the main causes of ill-health, physical inefficiency, and mental lethargy have been removed. "Stone-age people skipping a thousand years," somebody has said of some of the primitive Malays who go straight from their palm-thatched village homes into a modern army, a factory, or a mission school. But many of them are not so primitive. Buried in the jungles are memories of high civilizations that go back at least to the time of the European Middle Ages. Their steps from peasantry to modern economy are not so very different, after all, from those of the Calabrian peasant who lands on our American shore and a few weeks later drives a truck down one of our busy city streets. They are learning so fast that almost everything one reads about "native character" and "native ability" is out of date and, at best, only an amusing subjective impression.

Throughout the greater part of the region no single ethnic group today forms a large homogeneous society. Races and cultures are mixed up in colorful patterns of community life. A new tolerance is growing up and a new mental flexibility that makes possible ever more difficult adjustments to new conditions.

There are striking examples in tropical Asia of the ways in which groups branching from the same or related racial roots have adapted themselves to different environments and have, in the course of centuries, themselves become so different in looks and in modes of living that almost all appearance of kinship has disappeared. Some of them have so frequently adapted themselves to new conditions imposed by new rulers that at last they have become adapted to the condition of change itself. In some parts of the region the indigenous people have in a few generations helped to transform a backwater of world civilization into a demonstration center of progress; and that demonstration is still going on and evolving. All the customary laws, all the institutions, all the hereditary distinctions of status, all the beliefs, all the arts and lores, marvelously preserved in many cases, are now put to the test of a new kind of "opening up," very different from the opening up of the region for trade by the Merchant Adventurer Guilds and the East India Companies.

The present war has a special significance for Southeast Asia. It is a war for democracy and the four freedoms there, too; but especially it is a war for the minds of coming generations. Past wars have been for concessions of land and natural resources. This war is for the greatest of unused resources, for the spiritual freedom of the people.

XIII

CHANGING AIMS OF GOVERNMENT

NATIONALISM — in the broader sense in which that term is now commonly used — no longer confronts a solid opposition in Southeast Asia. The two dominant imperial powers of the region, Great Britain and the Netherlands, now accept it as an inevitable concomitant of their own major policy. Both accept the newer principle of " partnership" in the relations between mother country and dependency as an extension of the older principle of "trusteeship." Both claim that for some time the welfare of the native people has been the first concern of their colonial rule, and that the term "welfare" must be understood as including a gradually expanding participation of the colonial people in their own government. That progress in this direction has not been more rapid they explain with the necessarily slow growth of civic responsibility and the wide gulf that still exists between native attitudes and the requirements of modern rule. Moreover, the development of instruments to speed that growth, especially of schools, has been held back by a low productivity and a correspondingly inadequate public revenue. The discrepancy between aims and means became pronounced during the years of economic depression and the threat of war.

One may well accept these explanations and expressions of purpose and yet believe that in the years to come it should be possible to convert trusteeship into partnership at a much more rapid rate. There can be no return to the proved insecurity of the old colonial system; safety lies in the achievement of that community of interest which rests not only on the consent of the governed but on the active collaboration of all classes and all ethnic population groups in the building of a strong state. Such provisions as exist today in the dependencies to consult the wishes of the people on matters of vital importance to them do not correspond to the ability which they have already attained to judge issues that affect them and to arrive at reasonable decisions concerning them. This to some extent is true of all classes, though the range of issues that concern them will be greater in the case of Javanese industrialists or Burmese rice merchants than in the case of Papuan tribesmen or of "shifting cultivators" in the Malayan jungles. The existing beginnings of representative government do no justice to the earnestness and competency with which the indigenous farmers of all the countries manage their own affairs within the limits in which they are free to do so.

Too sudden and all-inclusive a change from one political status to another may well be disastrous to good government; but an undue prolongation of the transition stage between wardship and self-determination also has its dangers. Under the colonial system, commerce, shipping, and other elements of external economic strength have assumed an importance in the thinking of governments out of all proportion to the more intimate problems that press on the lives of the great majority. Even today, those spokesmen among colonial administrators who have shown themselves sympathetic to native demands for self-rule often seem concerned more with the status of the relatively small indigenous and alien Asiatic elements that are close to the ruling class and have already achieved a considerable independence from the old traditional social order than with the status of the masses which are quite remote from modern life even when they are to some extent dominated by it. We have, of course, the same tendency also in independent states which may go far toward liberalizing the franchise for some parts of the population and calling its members to every kind of administrative role, yet keep other parts of the population deprived of even the most elementary civic rights. The great difference is that in a colonial country the wholly disfranchised groups tend to be the great majority. When in such a country the welfare of the common people is a conscious and strong element of policy, the greater interest of the politically vocal groups in foreign trade and outer strength produces a dualism of political and administrative purpose which creates many difficulties. The colonial society is conceived as being divided into two sections with separate economies, one related to the world at large and dealing in large figures, the other "native" and economically of little importance to the outside world.

It is true that native economy, native law, native religious beliefs, and native production for native use can become exceedingly troublesome to the colonial government; but they are not allowed to encroach upon the chief area of imperial concern, the dependency's contribution to the trade, the raw-material resources, the financial strength, perhaps also the security, of the mother country.

In Southeast Asia the typical colonial picture is complicated by the inclusion of countries in different stages of dependence. In fact, the word "dependency" which not so long ago was extensively used in the literature because the word "colony" was held to misrepresent the relationship and gave offense, has now itself ceased to be respectable; writers who defend imperial systems often protest that such territories as Burma, the Netherlands Indies, the Philippines, or even Malaya are not dependencies any more than they are colonies. We need not here go into distinctions of political phraseology; but it is important to note that the unpopularity of imperial relationships has gone far enough in some quarters to make others, although they see nothing wrong in them, prefer to avoid a vocabulary that arouses so much antagonism. It would not be surprising if as a result of the post-war shifts in imperial responsibility all colonies were henceforth to be described as "mandates" — on the ground perhaps that at least in principle the right to their government has been conferred on the metropolitan power or at least confirmed by some external world authority.

This is not the place to describe in detail the governments of Southeast Asia or to examine the substantial benefits that have often accrued to other countries which had free access to economic opportunities in the colonies without sharing in the responsibility for their management or defense. Other writers have dealt at length with these subjects. But a note of warning is needed lest some reader should have an exaggerated notion of the actual power of the nations whose flags wave over the public buildings. Some of the dependencies are made up of colonies directly administered, of protectorates nominally self-governing, and of units in an intermediate stage not easy to label definitely. In several instances the occupation of the whole territory which on the map is colored red for Britain, yellow for the Netherlands, blue for France, and green for the United States is quite recent, and while law and order were maintained in every part of the territory claimed, the organs and activities of administration in the interior were often little more than an occasional visit from a magistrate.

Government and Social Welfare

Our concern here, recognizing these limitations on the actual exercise of administrative power, is with the ways in which the various systems and policies of government affect the fortunes of the native people, help or hinder the satisfaction of their normal desires, and keep in step with or remain behind the rising ambitions of those who have come in contact with modern ideas. But good government in a tropical region where a large part of the population still dwells mentally in the pre-industrial era obviously means something different from good government in a region far advanced in the mastery of modern techniques. In some respects, it is true, an Eastern government with modern standards has difficulties similar to those a Western government has at home when it rules over a population made up in large part of backward aborigines. The problems of Thailand are not so different from those of Bulgaria, the problems of the Philippines from those of Bolivia. Even such countries as the United States and Canada, with their large population groups only a few decades removed from an illiterate European peasantry, face cultural complications in the administration of their laws. Such governments if their rule is not to be overweighted by the interests of the more advanced population groups must seek to secure the active co-operation of the more backward ones in all their programs of economic and social advance. They may even go out of their way to provide such opportunities.

The field of public health has in Southeast Asia been largely instrumental in gaining the confidence of even the least progressive indigenous groups. Its benefits are direct and can easily be appreciated. Administered with due regard to prevailing beliefs and customs, it permits the introduction of innovations in social organization for practical ends. On the other hand, a sudden transition from a traditional economy of barter to a money economy or from established co-operative labor arrangements to wage labor may have disruptive effects that cannot be entirely foreseen. Health and long life are matters of common interest. What seems like indifference to hygiene may be no more than a compound of ignorance and of hopelessness in the unequal struggle between human ingenuity and the demons that lurk in swamp and jungle.

There will always be differences of opinion as to the extent to which a government is justified in public-health expenditures on behalf of classes or population groups which contribute little to the public revenue or which cannot, without even greater expenditures, be permanently lifted out of the physical and mental environment which breeds disease. Large employers may be assumed to have an interest in the physical efficiency of the village groups from which they draw their labor; but when the potential labor supply seems practically inexhaustible, the prospect of an immediate addition to their expenditure — whether direct or through taxes — may weigh more heavily with them than the inefficiency of which they complain. Cost of production still is a ledger item in private industry that cannot in part be charged against increased future profits. Especially when public health campaigns are directed against contagious diseases or a high infantile mortality, the benefits to the employing class are too remote to be of economic interest to it. The more influential groups in a colonial or semi-colonial country will usually protest against a large increase in such public expenditures.

In the Netherlands Indies, with practically no recourse to immigration to man the big estates and factories, a fully developed system of public-health provision is to be expected. In British Malaya, where the large employers until recently relied for their labor supplies almost exclusively on recruiting abroad, the state does less — and progressive and humane private enterprises are obliged to assume a larger responsibility. The cost of supporting worn-out Tamil contract laborers has hitherto fallen mainly on their compatriots in Madras. Yet the differences from country to country are not perhaps as great as might be expected. Colonial governments, even with the best intentions and with ample public support, never have enough funds to do the indispensable minimum that would be expected of them if the whole population were European. They take credit in their public-health reports for services and for "improvements" so basically necessary that in any modern self-governing country they would be taken for granted. In short, the standards of public health provision in any colonial country — and those of Southeast Asia are no exception — are far below those in efficiently governed independent states.

Generally speaking, health conditions in tropical Asia are bad. They are bad because the public health authorities cannot control some of the major sources of contagion. For example, economic opportunity has drawn vast populations to malaria-infested lowlands that should not have been settled at all. Swamps and jungles sometimes remain unreclaimed even close to centers of population because it would cost too much to drain or clear them. Above all, the grinding poverty of a large part of the population means that diseases of malnutrition are rampant. So, of course, are many other diseases caused by want. The idea has long prevailed that tuberculosis, until recently our most dreaded poverty disease in the Occident, is absent from the tropics. This is not so. "Tuberculosis in all its forms, and especially as a lung disease, is very prevalent throughout the country," says a report from Netherlands India. In Thailand, both the tuberculosis death-rate and infantile mortality — the two indices often used to measure poverty and overcrowding in the Western world — are exceptionally high. Rangoon has the second-highest death-rate from tuberculosis in the world. One out of every four children born in certain parts of Burma dies in infancy. In the Philippines, despite great advances in preventive hygiene, tuberculosis accounts for more than one-sixth of the total number of deaths, and its incidence is rising. The death-rate from the disease is five times that in the state of New York.

Malnutrition and overcrowding, the twin causes of ill-health, are so widespread in Southeast Asia because the phenomenal growth of its population has not been accompanied by a corresponding growth of wealth — at least of wealth available for the people's use. In some areas there has not been a corresponding growth of production, so that the drain of wealth is not the main cause. In Java, for example, the increase in food production has not kept pace with population growth, although dry lands have been irrigated and methods of rice cultivation have been intensified. The population of the island has doubled several times in the course of a single century, chiefly because internal strife was eliminated. Yet a high infantile mortality shows that the population might have grown even faster if the rate of food production could have been still further raised, at the expense of industrial export crops.

Lack of modern methods of production, superstition, incontinence, and other factors reflecting unfavorably upon the people have been emphasized by Occidental observers as the causes of a growing maladjustment between population and resources in the Asiatic tropics. Causes unfavorable to the reputation of governments have been minimized. But perhaps a fairer and more discerning judgment could be reached if the facts were weighed objectively without attempting to cast blame on anyone. A circumstance which then emerges as a major cause is the incompatibility of a native economy of self-sufficiency with a national economy centered upon foreign trade. When the owners of a large enterprise are of a culture different from that of the indigenous population, the discrepancy between the pursuit of their own interest and that of the native welfare is bound to be great. For centuries, the people, with their traditionally high birth-rates, were made the tools of enterprises that

had almost no incentive to protect them against the consequences of their adherence to outdated social attitudes. The
masses are starved and diseased today not because of their
own shortcomings or those of their present rulers but because nothing has been done for generations to discourage
their multiplication, and nothing until recent times to insure the millions their daily bread.

It may be objected that malaria, the most widespread
and perhaps the most destructive of all diseases in Southeast Asia, has nothing to do with poverty, that it strikes rich
and poor alike wherever the environment permits the
breeding of the Anopheles. Nevertheless, one cannot read
the voluminous reports on the control of malaria in tropical Asia without seeing the connection. The point is made
in a report of the League of Nations Health Organization
on rural health in eastern countries, held in Bandoeng in
1937, that "the physical debility and mental apathy of ma-
laria-stricken peoples will not permit them to respond to
a general public-health program." But it is just as true to
reverse the statement and to say that malaria takes its heavi-
est toll where the people have been enfeebled by exhaustive
work in a hot and humid climate and by an insufficient diet.
The League reports that "the greatest obstacle in the way
of malaria control is the fact that such measures as the use
of oil, Paris green, or drainage, cost more money than the
rural communities can raise." If this is so under the pressure of governments anxious to do their part, it must be
equally true that preventive measures have not developed
spontaneously in the infected areas because the people
there never have lived other than from hand to mouth and
their homes have never been constructed to keep them
comfortable, since even that has been altogether beyond
their means.

Debility and want are responsible for many of the alleged
moral failings of Indonesians and Malays which the apolo-

gists for exploitatory regimes have adumbrated in so many volumes. Physical weakness and a low metabolism are not, of course, in themselves responsible for moral qualities, any more than is a tropical climate. But the high standards of behavior which have evolved in the course of social living for many generations suffer and may even break down when environmental conditions deteriorate and a sense of injustice or frustration combines with hunger and neglect to lower both the physical and the moral resistance. Thus poorly balanced diets, neglected homes, carelessness in hygiene, over-indulgence when the occasion permits, are linked with disease and irresponsibility in a vicious circle. Fissures develop in the social organization; customary law and the advice of the elders are treated with disrespect. We are conscious of such deterioration in the mores when it occurs suddenly after a major catastrophe — as, for example, in Germany after the last war. It is more difficult to recognize it when it grows slowly over several generations, as it did in the case of the American Indians. That it can be arrested when recognized we have ample proof.

In recent years, social scientists have paid more attention to the relation between changes in material circumstances and the emotional life of individuals and groups. A good deal has been written about the sex customs of Asiatics, but in their case it is often falsely assumed that the observed attitudes and habits are static. Only glimpses are given us in the literature of what happens to courtship and family life, and to the mores associated with sex when a modern school system breaks in upon the established sanctions of behavior, when money prestige has come to challenge the prestige of age and experience, when large-scale enterprise pulls youth out of the self-sufficient farm family or tempts it from the relative security of old-time farm practices. Only gradually in recent times has some sort of normal family life been re-introduced on the plantations. For some generations the native or alien Oriental labor groups recruited to work on them were herded like cattle; and the resulting demoralization still has its effects.

We should know a great deal more also in another neglected field of psychological study — the emotional and hence the social by-products of hunger. Famine is not, of course, a modern phenomenon introduced by the exactions of foreigners in tropical Asia. Despite the lavishness of nature, catastrophes and wars of conquest have taken their toll throughout history. But the colonial expansion of the West contributed to the rise of land values in the sections favorable for the production of commercial crops; it encouraged the growth of population, for long periods took more in taxes than it put into the colonies, and introduced a cleavage between classes that led to absentee landlordism and onerous new charges on the native economy. The substitution of money payment for barter in itself was a disturbing influence since it created indebtedness on the one hand and an ever-increasing demand, on the other, for new articles of consumption that had to be imported and added to the drain of exports.

Differences in the ways which the different ethnic groups of Southeast Asia have adopted to adjust themselves to the new demands made on their economy through the influence of modern enterprise have sometimes been explained with racial characteristics, and sometimes also with reference to the character of the inherited culture. Tagalogs have been drawn into modern society in one way, Ilocanos in another. A dozen different ethnic groups in Celebes show a dozen different forms of response to the demand for taxes. But the greatest influence on these various reactions undoubtedly has been the relative sense of security enjoyed by the various groups. Where hunger and want are just around the corner, simple-minded people find it difficult indeed to abandon the modes of behavior, the methods of production, the religious sanctions, and the accustomed forms of organization, through which they have survived in the past. Where the resources are more prolific in relation to the population's needs, people are more receptive to new ideas.

One might expect the inhabitants of a barren hill country in the Shan States of Burma to be more conservative than those of the rich river deltas where the soil yields several crops a year. But actually, with a population density adjusted to the local resources, some of the hill people have been more easily led into the adoption of modern ideas than were the frightened denizens of overcrowded rice-growing communities, for whom even the smallest departure from tradition in their main economic activities might mean the death of whole villages. One cannot sufficiently stress the intimate relation between physical well-being and mental receptivity.

Schools or No Schools?

This brings us to the second great area of governmental concern in native welfare — that of education. Of no large population in Southeast Asia can it be said today that it is "steeped in tradition" — as that phrase was understood a generation ago. Everywhere the schoolmaster has established himself at least in the larger towns; everywhere contacts outside the tribal boundaries have grown to the point where many inhabitants have directly or indirectly experienced something of the material culture of a different world.

The peasant in Malaya or Indo-China who for the first time travels on a bus shows much the same wavering between fear and delight as any other simple person would in the same circumstances. In an astonishingly short time the timid jungle dweller who has never been far from the barnyard noises of his native village will have become a disciplined and courageous soldier, provided that his experiences at the barracks have enough pleasurable elements to outweigh his fears. But too often the poor peasant's and woodsman's contacts with modern civilization are those of the simpleton who is fleeced of what he has and of the defenseless person who is robbed. His reaction will be different. His emotions will pull him back into the safety of the familiar environment with its sanction of "what has always been," with its satisfying ritual. His reason will tell him that to be safe he must master that new knowledge which, in the hands of others, makes him a victim of their greed. He, too, will seek that new power if he thinks and talks with others about it; but his search will be more circumspect and easily arrested by new dangers.

With all their consideration for native traditions, modern governments in tropical Asia cannot but aid the necessary adjustment: their task is to break the hold of the ancestors on the living generation, but not to break the integrity of that generation's emotional life, its spirit. Whatever may have been thought possible in the earlier stages of contact between East and West, we now know that it is utterly impossible to train human beings to function efficiently in modern phases of the national life while they remain tradition-minded in the so-called native — more correctly, unattached, neglected — phases. There is a cultural pluralism in all modern societies, a healthy expression of the flux between nations and continents that characterizes the age we live in. But the so-called cultural dualism of the colonies is balanced precariously between two ways of life that permit no easy harmonization. The cultural growth of the indigenous people could be directed toward that realm of attitudes, habits, beliefs, and practices which the master race, from the standpoint of its own security, considers desirable — but only if all the rest of that realm also were opened to the people by means of suitable incentives. You cannot

have the attentiveness of the modern servant, the ingenuity
of the modern mechanic, the efficiency of the modern clerk,
unless you are willing to concede the rewards, material and
emotional, that go with a satisfying functioning in our complex, highly organized modern economic life.

The attempt to bring the brown man of the tropics into
the realm of world economy on a basis of free participation
and adequate compensation cannot succeed if at the same
time he is to be held within the confines of his traditional
culture. The area in which he can express his cultural
heritage, in which it is possible for his theocratic and even
animistic ideology to prevail, without unfitting him for participation in the modern side of the dualistic set-up of the
colonies, is shrinking fast. Visit the temples and mosques,
the shrines and monasteries, and you will find that they are
not impervious to the winds of new learning. Even there, in
the citadels of old Asia, a transmutation of values is taking
place. In order to hold contemporary youth the religious
teacher must be ready to answer personal problems that
did not exist in former times, must know something of the
world without the hallowed precincts of the institution if
only to counter forces of which he does not approve.

In every-day life, the religious leaders no longer find it
possible to insist on the observance of every last rite, every
holiday, every dietary prescription; like our own religious
teachers in the West they insist more and more on the essential virtues. There has been a great decrease in the number of pilgrims to Mecca during the last pre-war decade.
Although this is sufficiently explained by the economic depression, it is also true that despite the rising tide of nationalism there has developed some sort of Mohammedan
equivalent of a movement "Away from Rome." Intermarriage between believers and non-believers is more frequent.
In their moral teaching, the exponents of the great faiths
are coming closer together. Popular disapproval of cruelty

is gaining; the status of womanhood is rising; and in many
places the trend toward common sense and mutual tolerance in human relations is strong.

It follows that there is no longer the sharp contrast between the religious and the secular systems of education
which existed when the one served exclusively the conservation of the cultural heritage and the other the purpose of
fitting its pupils for modern life. Indeed, there are now inevitable cross-purposes in the school policies of colonial
governments. Looking at the economic turnover in pre-
war years of such countries as Indo-China, Netherlands India, or British Malaya (not the respective budgets), it can
hardly be contended that popular education occupied a
prominent place in the national finances. In each of these
countries there were those who complained that the educational system existed largely for the purpose of discourag-
ing a thirst for modern knowledge. This criticism is not
perhaps objectively valid but significant for the attitude of
ambitious youth, especially in the more affluent indigenous
classes.

The educational problem in colonial and semi-colonial
countries is, of course, the same in one respect as that in
other countries with a strong class division: how to make
inexpensive talents available for many tasks that require a
certain amount of knowledge — literacy, for example —
and yet not stimulate intellectual curiosity to the point
where members of the lower classes might aspire to functions in society which the upper classes wish to reserve for
themselves. This dilemma is obscured by a thousand di-
versions in a thousand reports, but it is unmistakable once
the concrete questions which such reports raise and discuss are analyzed. One may also paraphrase it by asking
the question: how may the human mind be freed from
ignorance and superstition to a certain point and then be
arrested?

One of the many Indonesian private schools built since 1920. Here children are taught subjects that are useful for modern living, but in the Malay language and with emphasis on the local culture heritage.

China's greatest asset in Southeast Asia. The largest population group in Singapore, the Chinese also do the most to provide their children with a modern education.

Formation of a queue before the public pawnshop was a daily occurrence in Javanese cities during the years of economic depression.

Thai, Chinese, and American films are shown in the capital of Thailand. The American ones are the most popular.

The typical answer given to this question in colonial Asia was to go ahead as far as necessary to produce the required degree of ability and specific knowledge, and then simply to cut off all opportunity for further learning. To justify such a procedure it was only necessary to proclaim that, alas, the native people are so constituted that they can never reach real mental maturity: they progress to a certain age of adolescence (sometimes the age of twelve is named, sometimes that of fifteen) and then suddenly drop off, retaining only with difficulty a little of the knowledge acquired up to that point. A French educator in Indo-China assured me that, among the Annamese, there was not only standstill but a rapid decline of mental capacity about the age of fifteen. Of the Javanese it is said that they are precocious and may outstrip European children of their own age; but after adolescence they become dull and unreceptive to new ideas. (Similar statements are often heard in the United States about Negroes or Mexicans — sometimes also about other minorities. Elaborate mental tests are cited in proof, but in these no allowance is made for differences in social background and the respective degrees of encouragement and discouragement experienced by students of the different groups.)

There are also some who, on the contrary, deplore all the evident eagerness of the colonial people for learning — on the ground that it can only lead to discontent and eventually to social unrest. The evidence which they present is not very scientific: the "veritable passion for learning" which a Philippine educator said he had observed was found, on further questioning, to be mainly a desire of members of certain classes to pass examinations so as to become eligible for the civil service. Sometimes it is an emotional reaction to the pressure exerted by the authorities to steer native students into vocational courses where their opportunities of rising to political prominence would be small. The existing disproportion in several countries of Southeast Asia between graduates of high schools or colleges and suitable jobs does not show that there are too many schools, or even enough. It merely shows that too many students are trained for professions that are not under present circumstances open to them. It is no longer true, whatever may have been the case a generation or two ago, that indigenous students in Southeast Asia study *only* for a diploma and the status of gentlemen. Many among them are imbued with genuine and not too extravagant professional ambitions; many are inspired by genuine humanitarian or patriotic ideals.

In recent years, vocational outlets for educated natives have increased. The greater variety of vocational choices among those who have received a higher education results from an increase in the vocational requirements of large-scale enterprises and the growth of cities. The old-time employer had little interest in popular education. It cost money, imposed troublesome prohibitions on the employment of children, created tastes that led to demands for higher earnings, and made labor less docile. But the more enlightened manager desires more "docility" — in the original meaning of the word: a teachability which presupposes at least a small amount of schooling. Valuable properties are in danger of damage through ignorance. Processes of production are more intricate than they used to be and require the workers' intelligent co-operation. Competition has become keener and, wherever possible, it is desirable to substitute indigenous or alien Asiatic for European skilled labor and sub-management.

No educator in the world can give these modern employers what they want without giving them something more: a self-respecting working class that wants some of the good things of life which technical progress makes possible. Hence, when they express much concern over the "inner conflicts" of native society, the more conservative colonial administrators often display their own. If the dual economy is to be maintained, there must be a ruthless repression of cultural advance. But it is already too late for that. The apparatus of living, even in the tropics, has become too involved to be managed by pre-industrial policies. Only a large forward step toward internal democracy, whatever the external form of government, can insure social harmony.

A New Trend in Colonial Policy

The examples taken in the previous pages of this chapter from the fields of public health and education must suffice to indicate the author's conviction that "good government" is not practically possible within the framework of colonialism.

There is no simple contrast between efficiency and inefficiency, success and failure; but always the question must be asked: efficiency in what, success for whom? It is of the very essence of colonial and semi-colonial government that its policies are dominated by large economic interests. These interests may not be hostile to, and temporarily may even coincide with, a genuine desire of the authorities to give the native welfare precedence over other claims. But there can be no permanent and complete integration of purposes so opposite, even in Malaya and in the Netherlands Indies with the proved humanitarian sincerity of the respective governments. Colonial empires, under whatever name, remain the largest and most complete demonstration areas of class government because in them class differences are reinforced by differences in color.

The British Labor Party in a recent declaration demands abolition of the color bar "in every shape or form" in territories for the laws and administration of which Parliament is responsible. This means trusteeship in its most absolute form, where the trustee no longer even indirectly seeks to advance the interests of his own kith and kin, in whose behalf the colonial obligation was assumed in the first place. One might put aside declarations of this sort as expressions of idealistic sentiment that bind nobody were it not for the fact that the British Government, largely under the urge of organized labor, actually has established a Colonial Development and Welfare Fund for the promotion of education and health and to aid economic developments of primary importance for the welfare of the native peoples. Indeed, like the Netherlands Indian Government, it has already accomplished a great deal in the improvement of native industries and native farming that is manifestly not designed for the profit of the European investors and business interests. Actions of this sort are either short-lived compromises or indications of what amounts to a revolution in colonial policy. If they are manifestations of a native-centered policy an entirely new orientation of basic attitudes toward imperial relationships must follow.

This is not the place for a discussion of colonial theories, but it is worth noting that several of the metropolitan governments have already proclaimed that the Atlantic Charter necessitates no drastic change in the policies which they have pursued in their dependencies for some time. According to them, all that concerted international planning can do is to speed a process of transformation already well under way. This view is strengthened by the insistence that a joint international guarantee for peace and order in the colonial regions of the world must take the place of the protection hitherto afforded by imperial systems or commonwealths. Even before the present war it was evident that the era of international rivalry in the exploitation of dependent territories and subject peoples as mainstays of the power of great nations was over. Subject and dominant peoples alike, throughout the world, felt in need of a stability in their economic life which only a genuine pooling of their interests could bring about. With the aggressive movement of colonial expansion which the Axis powers alone strove to revive there is dying the hopeless compromise of conflicting purposes that characterized the era of "ethical" colonial policies.

It is true that in some quarters there still lingers the concept of empire made up in part of aggressive, modern population groups chiefly interested in mass production for an international market, and in part of a native population, segregated as much as possible for its own protection. The "museum" idea of pre-industrial cultures and of the appropriate policies for preserving them arose when socially sensitive Westerners first became aware of the brutality of the systems of administration in far places. With their uneasy social conscience combined the uneasy aesthetic conscience of those who saw the old cultures with their ancient arts go down under the wheels of modern industry, as it invaded country after country with its leavening and skill-destroying mass products. Leave the indigenous peoples alone, was a cry that found a ready echo in the minds of those owners of large estates, mines, and other modern enterprises, who could use a humanitarian motive to support their preference for the more efficient imported Indian or Chinese labor. It was also helpful as an argument to those who wished to obstruct movements of independence — on the plea that the charming ways and the beautiful arts of the aborigines surely were going to be destroyed if dominant and economically aggressive native groups were to gain the right to rule over them.

Under the impact of the present war all the soiled and shopworn arguments for "adjustments" between the incompatible interests of native groups and their exploiters are exposed to the public view for the self-delusions they are. Foreign domination in the spirit of trusteeship cannot also be foreign domination to preserve a valuable "possession" in behalf of European investors. Administration of a dependency with a view primarily to its trade and resources cannot also be administration for the purpose of bringing about self-government at the earliest possible time. Competitive production for the world market is not production of highest economic benefit to the native people — except to the extent that they demand imported commodities to enrich their standard of living. Mass production at low wages makes for an excess of exports over imports; a "favorable balance of trade" is achieved in the nonsensical meaning attached to that term by those colonial economists who see its highest attainment when the indigenous people are deprived of all they have, their natural resources, their labor, their freedom, and their happiness.

It is against these misconceptions and false doctrines that enlightened world opinion is now turning. A speeding up of production with cheap labor in the tropics benefits the Occidental peoples no more than does sweated labor at home. Most of the Western countries have taken steps to exclude immigration from the Orient so as to protect their workers against the competition of sweated labor. But the competition offered by the products of that cheap labor continues, reducing employment in the countries with higher living standards and at the same time precluding an expansion of the market for their own products to the millions of Asiatics who hardly as yet are customers for manufactured commodities at all. In spite of the greatly expanded producing capacity of the industrial countries after this war, the workers are doomed to a period of severe unemployment unless the one colossal gap in the world's economic interrelations is closed — that is, unless the millions yet living in a pre-industrial stage of development are freed from the shackles of their abysmal poverty and helped to enter the world market as consumers.

There is, in short, no possibility of economic recovery

after this war if the world as a whole continues to be divided into two sharply distinct branches of the human family: those who participate in modern production and are on the way to attaining modern standards of consumption; and those who "potter" in the fields of a precarious self-sufficiency, occasionally work at starvation wages, and are closer to the stone age in their living standards than to the age of the *Ladies' Home Journal*. Political freedom is secondary; freedom from want is the first plank in any reasonable international program of emancipation. It cannot be attained without effort that takes time — but it comes first, just the same.

There is *prima facie* need, then, for some form of international, interracial, and intercultural co-operation to strengthen the tendency already at work in the colonial systems — feebly in most but more pronounced in some — to rid themselves of an untenable duality of purpose and policy. One may find fault with the language used by this or that advocate of a new international system. The British Prime Minister is not alone in believing that the British Empire is not yet ready for "liquidation." But those who sincerely desire a basis of assured peace when the present disturbers of the peace have been beaten do not, for the most part, differ in their ideas about the prerequisites. No better proofs of this are needed than that of the United Nations' common statement of war aims, and again in the report of the United Nations' Conference on Food and Agriculture. There are diehards in all countries who will to the last oppose measures that menace their special privileges. But they can be defeated by a combination of democratic and forward-looking forces. Just what that combination may be in the part of the world with which we are here concerned will be considered in the next and last chapter.

XIV

POSSIBILITIES OF REGIONAL COLLABORATION

As THE active campaign for the re-occupation of Southeast Asia begins, the trend in policy discussed in the last chapter assumes a new international importance. That trend, formulated as a war aim, becomes the weapon most relied upon to insure the adherence to the United Nations of the indigenous peoples of all that region. There is no longer any question that the Atlantic Charter, to which most of them subscribed, is intended to be global in scope, though some difference in judgment is permissible as to means and as to the time that must be allowed to reach self-government.

When read in conjunction with other parts of the declaration, "the right of all peoples to choose the form of government under which they will live" is conditioned but not limited. Among other things, there must be an orderly procedure, internationally guaranteed, providing safeguards for such international rights and obligations as free access to trade and raw materials, freedom of the seas, and general mutual protection against aggression. The procedure for attaining self-government must be in harmony with "the fullest collaboration between all nations in the economic field with the object of securing, for all, improved labor standards, economic advancement, and social security." This alone would seem to preclude a sudden severing of existing economic bonds that have served to guarantee the livelihood of a large part of the colonial population. Nor can these purposes be fulfilled by simply re-apportioning colonial possessions between "have" and "have not" countries.

Positively stated, the Atlantic Charter, as amplified by subsequent declarations of United Nations policy, requires of the imperial powers something more difficult even than the cutting off of some of their possessions or the grant to them of a more favorable status if they should choose to remain within the imperial system. The shift from "possession" — with the implicit right to exploitation — to "trusteeship," long conceded in principle by the larger imperial powers, is now seen as only a step from exclusive imperial control to some distant but nevertheless firmly envisaged world control. The transition period may be long. But in the interest of stability it must be one of definite and graded progress toward the goal; and at each stage there must be a clear-cut new conciliation between the old and the new policies that go with a change in the relations between sovereign and subject, between state and state. Objects which in theory may appear to be contradictory nevertheless must during this transition be combined in one set of purposes: imperial economic stability and resolute advance of native participation, solidity of the imperial structure and world security, regard for historic affiliations — in trade or language or administrative methods — and regard for growth of the area of international co-operation.

Obligation toward the whole world in the relations between the constituent parts of an imperial system is not new. Its violation, as under the Ottawa Agreement of 1932, has always proved disastrous in recent times. In many things, the field of international joint action and mutual responsibility is, of course, far more advanced today than it was at the end of the last war. One only needs to think of such matters as treatment of minorities, contract labor, protection of particular classes of people, allocation of quotas, currency agreements to uphold values, the network of trade agreements, public health provisions of various kinds, not to mention political and economic arrangements which recognize the principle of mutuality but which in practice have been much less successful.

In every instance the question arises how and to what extent such abrogation of absolute sovereignty — since that is what it amounts to — can be compensated for by an international security system. In view of the early events in this war, it may be questioned whether the imperial system really did afford any security; and in retrospect one may even wonder how it could ever have been supposed to do so. Nevertheless, within each imperial structure such mutual reliance did exist and contributed not a little to stability, smooth trade relations, and some protection for the indigenous peoples. The interdependence of areas, united in a single political structure, bridged climates and cultures and, imperfect as it was, tended to become less one-sided than it had been at the start. Through their common interest in the stability and improvement of the empire's economic structure, white and colored colonials, East and West, experienced a mutuality of interest, though fully conscious of their differences as producers and investors, as employers and laborers, as profiting and losing with high prices on colonial products, as members of an ethnic group held in subjection and as members of the ruling group. The area of common interest grew when white and colored colonials came more often to fulfill similar economic functions, as merchants, as producers, as bankers, as civil servants. Colonial economies started, as the native cultures did, from primitive collecting, passed through the phase of still somewhat primitive agricultural production until the processes of gaining wealth became so refined and specialized that it is possible to speak of great export "industries" in the dependencies. When that stage was reached, the caste system was bound to break down eventually because it was — and is — irreconcilable with the technical demands.

The Growth of Interdependence

If it had not been for the calamitous breach of the peace by a feudal Asiatic empire equipped with modern weapons, the social relations of the colonies of Southeast Asia would probably have been modernized by natural stages. And with the gradual interchanging and sharing of economic interests and functions on the part of natives and foreigners, colored and white, the political relations also would have changed; there would have been more and more recognition for the growing interdependence of the different parts of the empire and of the races that compose it. That slow democratization of the internal relations was given a new stimulus by the war. Even before the war, the more foresighted statesmen recognized the insufficiency of imperial defenses. Economic and political interdependence in an age of global strategy could not with impunity be limited by the historical accidents that determined the distribution of sovereignty the world over. A comprehensive international structure of mutual defense was necessary; but even that was not enough — there also had to be a joint advance in the opening up of new resources, a wider community of interest in the raising of those dangerously low levels of life and liberty which in this new era were liable to become hotbeds of spreading discontent. The imperial powers, with all their long experience in the constructive solution of administrative problems, no longer could cope with the ever-growing disparity between the demands of world opinion — including that in their own home countries — and the political and social *status quo* in their dependencies.

It is not because of the present war but as an outcome of

developments much longer in the making that the imperial powers must relinquish some of their sovereign powers if they themselves would survive and prosper. They know it and do not attempt to resist the inevitable. All they ask is that the eventual integration of the separate imperial and commonwealth organizations in a larger world organization shall not be over-hasty — with incalculable risks to material and cultural values now supported by the sovereign authority of states; that it shall proceed without detriment to the safety and welfare of those politically untrained peoples whose protection presents for the mother countries a sacred obligation; that the transformation of this trusteeship into a partnership, watched over by a larger international board of guardians, shall not be interrupted by irresponsible outside interference.

Without a reliable world organization, the "demolition of the colonial system" is hardly a constructive proposal. A dissolution of the existing colonial empires would only produce the most dangerous kind of regionalism. Instead of an intricate network of common interests spanning wide differences in race, religion, technical achievement, social custom, language, and livelihood, there would be created political structures — perhaps loose federations at first, tending to become empires under the hegemony of some strong power within the region — unified in some of these respects and in stark opposition to other such regional structures elsewhere. From the undeveloped but growing community of interest between Occidental and Oriental peoples, more in particular, there would be a return to the fanaticism of the middle ages: a racially or culturally more homogeneous East would challenge the world leadership of the West. For this reason if for no other, sincere defenders of the colonial system tell us, it would be folly to give up the relative security which the mutual responsibilities within the far-flung Occidental-Oriental empires afford before a global security system has evolved, and this in established practice with all the necessary implements of control — and not only on paper.

Speeches have been made in the British Parliament complaining about the thoughtlessness of Americans who discuss "independence" in such regions as Southeast Asia without regard to the difficulties which the dissolution of the colonial systems would entail. In other parts of the world this caution, unfortunately, has given the impression that the leading political circles in Great Britain — and in other metropolitan homelands, too — did not take the Atlantic Charter seriously enough. Reasonable persons, even among those most ardently working for world democracy, do not advocate a sudden change and are not inclined to quarrel too much over the length of time it must take to accomplish the purpose; but they do insist that self-rule — economic and social no less than political — *is* the avowed common aim to which all colonial policies henceforth must be bent. That aim does not preclude the continued operation of scattered imperial commonwealths if their survival seems best suited to guarantee order and to insure progress; but it involves a definite if graded advance of hitherto dependent peoples in representative government. A "token" of democracy, that is, a parliamentary type of legislation with very limited powers and an even more limited franchise (as in Burma), may in some instances have to do at first. But from the start provision will be needed to facilitate a gradual widening of both the powers and the franchise, until complete autonomy has been attained. Those who take this view are well aware that such a process has not yet matured or even been assured in all of the supposedly self-governing countries of the world — not even in the United States which speaks so loudly for democracy and yet permits large minorities to be kept disfranchised solely on racial grounds. But the purpose of mending matters is gaining ground. To quote President Roosevelt, who in turn was quoting Thomas Jefferson (April 14, 1943):

> "He believed, as we believe, that men are capable of their own government, and that no king, no tyrant, no dictator can govern them as wisely as they can govern for themselves."

This book happens to be about Southeast Asia; were it about some other region, it would be evident that other nations, too, have yet to travel a long way before they can be said to have put their democratic principles into practice. However, there must of necessity be wide variations in methods and programs before that is accomplished. It would be folly to forecast without the most careful local studies how the Indonesians, the Malayans, the Annamese, the Burmese, and others, under the conditions that dominate their economic and social life, can best be helped to achieve full autonomy. All we can do here is to consider some questions that affect the process as a whole and the fortunes of all the diverse peoples that make up the population of Southeast Asia.

The colonial powers now established there share with each other and with other powers the right to determine the future political status of their subjects. They will retain the exclusive right of sovereignty and of administration, but some of their unfinished colonial tasks will merge in the larger setting of a world organization. That in permitting any kind of world authority to influence its policies and practices a government incurs risks goes without saying. But against these must be set the even greater risks of continuing imperial rivalries unmodified by international agreements — rivalries which in themselves make for reaction and timidity in the grant of civil rights. No great outside power, like the United States or the Soviet Union, will want to guarantee the security of political structures the purposes of which are inimical to their own principles. This matter, indeed, is so important that, unless recognized in time, the whole idea of international mutual guarantees for the perpetuation of existing sovereignties and imperial relationships may prove illusory. At least a minimum of political reconstruction has to be assured.

Southeast Asia, again to restrict the argument to the region considered in this book, abounds in anomalies of political map-making. For example, northern Burma and northern Indo-China contain highland areas and population groups that have more in common with each other and with similar areas and populations in Thailand than either has with the particular country of which it is a part. Southern Thailand is separated from Malaya only by a historical accident which should not determine for all time the political affiliation of these neighboring and related peoples; but the clumsy rectification attempted by the enemy in handing four of the most purely Malay states with a population of about a million over to Thailand will not do. Although the Netherlands Indian Government, by adopting the name "Indonesian," long infamous because of its nationalist connotation, has tried to emphasize the unity of its heterodox population, clearly in Borneo its subjects are closely related to those who live under the British flag, and some of the peoples of Sumatra are in race, culture, and economic status more closely related to Malaya than to Java or Celebes. The Mohammedan Moros of the Philippines have far more in common in their history and culture with the coast Malays of Borneo than with, say, the Tagalogs. The great Chinese minorities of Cochin-China, Thailand, Malaya, Java, and the Philippines, can hardly be expected to become completely de-sinified in their feeling and thinking. More important still, the question has been raised: why should the nationless peoples of the region — those assumedly backward groups which have never been given even the smallest share in the government of the state that rules over them — have to go through the long and tedious process of becoming national citizens, with all the mutual exclusiveness and arbitrary fixation of social interests which that implies? Must European history be repeated and Southeast Asia be subdivided into so many independent states, each composed of a multitude of tribes with conflicting interests? Or can the region's present political immaturity be turned to good account by leading these millions of unschooled peasants straight from their relative isolation into a more inclusive co-operative commonwealth?

We are so accustomed to think of nationalism in relation to incorporated states that it is difficult for us to visualize nations which for scores of generations have been dispersed. After the last war, the existence of such nations in Europe led to the somewhat arbitrary fixation of boundaries between newly recognized states, each equipped with full sovereignty. After this war, many hold, it should be possible to devise a scheme more in conformity with the actual situation. And this especially in the new areas of materializing nationalist aspirations. Why should the people of Celebes, of Mindanao, of Laos, and of the Chin Hills in Burma have to go through the process of acquiring a political national consciousness for which the predisposing traits are entirely lacking in their experience? And is not in our own lives the power of the political state challenged today by other law-giving institutions in ways wholly alien to the thinking of the signers of the Constitution? The life of the Burman or the Indonesian is ruled even more than our lives are in the West by economic bonds that have the force of law. Why squeeze it into the formulas of an outdated political kind of thinking?

No one who contemplates with detachment the debacle of nineteenth-century nationalism in the present global war will wish to re-establish it on an even grander scale. He will not wish to see additional millions, hitherto held in subjection, achieve independence in the orthodox meaning of that term. He will rather stress the fact of interdependence.

Organs of International Collaboration

Giving full weight to the arguments for continuing the present political affiliations — with only such border adjustments as may be mutually agreed — there is need for greater international unity in matters pertaining to native welfare; and this includes considerations of external trade, of military and naval security, of communications and of shipping, as well as the more narrowly conceived elements of prosperity and the good life. To bring about such unity without doing violence to the separate needs and aspirations of the peoples of Southeast Asia means a departure from that cautious political isolationism which has ruled the relations between the colonial powers. Some of their leading statesmen shudder at the very thought of having to submit their legislative plans and administrative programs to joint organs of international authority less intimately acquainted than they are with the conditions out of which these proposals spring. But the necessity for sharing experience and counsel is no longer open to question. The sad decay of the mandate system, which in its main lines was well-conceived, illustrates how easily an instrument of international policy can fail of its purpose when the ghosts of national selfishness pop out of every imperial cupboard. A joint instrument of watchfulness, fully equipped to enforce international agreement, alone can render safe a divided exercise of authority by the different sovereign states.

There are in Southeast Asia a number of especially attractive possibilities for the functioning of joint organs in behalf of either some or all of the governments in that region. Such agencies, however, as history has shown, will function successfully only when the various governments fully recognize the advantage of making common cause with their neighbors and with other interested powers. With the existing state of jealousy, it may be necessary at first to limit the activities of such agencies to study and advice. Colonel Oliver Stanley, the British Colonial Secretary, speaks of a network of regional commissions for consultation and collaboration. To avoid even the appearance of the much-feared "super-government," they need not, to begin with, be bound together under a single administration. The different governments would continue in most things to act independently — until perhaps at some future time a partial overlapping of authority and the magnitude of the total area of joint activity already achieved would produce a strong call for greater cohesion.

Only in one respect would there seem to be an immediate necessity for a joint regional administrative organ in Southeast Asia: after the recapture of the mandated areas, their government may perhaps best be entrusted to a single responsible agency. That agency need not introduce the principle of direct administration by an international authority global in scope; instead, it may well represent the joint authority of the governments in the region and those with special interests in it. Taking over at the start the Japanese mandates in Southeast Asia — the Marianas, the Carolines, and the Marshall Islands — such a joint authority may eventually prove so efficient that some of the governments may voluntarily wish to relegate to it the administration of marginal territories inhabited mainly by politically immature aborigines. This might take place, for example, if obstacles to the attainment of independence should arise from the inclusion in the population of a given territory of considerable minorities that have no confidence in the disinterestedness of the politically more advanced and active groups.

Again, limited areas might be subjected to that joint authority for the special purpose of administering refugee settlement or other joint settlement projects.

Other fields in which the desirability of greater international collaboration has long been felt are those of intra-regional migration, combat of lawlessness (smuggling, piracy, slave traffic, drug traffic), regulation of shipping lanes and communications, control of epidemics and other public health matters. To begin with, there is, of course, the enormous joint war task itself and with it the task of shifting from military re-occupation to the re-establishment of normal civil government. In some instances this will entail operations which the home government — for instance, France in the case of Indo-China — may find it difficult to carry through without help. Connected with re-occupation are also the relief and rehabilitation activities now being planned by the United Nations as part of the war effort but likely to involve programs lasting far into the post-war period of international collaboration. Although some of the governments in Southeast Asia will wish and be able to carry out these lengthy and involved tasks under their own unaided and undiluted authority, there will be need for much sharing of limited resources and avoidance of friction through the adoption of parallel policies.

Thus the need, only vaguely sensed in the past, for a more functional international machinery of co-operation will be evident and even urgent in the days to come. But the very multitude of the tasks that call for joint effort shows that it will not be enough to set up joint international agencies — perhaps, in some distant European city — with the whole world for their field of administration. The case for a regional set-up is much clearer today than it was ten years ago, and is especially clear in Southeast Asia. A central international authority may be successful in running an international weather reporting service or an epidemological reporting service, but it could hardly go very far in the adaptation of joint international policy to the welfare and progress of particular population groups from the tropics to the Arctic Circle. A regional council, more representative of the governments with special interests in a given region, would be more intimately informed of needs and possibilities and could act more promptly. Among matters likely to benefit from a regionalization of international authority are allocation of production quotas, regulation of shipping and of international migration, enforcement of international labor agreements — just to mention some fairly obvious examples.

Such a plan would not involve a federalization of the existing colonial governments — a step that is dreaded by many statesmen as opening the door to uncertainty as to where authority lay in a given case, and for which that part of the world probably is not yet ripe. It would do little more than expand and systematize a collaboration which, in some respects, is already well-advanced, and assign responsibilities in the marginal area between manifest national and partly international concerns. Most of these agencies would, of course, be affiliated also in international organizations with others operating similarly in other regions.

It is difficult to see how, without some such organization, could be met the world-wide demand for a greater recognition of the interdependence and mutual responsibility of nations. It would not supersede existing structures of government; it would not break into the established relations between Indo-China and France — which the United States has promised to respect — between Indonesia and the Netherlands, or Malaya and the British Commonwealth. It would not detract from the political independence of Thailand or stand in the way of an early realization of independence by Burma and the Philippines.

Joint agencies, equipped at the start with no more than advisory functions, may be expected, as confidence in them grew, gradually to develop some administrative organs, without power of legislation, receiving their directions from international conventions duly ratified in the participating countries. Being related to regional needs, such conventions would be more specific than those adopted for and by a globe-encircling group of nations. They could correspondingly be applied more directly, and their application could be supervised with greater respect for local differences in conditions.

Whatever else they may do, instruments of regional cooperation are necessary to the fulfillment of the declared war aims of the United Nations in so far as they affect the relations between colonial powers and subject peoples. Just because no reasonable person will demand the immediate enfranchisement of all dependent peoples irrespective of their competency for self-government, democratic world opinion must insist that the progress toward the realization of that end be implemented with something more than vague promises. There would seem to be need for a system of internationally administered tests by which may be ascertained from time to time whether a given colonial power has, in its policies and practices, provided its subject peoples with adequate opportunities for the achievement of a given stage in its guided advance to self-determination. The number and nature of these stages would necessarily differ for different population groups; and it is largely for this reason that a regional body, acquainted with all the facts and in a position to make intimate local studies, is in a better position to supervise the procedure than would be a distant world organization.

In principle, the setting up of a regional council, to coordinate such activities as those mentioned, has already unofficially been agreed upon by the governments primarily concerned. On such a council they will be reconciled to see represented not only the colonial powers with direct responsibilities in Southeast Asia but also the independent states of that region and perhaps also other powers with no direct responsibilities for government there. The success with which some nations have solved their minority or nationality problems in other parts of the world would be reason enough for including their representatives in an advisory capacity. The subject peoples themselves should also receive some representation, not so much for the purpose of pressing their political claims as to insure that the experience and desires of the population groups most intimately affected will be given due weight.

While for the sake of clarity it has been argued here on an earlier page that the object of an early attainment of self-rule is distinct from the object of native welfare as pursued by all modern colonial governments, obviously the two aims are related. The development of self-governing institutions in the colonial areas of the region necessitates a corresponding social and economic advance.

Common Problems of Livelihood

In another study (*Freedom and Welfare in Southeast Asia,* New York, 1942) the present writer has outlined a three-dimensional regional organization that would give broad recognition to the need for concerted action in the political, economic, and cultural fields. Only a few samples can here be given of the sort of thing that may best be achieved in each of these fields by pooling both the resources and the resourcefulness of the various states.

In the improvement of economic conditions a stronger accent on intra-regional trade would play its part. This, however, at best cannot assume large dimensions because the major products of the different countries in Southeast Asia are so similar, and will be still more similar perhaps if greater emphasis is laid on food production and if each receives additional stimulus to develop industries for the production of simple consumer goods. Specialization will follow in time; but if one country of Southeast Asia were permitted to become a principal supplier of manufactured goods for the others and these had to pay for their imports with agricultural and other raw materials, there would remain the same inequality in economic status that has burdened the whole region in the past when it had to look for its manufactured articles to the Occident, to India, and to Japan.

More important as a matter of common economic interest, therefore, is the establishment of joint controls over those exports in which many of them share and on which many of them depend for a large part of their national income: rice in the case of Indo-China and Thailand; rubber, tin, coconut, various textile fibers such as kapok and jute, sugar, tobacco, and many more. When governments so largely control trade, the automatic checks of free trade no longer operate. Both production and international exchange must be jointly controlled if an equitable market is to be maintained. The Sleeping Beauty of the fabled wealth of the Indies can be awakened only with the aid of extra-regional capital and extra-regional markets. A joint regional council would represent the interest of all the colonial peoples in a fair apportionment of the free capital and of the free markets of the world under whatever more inclusive world organization may grow up after the war to get trade going again. It would also represent the region as a whole in the important matter of shipping connections with the rest of the world and would endeavor to substitute a combined adequate service for the separate, competitive and wasteful services rendered in the past by the various shipping companies under the impetus of the aggressive commercial and political policies of their home governments. Thailand and the Philippines would benefit as much from an ordering of the region's external economic relations as would Malaya or Timor.

No international body can directly affect the distribution of profit between capital and labor. But it can bring about a substantial rise in the consuming power of the people through measures designed to raise the value of per capita production; for that means the use of more capital in the relation to labor power and involves the international flow of credit. No country desires to play the part of large-scale exporter of raw materials while it depends for manufactured goods entirely on imports, because that means inability to accumulate savings and, in the long run, domination by foreign capital. Industrialization as the answer to the central economic and political problem of Southeast Asia does not, however, mean that there must be a uniform and hasty adoption by all the region of grandiose plans for the building up of a rounded industrial system. The need, as we have seen, is for a diversity of industrial developments and for a rate of speed in their achievement that is adjusted to needs and resources. Some of the countries will think primarily of military and naval defense; it will depend on the degree to which they can rely on an international security system whether other plans must be subordinated to this. A regional economic organization could prevent a scramble for foreign capital in which enterprises promising the highest returns rather than the respective long-range requirements of a regional economic reconstruction would determine the flow of investments.

From the international standpoint it is important that means of transportation (including shipping, aviation, railways and roads), basic agricultural developments, proper use of mineral and forest resources, and a socially advantageous employment of the available labor power receive precedence over speculative booms in the manufacture of consumer goods. The rise in standards of consumption, while steady, cannot with safety be allowed to be much swifter than the rise in production. The building up of native capital and native enterprise is necessary for a stable economic future of all tropical Asia. The growth of small industries, designed to satisfy with local raw materials and local labor those consumer demands which still are in the main part of the traditional ways of life, can best be insured in combination with a rounded agricultural life. Therefore a regional planning in which the production of commercial crops takes its proper place with native farming for local consumption and with the supply of raw materials for native crafts and incipient small industries is more advantageous than a separate planning by each nation and each colony for its maximum share in world trade.

There is need, then, for a central economic organization for all of Southeast Asia, staffed with the best experts to be found, impartial in its supply of technical and financial assistance, financed from a joint development fund which would also administer outside governmental loans. Such pooling of plans and, to some extent, of resources, would go far to advance the well-being of the region as a whole. Greatest beneficiaries would be those population groups that have suffered most in the past from exploitation or simply from neglect. A regional international organization for that purpose would not supersede the authority of the separate governments but would strengthen it. By providing an element of security, it would make it easier for each of them to draw into every kind of enterprise and into every kind of administrative responsibility representatives of the native peoples, as part of their training for self-rule.

Among specific tasks for such a regional organization, in addition to the administration of a joint development program, mention has already been made of supervision of labor conditions in large enterprises in so far as these are subject to international conventions. This control would extend to the employment of contract labor, and insure the minima of safety and protection established under international labor codes.

Migration and land settlement are other areas of joint concern when they involve the movement of workers between separate political units or, as has previously been suggested, the creation of joint reservations and settlements for special purposes. It is possible, through joint planning, to even out some of the great disparities in population density in relation to the supporting capacity of the land. There are also possibilities of large-scale temporary intra-regional labor migration which would help to increase production and to relieve population pressure.

In connection with all such new enterprises, a regional set-up, mainly concerned with welfare and advance toward responsible self-rule, would stress all those types of organization that provide training in self-determination. It would encourage co-operation within class limits and a widening participation of native labor with management and with public authorities in the administration of productive and welfare activities. In this way, a valuable contribution would be made not only to social peace but also to the formation of habits of collaboration between members of different racial and culture groups. What is here proposed does not imply a huge program of improvisation. There is a good deal of experience to draw upon.

The "Quenchless Indispensable Fire"

This brings us to possibilities of greater inter-cultural collaboration by means of perhaps yet other types of regional joint agencies. So-called nationalist movements sometimes are little more than aspirations toward a wider sharing of rights and responsibilities than the narrow tribal and community organization allows. A cultural nationalism ceases to be dangerous when it has constructive tasks to perform that permit co-operation between one ethnic group and another. Only its frustration, through an attempted isolation behind the ramparts of the separate tradition, leads to a negative and destructive attitude toward government. The cultural awakening of the peoples of Southeast Asia, expressing itself mainly in new demands on the school system, in the first place affects the separate governments. But a regional organization can do much to limit the area of inter-cultural conflict by providing for joint deliberation of common difficulties, by bringing seemingly local issues into the focus of a larger setting, and by bringing outside world opinion to bear on problems that can only be solved as a part of larger problems involving the relations between great religious bodies, schools of thought, and culture traditions not limited by political boundaries.

Movements described as "nationalist" often are essentially religious. Some, as we have seen, represent a revolt of youth, some combine a democratic urge with reverence for inherited customs. "Nationalism" is, in fact, a misnomer — made unavoidable in our discussion by the word's accepted use. One could imagine a sort of cultural parliament for the region which would settle some of the outstanding disputes in the relations of the religious bodies with each other and with the governmental authorities and thus make for mutual understanding. Such a deliberative body would have only advisory powers, as far as the governments were concerned, but might contribute a great deal of sound advice on the harmonizing of native and metropolitan law, on cultural conservation that does not stagnate, on school questions, on the development of a common regional auxiliary language, on the protection of religious pilgrims, on the campaign against rackets in the guise of religious movements, and on many other matters that intimately affect the lives of millions of people. Here also, a joint attack on problems common to the different political units of the region would provide priceless opportunities for the training of native leadership.

A regional cultural council would create an atmosphere of tolerance between people of many faiths and many tastes and ideas sanctioned by antiquity. It would keep the various governments informed of changes in customs, habits, ideas, rites, and organization, changes which, unattended to, might come into conflict with the law. It would reduce misunderstanding and neglect of cultural factors. It would make easier a large forward step of all population groups and their government toward that economic and political co-operation which, after the war's disruption of orderly government, will be so necessary for the re-creation of inner peace and stability.

Enough has been said, perhaps, on earlier pages, about the possibilities of greater political co-operation in Southeast Asia to make it unnecessary here to discuss how a political joint council for the region would function and what might be expected from it. There is reason to hope that a clear and definite set of principles for regional political organization will before long emerge from the joint counsels of the United Nations. Only one thing need here be stressed. It arises from a discussion here that has been more concerned with the welfare of the native people than with any other aspect of the future of Southeast Asia: every forward step in international collaboration between countries with so great a diversity of conditions and historical experience as those of this region requires a corresponding differentiation of functions. To hope that a single regional council or commission, responsible to a single world organization, will be able to deal adequately with all the diverse problems of the region that have here been named, and many more, is bound to produce disappointment. Only a new departure separating as far as possible the different

responsibilities along functional lines can produce the
needed practical results.

It may be objected that too elaborate an organization —
the establishment of three separate co-ordinate regional
bodies as suggested above — would produce additional friction and invite additional opposition. But the contrary is
more to be feared. All the governments of Southeast Asia
are hostile to forms of international organization that
threaten to impose restrictions upon their freedom of action. They oppose everything in the nature of a full-blown
federal super-government. But all these governments may
be expected to welcome an array of separate joint organs,
and organs of world collaboration, that are designed for
specific jobs without reducing the area of political power.
Most of them have in the past willingly collaborated with
the International Labor Organization, with the Health Organization of the League of Nations, with numerous bodies
created to effect specific common purposes — and are willing to go considerably farther in these directions. The
world economic depression of the 'thirties has shown them
that economically their very existence depends on making
joint cause in the basic insurance of livelihood for their
peoples. Japan has shown them that even incorporation in
a strong empire does not suffice to guarantee their freedom.

This is not the place further to develop the opportunities
and the difficulties of producing in Southeast Asia a living
peace — a peace in which no hand lies heavily on any group
of people aspiring to new heights. Neither these pages nor
any other writing in these clouded days of strife can show
all the way. We can only discuss the general direction in
which that peace is to be sought. In tropical Asia, Occidentals who look to the future of human relations are handi-
capped by ignorance and also by a cultivated misunderstanding. Americans have learned to see Eastern Asia almost
entirely through the eyes of Europeans — and of a particu-

lar class of Europeans at that, those who have benefited
from ownership and rule in that distant part of the globe.
We have spoken of the far western outreach of our hemisphere as the "Far East"; we have accepted the most reactionary European colonials' appraisals of lands and peoples.
We have accepted, for example, a judgment of the indigenous people as "lazy" when they were merely too busy
in their own rice fields and gardens to be lured by the bid
of the foreign-owned plantations. Our travellers and ex-
hibitors, motion picture producers, and fiction writers have
taught us to regard the most primitive tribes as representative of populations composed of many millions of hardworking peasants. Our school geographies not so long ago
pictured "the races of man" in quaint barbaric splendor
and only the white man garbed in speckless linen. In short,
our remoteness and our appetite for romantic nonsense
have not permitted us to know what the brown and yellow
people of the world are really like. Today we know at least
this about the dwellers on the wide plains, in the rugged
hills, and on the thousands of islands of tropical East Asia:
about equal in number to the population of the United
States with its dependencies, they are our comrades; we
need their help to build a better world.

INDEX

TYPE NOTE

The text of this book has been set on the Linotype in a type-face called "Baskerville." The face is a facsimile reproduction of types cast from molds made for John Baskerville (1706–1775) from his designs. The punches for the revived Linotype Baskerville were cut under the supervision of the English printer George W. Jones.

John Baskerville's original face was one of the forerunners of the type-style known as "modern face" to printers: a "modern" of the period A.D. 1800.

The typographic scheme and the binding design are by W. A. Dwiggins. The book was composed, printed, and bound by The Plimpton Press, Norwood, Massachusetts.